The Author's Inheritance

The Author's Inheritance

Henry Fielding, Jane Austen, and the Establishment of the Novel

Jo Alyson Parker

Northern Illinois University Press
DeKalb 1998

Published by the Northern Illinois University Press,
DeKalb, Illinois 60115
Manufactured in the United States
using acid-free paper

Design by Julia Fauci

Library of Congress Cataloging-in-Publication Data
Parker, Jo Alyson, 1954–
The author's inheritance : Henry Fielding, Jane
Austen, and the establishment of the novel /
Jo Alyson Parker.
p. cm.
Includes bibliographical references and index.
ISBN 0-87580-239-7 (acid-free paper)
1. Fielding, Henry, 1707–1754—Authorship.
2. Inheritance and succession in literature.
3. English fiction—History and criticism.
4. Austen, Jane, 1775–1817—Authorship.
5. Authority in literature. 6. Women in literature.
7. Fiction—Authorship. I. Title.
PR3458.A9P37 1998
823'.5—dc21 98-12957
CIP

Chapter 4 contains an adapted version of the author's article, "Pride and Predjudice," *REAL: The Yearbook of Research in English and American Literature* 7 (1990): 159–90. Used with permission of the publisher.

In memory of my father,

Joseph Julian Parker (1923–1996)

Were we too busy to notice the day?

CONTENTS

ACKNOWLEDGMENTS

ALTHOUGH THIS STUDY DEALS WITH Henry Fielding's and Jane Austen's struggles to establish their literary authority, I wish to begin by divesting myself somewhat of mine. My name appears on the title page as sole author, but those whose names follow can in many ways be deemed coauthors. Their recommendations, comments, and suggestions helped bring this book into being. My first thanks go to my mother, who gave me a copy of *Pride and Prejudice* when I was twelve years old and thereby sparked my interest in Jane Austen. I must acknowledge also the director Tony Richardson, whose inspired film version of *Tom Jones* prompted me at an early age to discover the genius of Fielding, launching me on the ambitious summer reading project of the novel itself.

Early drafts of the book benefited from the careful readings and thoughtful suggestions of Homer Brown, Murray Krieger, and Harold Toliver. Homer helped me to go beyond my comfortable assumptions about the eighteenth century. Murray ensured that my theoretical pronouncements were properly grounded. Hal prompted me to think in terms of an ongoing literary tradition and kept me from committing too many stylistic lapses. I am grateful to Eileen Cohen and Richard Fusco for reading drafts of the manuscript as it neared completion. Eileen's insights enabled me to hone the overall argument. Rich's editorial suggestions were invaluable. Although I sighed over the red ink he spilled over my pages, I am indebted to Rich for honing my style and keeping my argument on track. Kelly Hager, Paul Levitt, Laura Runge, and Lynda Wiggens read individual chapters of the manuscript, and the book has benefited from their incisive comments.

I owe thanks as well to several people who have directly enhanced my understanding of eighteenth-century literature. Robert Folkenflik's graduate course on the eighteenth-century novel gave me a critical understanding of the period and the genre. John Allen Stevenson graciously allowed me to sit in on his course in the eighteenth-century novel, providing me with new insights. I am grateful to Caroline Woodward for suggesting texts that gave me a new understanding of gender issues during the period.

Many people helped in other, no less valuable, ways. I am indebted to Robert Anthony, Martin Johnson, and Susan Bean for helping me through the publication process. Jack Balas, Lois Cole, Sue Daney, Owen Gilman, Wes Hempel, Katie Palmer, Kevin Parker, and Claudia Putnam provided various forms of moral support and encouragement during the writing process, and for this I thank them. As I teach my students, they teach me as well, and many of their sharp observations have found their way into this book. I thank Jerry Bandyk-Hill for providing crucial secretarial support. The librarians at Saint Joseph University's Drexel Library have been consistently helpful. I am especially indebted to those hard-working individuals in the Interlibrary Loan Department. I am grateful to the Board of Research and Development at Saint Joseph's University for giving me a summer research grant, which aided me in completing the book. An early version of chapter 4 appeared in *REAL: The Yearbook of Research in English and American Literature* 7 (1990): 159–90, and I thank the editors for allowing me to reprint it here.

My deepest thanks go to the two Weisserts in my life, Tom and Lizzy. Tom has been with this project from the beginning—reading, criticizing, suggesting, encouraging, and always sustaining. Lizzy appeared in my life as I was partway through the project. She has been developing as it has, and it has been my pleasure to watch my actual offspring and my literary offspring grow together. As she joyously embarks on her first reading experiences, she reminds me that it was my own love of reading that brought this book into being.

NOTE ON PRIMARY SOURCES AND ABBREVIATIONS

REFERENCES TO THE WORKS of Fielding and Austen are included in the text. When possible, for the works of Henry Fielding, I have used the Wesleyan editions (Wesleyan University Press, Watertown, Connecticut), which include the following: *Amelia*, ed. Martin C. Battestin with textual introduction by Fredson Bowers (1984); *The Covent-Garden Journal; and, A Plan of the Universal Register-Office*, ed. Bertrand A. Goldgar (1988); *An Enquiry into the Causes of the Late Increase of Robbers and Related Writings*, ed. Malvin R. Zirker (1988); *Joseph Andrews*, ed. Martin C. Battestin (1967); *Miscellanies, by Henry Fielding, Esq.*, ed. Henry Knight Miller (1972). *The History of Tom Jones, a Foundling*, eds. Martin C. Battestin and Fredson Bowers, introduction by Martin C. Battestin (Oxford: Wesleyan University Press, 1975), is in two volumes. The text of *Shamela* is from the New American Library edition of *Pamela*, ed. John M. Bullitt (New York: New American Library, 1980). The text of *A Journal of a Voyage to Lisbon* is from *Henry Fielding: Miscellaneous Writings*, vol. 1 (New York: The Literary Guild of America, 1937). The text of *Jonathan Wild* is from the Penguin edition, ed. David Nokes (Harmondsworth, Middlesex: Penguin, 1982).

For the works of Jane Austen, I have used the Oxford editions, which include the following: *Minor Works*, ed. R. W. Chapman, volume 6 of *The Works of Jane Austen* (Oxford: Oxford University Press, 1986); and, from *The Novels of Jane Austen*, ed. R. W. Chapman, 3d ed. (Oxford: Oxford University Press), volume 1, *Sense and Sensibility* (1933); volume 2, *Pride and Prejudice* (1965); volume 3, *Mansfield Park* (1934); volume 4, *Emma* (1933); and volume 5, *Northanger Abbey* and *Persuasion* (1969). I have also drawn upon R. W. Chapman's edition, *Jane Austen's Letters to Her Sister Cassandra and Others* (London: Oxford University Press, 1952).

ABBREVIATIONS USED PARENTHETICALLY IN THE TEXT

Am *Amelia*

CGJ *The Covent-Garden Journal; and, A Plan of the Universal Register-Office*

Em	*Emma*
JA	*Joseph Andrews*
JVL	*A Journal of a Voyage to Lisbon*
JW	*Jonathan Wild*
LIR	*An Enquiry into the Causes of the Late Increase of Robbers and Related Writings*
LSC	*Jane Austen's Letters to Her Sister Cassandra and Others*
Misc	*Miscellanies, by Henry Fielding, Esq.*
MP	*Mansfield Park*
MW	*Minor Works*
NA	*Northanger Abbey*
Pam	*Pamela* (Bullitt edition)
Per	*Persuasion*
PP	*Pride and Prejudice*
Sham	*Shamela*
SS	*Sense and Sensibility*
Tom	*The History of Tom Jones, a Foundling*

The Author's Inheritance

Introduction

Establishing Genre, Establishing Gender

Between the work of the four great novelists of the mid-eighteenth century and that of Jane Austen and Scott there are no names that posterity has consented to call great.
—J. M. S. Tompkins, *The Popular Novel in England*

Women cannot write monologues; there must be two in the world for one woman to exist, and one of them has to be a man. —Myra Jehlen, "Archimedes and the Paradox of Feminist Criticism"

AN INTRODUCTION is particularly appropriate considering that my initial impetus for this book was the "introductory Writing," or prefatory chapters, that Henry Fielding intersperses throughout *Tom Jones*. Since my earliest encounters with the text, I had puzzled over the connection between these seemingly nonfictional elements and the fictional narrative of Tom Jones's fall and rise. Appearing at a time when the very concept of the novel had yet to crystallize, they served as a gesture toward legitimation—even self-canonization—and they prompted me to consider the nature of authorship and authority in the upstart novel form. How did writers attempt to establish the legitimacy of this new genre—a genre that, unlike others, did not speak mainly to a privileged class and often flaunted its independence from tradition? Furthermore, what was the connection between the novel's authority—both the individual novel and the genre—and the discussions of moral authority that played such a significant role in many eighteenth- and early nineteenth-century texts? What was the connection between the inheritance plots, so prevalent in early novels, and notions of a literary inheritance, which were also prevalent? And did the female writer employ different sorts of legitimating strategies than her male counterparts? It was out of these questions that the following study evolved.

In order to provide a provisional answer to these questions, I focus on several texts by Henry Fielding and also on several by Jane Austen, the first significantly canonized female writer, alternating their texts so as to set up a dialogue between them. Juxtaposing Austen to Fielding, rather than looking at each writer in isolation, enables me to explore the distinction between a male claim to authorship and a female one. As Myra Jehlen argues in "Archimedes and the Paradox of Feminist Criticism," we can more accurately evaluate women's writing—and, I would add, men's—when we look at each in the context of the other.[1] The alternation of texts highlights the writers' divergences as they cover the same ground, thus bringing to the fore the role played by gender in the establishment of the novel genre. Austen's texts serve as misprisions of Fielding's, exploring gender inequities that he ignores or takes for granted.[2]

The traditional narrative of the novel's origins and history serves as a springboard for my study. That narrative has gone something like this: the eighteenth century produced four or five "great novelists," and nothing of note occurred until Jane Austen stepped forward to assume her joint inheritance from Henry Fielding and Samuel Richardson. Richardson and Fielding have generally been regarded as the originators of the novel genre in England, with Defoe playing the role of important protonovelist and Smollett and Sterne continuing the great tradition, although not significantly building upon it. It has been claimed that, after the death of Smollett, the novel declined into "tenth-rate fiction," a mere "form of entertainment," regaining its pretensions to aesthetic value only when Jane Austen and Sir Walter Scott appeared on the scene.[3]

Ian Watt's *The Rise of the Novel* (1957) has been especially influential in putting forth the great-men-followed-by-a-great-woman history of the novel, maintaining for nearly three decades a virtual hegemony over theories accounting for the novel's ascendance and import in eighteenth-century England.[4] Watt argues that the joint efforts of Defoe, Richardson, and Fielding made the novel viable as a genre and that Jane Austen successfully synthesized Richardson's "realism of presentation" with Fielding's "realism of assessment." Certainly Watt's importance cannot be overestimated. His analysis of the influence of the rising middle class and feminine sensibility upon the novel, his distinction between realism of presentation and realism of assessment, his trenchant discussions of the works of

Defoe, Richardson, and Fielding—all have aided in our understanding of what a novel is and does. Even if we quarrel with some of Watt's premises (such as his devaluation of Fielding or his insistence on novelistic realism), we cannot dismiss them as ungrounded.

Within the past decade or so, however, the traditional narrative has undergone significant revision. Watt's study has in fact served as a point of departure for many of these revisionary, and perhaps equally influential, theories of the novel's rise. Michael McKeon's *The Origins of the English Novel* (1987) has caused us to reassess Watt's central notions that the rise of the novel coincides with the rise of the middle class and that the novel's strength lies in its formal realism. McKeon argues that the novel emerged out of the epistemological and moral instabilities that characterized the late seventeenth and early eighteenth centuries; rather than serving to reflect middle-class interests in a primarily realistic manner, it served to mediate between the conflicting forces of romance and realism and of aristocratic and mercantile interests.[5] But, despite its revisionary nature, McKeon's study cannot escape from the great-man notion of the novel's beginnings; like Watt, he concentrates on Defoe, Richardson, and Fielding, the only significant addition being the rather quirky one of Jonathan Swift.[6]

Although McKeon ignores, for the most part, the significant role women played in "originating" the novel, others have begun to focus on the contribution of female writers to the establishment of the novel and the mutual exchange between the formation of genre and the formation of gender. The critical premises that have led to the dismissal of so many novels—particularly feminocentric ones—as "tenth-rate" have begun to be reevaluated in light of new historicist and feminist theory.[7] Jane Spencer's *The Rise of the Woman Novelist* (1986) and Janet Todd's *The Sign of Angellica* (1989) foreground women's achievements in the novel genre and explore their various responses to the imperatives of a patriarchal culture. Nancy Armstrong's *Desire and Domestic Fiction* (1987) discusses the rise of female authority in the novel, arguing that the emerging genre of the novel, like that of the conduct-book, inscribes values within the domestic woman. Patricia Meyer Spacks's *Desire and Truth* (1990) examines the way in which a struggle over a male and a female truth is played out in the novels of the eighteenth century. And Susan Lanser's *Fictions of Authority* (1992) provides us with new tools for assessing the female voice in the eighteenth-century novel.[8] Such studies ensure that the eighteenth-century novel can no longer be, in Armstrong's words, "represented as the history of male institutions."[9]

By focusing upon several novels apiece by Fielding and Austen, I may appear to reinforce the view that they are founders of the novel and that their texts are authoritative formulations of the gender. My aim, however, is not to perpetuate the traditional narrative but to examine its underlying assumptions about literary authority, aesthetic value, gender, and their intersection. I thus explore the textual strategies that Fielding and Austen employ to establish literary authority.

My choice of these two figures, separated by a half-century during which the novel flourished, is not an arbitrary one. According to the traditional narrative, Austen's work is generally regarded as the culmination of two vital strands of the eighteenth-century novel: Fielding's omniscient ironic vision coupled with Richardson's psychological complexity.[10] In fact, the Richardsonian Austen generally gets the emphasis, as we can see from the studies tracing Austen's predecessors.[11] No doubt this tendency derived from the novel's increasing emphasis on psychological complexity during the nineteenth century and the resulting critical elevation of it. The Richardsonian strain—especially as filtered through Fanny Burney—is a vital one for Austen, and a viable dialogue might be set up between Richardson and Austen as well.

Austen's indebtedness to Fielding, however, is more apparent and more fruitful for my purpose. Ostensibly, Austen seems to owe little to Fielding. In the "Biographical Notice" affixed to the posthumous edition of *Northanger Abbey* and *Persuasion*, Austen's brother Henry made clear that his sister preferred the moralizing Richardson to the ribald Fielding:

> Richardson's power of creating, and preserving the consistency of his characters, as particularly exemplified in "Sir Charles Grandison," gratified the natural discrimination of her mind, whilst her taste secured her from the errors of his prolix style and tedious narrative. She did not rank any work of Fielding quite so high. Without the slightest affectation she recoiled from every thing gross. Neither nature, wit, nor humour, could make her amends for so very low a scale of morals.[12]

Of course, as Margaret Kirkham argues, the virtuous, sheltered Jane Austen may be a creation of the family biographers, so we do well to view Henry's pronouncement with some skepticism.[13] Nevertheless, in the letters, we find only one reference to Fielding, and a flippant one at that—Austen's sly comment that a gentleman wearing a white coat must have been trying to emulate Tom Jones.[14] In the novels themselves, the only Fielding reference appears in *Northanger Abbey* when the egregious boor John Thorpe proclaims that "Novels are all so full of nonsense and stuff; there has not been a tolerably decent one come out since Tom Jones, except the Monk" (*NA* 48). In the mouth of a fool, such praise is faintly damning. Thus, although we can assume that Austen read Fielding, we have no evidence that she considered him worthy of imitation.

Yet in significant ways, Austen's literary province lies closer to the expansive, comic one of Fielding than the circumscribed, sentimental one of Richardson. With Richardson we feel confined to a world of claustrophobic textuality, to the extent that references to the social milieu end up sublimated to the characters' obsessive efforts to define and assert themselves through letters. Fielding's novels, on the other hand, offer an inclusive rather than an exclusive vision; we have a sense of the vital interconnection between the individual and society, as well as the way in which these two forces work upon one another. Although they move increasingly toward an attempt to represent the workings of the characters' minds, Austen's novels never move into that solipsistic realm of sheer textualized "consciousness" that we find in Richardson's. Like Fielding's, Austen's novels concern themselves with the interplay between the characters and the society they inhabit, and, if her range is not as wide as Fielding's, Austen nevertheless gives us a pretty good idea of a social group that had a major impact on nineteenth-century British society. We have fortunately begun to shed our prior notions of Austen's limitation with regard to subject matter—the "two inches of ivory" assessment that has often led to qualified critical appraisals. To be sure, all her novels follow the oft-noted pattern of the arrival of an eligible bachelor or two in a small community and the subsequent pairings, partings, and re-pairings until the appropriate partners are matched. But this "limited" subject matter manages to touch on important issues of morality, gender, and class as Austen moves among the inhabitants of her country villages and manors.[15] Unlike Richardson, both Fielding and Austen put forward a comic vision of the societies with which they deal, the wry narrative voice that each employs allowing for a certain distancing so that social critique does not get reduced to dogma. More important, Austen recontextualizes significant themes and motifs from Fielding's novels so that she can legitimate a realm of female experience.

To make the half-century jump from Fielding to Austen seemingly ignores a vital tradition of feminocentric women writers who also engage Fielding's texts. Charlotte Lennox's *The Female Quixote* deals with a deluded protagonist similar to Abraham Adams in *Joseph Andrews*. Fanny Burney's eponymous, fatherless Evelina, searching for origin and legitimation, has affinities to Tom Jones. In *The Memoirs of Miss Sidney Biddulph*, Frances Sheridan deals with the trials of an exemplary woman confronted with an adulterous husband, such as Fielding does in *Amelia*. Yet, just as Fielding has been critically regarded as the first significant male novelist, so has Jane Austen been regarded as the first significant female novelist. They have each been canonized, and their prominence in the canon has much to do with the similar circumstances they faced as writers and the similar approaches they took to the problems—societal and literary—that each attempted to examine and resolve through fiction.

Fielding wrote his three novels at a time when the genre itself was being formulated or, perhaps more accurately, pieced together. It was a time of competing textual strategies and competing ways of assessing moral authority, both of which impacted upon the other. The decay of belief in the myth of aristocratic morality coincided with the decline of the romance genre, which the novel is often (and often too facilely) seen as replacing. McKeon's remarks upon this connection are pertinent: "the early modern period marked a critical turning point in the efficacy not only of romance but also of the social institutions with which we are likely to associate it, a point at which they began systematically to attest not to the concord but to the discord of internals and externals, of virtue, status, wealth, and power."[16] Fielding, I argue, puts his texts forward as resolutions to these problems. Throughout, however, he betrays his anxiety over the legitimacy of his textual strategies. The bastard hero of his masterpiece novel, *Tom Jones*, serves as a fitting emblem for the novel genre and for Fielding's complex relation to his own authorial vocation.[17]

By the time Austen began writing, the novel genre, with the help of such advocates as Fielding, had been more or less legitimized. Yet, despite the increasing acceptance of the genre itself, the very fact of authorship for the woman writer remained a vexed issue. The phrase "female author" is in itself something of a contradiction in terms; according to the *Oxford English Dictionary*, "author" and "father" had at one time been used synonymously. Writing was thus linked semantically and culturally to male prerogative. Before the rise of the novel, the world of letters had been almost exclusively male-dominated. In fact, there was a veritable genealogical continuity among texts, an inherited tradition passed down from male writer to male writer. Fielding, like many of his fellow writers, regarded himself as the heir of a noble authorial tradition; the density of his allusions, as parodic as some of them may be, bespeaks his connection to a long line of literary forefathers. The female writer had few foremothers upon which she could rely, and some of the few that she did have, such as Aphra Behn and Eliza Haywood, were vilified by the arbiters of culture. Too, as Susan Lanser points out, "when an authorial voice has represented itself as female, it has risked being (dis)qualified."[18] In the latter half of the eighteenth century, the novel was increasingly connected with feminine values, and this very connection undermined its generic legitimacy.[19] By the time Austen began writing, the popular, feminocentric novel was simultaneously being trivialized for the limitations of its subject matter and condemned for its corrupting influence on the female readers.

Austen displayed a consistent awareness of the vexed status of the novel genre. It is significant that during her lifetime she never affixed her name to her novels. In effect, by publishing them she acknowledged her desire to speak publicly, but by refusing to own them she acknowledged her uncertainty about the propriety of such speech. Her work overall, however, is a means for legitimizing such speech and serves to make a case for the feminocentric novel.

My strategy here is threefold: (1) I examine the plot of authorship that Fielding and Austen develop within their key works, a plot that is linked implicitly with the inheritance plots that are so integral to the novels with which I deal. (2) I trace the different approaches they adopt to establish literary authority and moral authority, concerns that, as McKeon points out, are "closely analogous" in that they "pose problems of signification."[20] As they address issues of authority, both writers often revise or at least call into question one of their earlier texts, as if acknowledging that solutions can be only provisional, never definitive. (3) I demonstrate how Austen reworks Fielding's themes from a female perspective, inscribing women in a tradition of the novel as she explores their societal influence and options. Ultimately, these three concerns dovetail.

The plot of authorship in the texts of Fielding and Austen is mapped, especially in the authorial *Tom Jones* and the authoritative *Pride and Prejudice*, by the inheritance plots upon which they rely. The inheritance plot is an integral part of the English novel in general, as Franco Moretti points out: "the recognition-inheritance pattern, virtually nonexistent in European narrative, is instead the most typical form of the English happy end."[21] Its prominence in the English novel reflects the societal and epistemological turmoil that gives birth to it. Although separated by half a century, both Fielding and Austen wrote during times of profound societal changes, changes that were registered in the particular preoccupations of their novels.

The century leading up to Fielding's birth as a novelist had witnessed a sustained assault on traditional forms of authority. A scaffold had exposed the fictionality of the king's pretensions to divinity. Within four decades of that cataclysmic event, James II was expelled from England in what Donald Greene characterizes as "the last time that there had been a serious attempt to change the basic terms of government in England by internal force."[22] Granted, as J. G. A. Pocock points out, "both the Restoration and the Revolution of 1688 could be represented as efforts to restore the fundamental law."[23] Despite this appeal to ancient tradition, however, the events of the seventeenth century had undermined the comforting belief that authority was innate and God-given. Throughout the first part of the eighteenth century, thinkers grappled with the question of what might now serve as a basis for authority.[24] The influence of the squire with his landed property was being challenged by that of the tradesman with his ready capital. According to Pocock, although "real property remained the assurance of virtue," in that property conferred autonomy and thus ensured against corruption, this assumption came increasingly into conflict with a burgeoning commercial establishment.[25] The authority of the church was being called into question and reconstituted by the deist challenge to revealed religion and by the nonconformist challenge to ministerial mediation. Women were finding a voice and defining themselves, rather than letting themselves be defined, with the novel itself enabling and encouraging such self-definition.[26] To some extent, all of Fielding's novels touch upon these issues.

Austen, too, wrote at a time of profound societal change, replete with challenges to traditional authority. During her writing apprenticeship, revolution in France sent shock waves throughout England, inspiring a consolidation of Tory values in the face of the Jacobin threat and prompting Austen's own reactionary response.[27] During the time Austen wrote professionally, England was embroiled in both the Napoleonic Wars and the War of 1812. This period saw the rise of what David Spring calls "the pseudo-gentry," those who had no landed property but who "devoted their lives to acquiring the trappings of gentry status for themselves and especially their children."[28] This definition encompasses Austen's own class and the class with which her novels deal. A "pressure for a renewed commitment to religious and moral principle," in Marilyn Butler's terms, occurred among them.[29] In the half-century after Fielding's death, women increasingly expressed and defined themselves publicly through novel writing, yet there was conflict over what might constitute appropriate forms of self-expression and self-definition. Although Austen generally eschewed direct allusion to the major political events of her day, her novels, like Fielding's, engage the ideological conflicts that beset her society.

The tendency of the recognition-inheritance pattern to tie things up neatly (a tendency Moretti deplores) points toward an attempt to mediate through fiction conflicts that may have been irresolvable in actuality—conflicts with which the novels of Fielding and Austen both explicitly and implicitly deal. In fact, we might say that the inheritance plot masks such conflicts. On the one hand, the neater the solution the less we are aware of the ideological contradictions. On the other, less aesthetically "finished" texts (for example, Fielding's *Amelia* with its unearned providential ending) often bring such contradictions to our attention.

Although a great many novels of the period feature inheritance plots, those of Fielding and Austen force us to consider the important societal implications of the "proper" disposition of property and the conflict-resolving tendencies of the happy endings they put forward.[30] All of Fielding's novels deal explicitly with a missing or dispossessed heir: (1) Joseph Andrews is a changeling, reunited with his true father only at the end of the text; (2) Tom Jones is the secret, first, and more beloved son of Squire Allworthy's sister, Bridget; and (3) Amelia is (unbeknownst to her for most of the novel) her mother's only heir, a fact that her wicked sister unsuccessfully hides. Although Austen's novels subtilize the romantic-quest structure of Fielding's, the issue of estate settlement initiates and culminates the action of the plots in each one except *Northanger Abbey*. Entailed estates threaten security, autocratic parents elevate younger sons over elder, affectionate yet pragmatic young women pin their hopes on the death of an elder brother, young men such as Frank Churchill form secret engagements in order to avoid being disinherited, and so forth. Although appearing in various guises, the inheritance plot in the novels that I examine is roughly similar: at the outset the protagonist, deprived of his or her rightful inheritance, must embark on a quest for security and position; by the end, he or she has been revealed or recognized as the proper heir and has come into wealth—or, at least, an elevation in social position.

Both Fielding and Austen draw upon and test out various permutations of the inheritance plot in an attempt to resolve the questions of whether moral authority resides in traditional hierarchical structures or needs to be substantiated through action. By the mid–eighteenth century, the myth that noble or elevated birth guaranteed noble behavior could no longer be taken for granted. Wherein did moral authority lie? The inheritance plot invariably demonstrates that the proper heir to a material estate is also the proper heir to what is, in effect, a moral estate. In other words, just as wealth and property are transmitted to the deserving, so is moral authority, the material estate thus continuing to serve as a repository of values, but one that must be earned. In *Joseph Andrews* and *Northanger Abbey*, Fielding and Austen work toward the notion that the individual must earn a position in society, but both are still feeling their way, uncertain whether to treat their main characters realistically or parodically. In the masterpiece novels, *Tom Jones* and *Pride and Prejudice*, the inheritance plot is foregrounded, both Fielding and Austen envisioning a seamless connection between earned and inherited authority. The inheritance plot is troubled in the succeeding novels, *Amelia* and *Mansfield Park*, signifying the writers' increasing doubts that the deserving—whether characters or writers—will get their rewards.

The preeminent position that the texts of Fielding and Austen hold in the canon owes more than a little to the ways they resolve this issue of transmitting authority—a vitally important matter for a nation caught in the struggle between conservative and progressive forces. Although deriving from an older archetype (the fairy tale), the inheritance plot grafts itself onto a realistic exposition of everyday occurrences.[31] Yet it retains vestiges of its fairy-tale origins in that, invariably in these novels, genteel birth will out—as clearly as it does when the princess feels the pea. The archetypal inheritance plot serves to deflect a potentially subversive critique into a conservative agenda. Featuring an outsider who eventually makes it into the dominant social class and, in so doing, makes that class into something better, novels of "making it" seemingly suggest that tradition-bound society needs an external force to change it. But the outsider turns out to be an insider all along, one who has previously not been recognized or acknowledged. If we refer to the archetype, we recall that Cinderella herself was no true scullery maid but a noblewoman forced into that position by her wicked stepmother and stepsisters. Although in *Shamela* and *Joseph Andrews* Fielding makes fun of her base origins, Pamela, the novel genre's first and foremost Cinderella, is not the daughter of lower-class servants but of an insolvent teacher—and by the end of the novel she seems to be something more than a daughter of Mr. and Mrs. Andrews.[32]

Fielding's and Austen's protagonists follow the disguised-insider pattern. Joseph Andrews is not the rustic Andrewses' son but the genteel Wilsons'; Tom Jones is legally and almost biologically just another Thomas Allworthy; and Amelia is always "the finest Woman in England of her Age" (*Am* 533); Catherine Morland is not the destitute fortune-hunter that General Tilney takes her for, but the worthy recipient of his son's affections; Elizabeth Bennet is a gentleman's daughter, unfairly deprived of the fortune that is her due; and Fanny Price is "the daughter that [Sir Thomas] wanted" (*MP* 472). The change needed by society comes not through the intervention of an outsider, but through the expulsion of someone from within—Blifil or Betty Harris or Lady Catherine or Aunt Norris—who has wrongfully usurped power and kept the true insider from being recognized.

"Making it" in these novels does not ultimately have Horatio-Alger connotations. Wealth is inherited—passed down to a deserving member of an established line—not earned through the efforts of the protagonist. The motif derives from aristocratic tradition, as Moretti remarks: "Although the bourgeoisie has always taken care of its wills and inheritances, the idea that wealth par excellence is something to be passed on from generation to generation, rather than being produced *ex novo*, is certainly far more typical of the landed aristocracy."[33] The inheritance plot is progressive in that moral worth is no longer simply assumed; the protagonist must demonstrate the moral authority that qualifies him or her as the heir. But overall the inheritance plot is based on a notion of continuity, not radical change, a tendency characteristic of comedy in general. The comedic plot may involve the creation of a new society, but this society marks not a rejection of the past but a partial return to it, the bad state of things at the outset having been a reversal of an original golden age.[34] As disciples of the comic muse, Fielding and Austen reinforce a notion of renewal based on existing grounds, attempting—through resolutions that satisfy both morally and aesthetically—to allay in fiction the insoluble conflicts of society. Fielding may have certain progressive tendencies, but he clearly champions the values of his class. Although Austen is generally a good Tory, her support of traditional values is more problematic, perhaps because of the marginalized position in which she found herself as a woman, yet overall, in the texts that I examine, like Fielding she makes a case for revitalizing rather than overturning the status quo.[35]

The working out and resolution of the inheritance plot dovetail with what I call the plot of the author. As Peter Brooks notes in *Reading for the Plot*, the word "plot" can often stand for a scheme or conspiracy, a definition that has relevance to our understanding of narrative plot: "in modern literature this sense of plot nearly always attaches itself to the others: the organizing line of plot is for the accomplishment of some purpose which goes against ostensible and dominant legalities of the fictional world, the realization of a blocked and resisted desire."[36] The plot of the author is the writer's scheme to establish the legitimacy of the novel genre and his or her own claim to be a legitimate heir of literary tradition. The writer's claim for the novel's literary authority is analogous to the protagonist's assumption of rightful position and, like that, indicates an uneasy alliance between the traditional and the new. We often find thematic reverberations between the happy fate of the protagonist and the (desired) happy fate of the text itself.

Superintending this plot of authorship is an author figure, which can range from the characterized author to a spuriously transparent neutral observer. In *Joseph Andrews*, *Tom Jones*, and to a lesser extent *Northanger Abbey*, we see characterized author figures commenting directly on the fiction-writing process. In *Amelia*, *Pride and Prejudice*, and *Mansfield Park*, the characterized author figure disappears, but the authorial voice still insistently mediates events and insists on its own authority.

By "author figure," I do not mean something along the lines of Wayne Booth's "implied author," which enables a certain set of values to be established within a text.[37] Although Booth's insights about authorial perspective have contributed to my understanding of the workings of narrative, his notion of the "implied author" suggests that there can be textual coherence and consistency, a realization of authorial aims. My notion of the author figure is more in keeping with what Michel Foucault calls "the author function," which "is to characterize the existence, circulation, and operation of certain discourses in society."[38] The author figure results from particular culturo-sociohistorical circumstances and provides us with the illusion that there is someone in control of the text, responsible for maintaining its coherence, directing its reception, and establishing who may speak and what may be spoken. When I use the names Fielding and Austen in my discussions of textual strategies, I refer not to the historical personages who engaged in the act of writing but to the author figures that they employed in establishing textual authority.[39]

The plot of the author is prominent in Fielding's novels, wherein magisterial pronouncements about what the genre should be and do intertwine with illustrative material. It is more complicated in Austen's novels, however, for in laying claim to authority Austen must both contend with potentially hostile existing terms and also negotiate for new ones. Whereas Fielding establishes his authority through an assured commentary that assumes a common set of values with his readership, Austen is far more cagey, ostensibly championing societal values while subtly playing with and off them. Austen's ambivalent feelings about traditional power structures stand out against Fielding's celebration of them. Although Fielding is less celebratory in *Amelia*, his more pessimistic position results from his desire to return to traditional values rather than his attempt to clear a space for a new sort of value system connected with women's concerns.[40]

Concentrating on three novels apiece by Fielding and Austen, I impose my own narrative upon their literary careers by grouping together similar works. The narrative I herein set up does not reflect some ultimate "truth" of Fielding's and Austen's literary careers; rather, it serves as a useful heuristic for bringing into focus the way the writers respond to and react against a literary tradition, including the tradition laid down in their own texts. In Part 1, I examine Fielding's and Austen's initial forays in novel writing. Each writer begins in reaction to prevailing literary modes: *Shamela* and *Joseph Andrews*, Austen's juvenilia and *Northanger Abbey*. These texts establish authority through a complex relationship to what has gone before. In Part 2, I examine the texts that have traditionally been regarded as Fielding's and Austen's masterpieces, concentrating particularly on the prominent inheritance plots in each. *Tom Jones* and *Pride and Prejudice* manage to combine progressive and conservative strains, providing satisfying resolutions that testify to the essential rightness of tradition. In Part 3, I examine the so-called problem novels, arguing that what troubles us in them is their inability to resolve the conflicts so seamlessly resolved in the masterpiece novels. *Amelia* and *Mansfield Park* highlight what was occluded in the earlier works, more vociferously espousing traditional values yet more clearly exposing their deficiencies.

As with any narrative imposition, I have followed a principle of selection that downplays or excludes much that is equally provocative, particularly in the case of Austen. Whether by choice or chance, *Amelia* ended up being Fielding's last novel, but after *Mansfield Park* Austen went on to write two very different novels and to make a good start on a third, each in its own way a response to contemporary conflicts. My particular choices, however, most clearly demonstrate the link between canonicity and comforting social vision.

To some extent the texts of two of our most canonized early writers ultimately maintain and uphold the status quo. Yet the texts resist the totalizing resolutions that such an agenda might entail. By attempting to mediate the culture it refracts, the novel genre enables us to observe and to understand this culture in ways denied by more totalizing discourses. As Spacks has observed, the authority of the novel genre consists of its ambivalent relationship to power: "authority belongs, finally, to authors, who may construct 'morals' for their fictions that obscure the operations of power, but who, in the mid-eighteenth century, consistently created fictions whose 'tendency' exposes power's omnipresence."[41] In attempting to mediate between conflicting forces, the novel genre necessarily brings conflict to the fore. Neither solely subversive nor solely prescriptive, it is both at once in varying degrees.[42]

Throughout each of these texts occurs a tense warfare between different ways of conceptualizing experience. Opposed metaphors struggle against one another, different discursive systems compete, characters act in ways inconsistent with their apparent purpose, and textual evidence belies authorial assertion. Some of the conflict is the result of the spillage, the gaps, inherent in language itself. Some is a reflection of the playfulness inherent in the fictionalizing process. But overall, the conflict stems from Fielding's and Austen's laudable inability to rest their cases. Revising the texts of others, revising their earlier work, both writers simultaneously reinforce the status quo and (however unintentionally at times) reveal its deficiencies. Their texts are matrices of cultural conflict. And their relative canonicity attests to the skill with which Fielding and Austen generally subsumed such conflict to the satisfactions of plot.

Part One

From Parody to Autonomy

CHAPTER ONE

Discovering Homer's Heir

"To write in any other way," said Don Quixote, "would be to write not the truth, but lies; and historians who resort to lies ought to be burnt like coiners of false money."
—Cervantes, *Don Quixote*

Fielding's purpose to ridicule *Pamela* produced the *History of Joseph Andrews*; and . . . a work was executed infinitely better than could have been expected to arise out of such a motive, and the reader received a degree of pleasure very different, as well as superior, to what the author himself appears to have proposed. —Sir Walter Scott, *Lives of the Novelists*

IN THE PREFACE to *Joseph Andrews* Henry Fielding grandly declares that he has undertaken a "Species of writing . . . hitherto unattempted in our Language" (10). Whether his claim is entirely justified may ultimately be beside the point. We have, after all, bought into it, granting this text the canonical status that he asserts for it and considering it—along with Samuel Richardson's *Pamela*—one of the first novels, a term that Fielding himself did not, and perhaps could not, use.[1] *Joseph Andrews* eloquently, if not always convincingly, bespeaks Fielding's notion that he is, in fact, engaging in a novel enterprise.

Shamela, Fielding's earlier foray into narrative fiction, is a parasitic text, a witty denunciation of moral and aesthetic deficiencies in *Pamela*. With *Joseph Andrews*, however, Fielding is no longer content with merely reacting negatively; he is ready to provide a counterfiction to *Pamela*—to affirm the alternative possibilities of a new narrative form. Although Richardson's novel ostensibly supplies Fielding with a moral theme and even a few characters, the real interest of *Joseph Andrews*, as its writer himself must have known, lies not with the hero's function as an exemplar of male chastity but with his problematic journey toward nomination, a journey linked to that taken by the text. Joseph Andrews may begin as Pamela's brother, but by the end of the text he discovers that his proper surname is Wilson, a name devoid of literary associations.[2] Gammer Andrews deceives her unobservant husband by substituting the child left by the gypsies for the daughter they kidnap. Fielding gives us a cuckoo in the nest as well. With its deceptively eponymous title, the text that tells Joseph's story would seem to claim kinship with Richardson's, but in telling Joseph's journey toward self-discovery, the text too is journeying toward its own identity, struggling to assert both its individuality and its status as a legitimate heir to literary tradition.

In essence, Joseph Andrews marks a beginning—a self-conscious attempt to define and present a kind of writing "hitherto unattempted." As with all would-be origins, however, it can neither shake off the past nor seamlessly assimilate the old to the new. Fielding is torn between establishing a new generic lineage and demonstrating his text's affiliation to traditional genres. His critical commentary lacks a clear agenda, serving more as apologia than aesthetic manifesto. He veers between parasitic parody and autonomous "originality," and he struggles as he tries to adapt the casual circumstances of the picaresque to the causal structure of the unified plot, not yet having conceived of the developing protagonist whose journey will give him a chance to prove himself. The romantic birth-mystery motif is clumsily appended to the text, indicating Fielding's irresolution over the meritocracy-versus-aristocracy debate. Yet despite the inability to integrate diverse materials and aims, *Joseph Andrews* serves as a fascinating trial run for Fielding's theory of the novel. Its very contradictions bring to the fore the conflicting assumptions about class, gender, and moral and literary authority that give rise to the new genre.

We can appreciate Fielding's self-consciousness about the novelty of his enterprise when we compare *Joseph Andrews* with the roughly contemporaneous narrative *Jonathan Wild*.[3] It is interesting that, in discussing the thematic content of *Jonathan Wild*, Fielding invokes the same generic classification (history) and the same Aristotelian criterion (probability) that he would specify for his novels: "This is the doctrine which I have endeavoured to inculcate in this history, confining myself at the same time within the rules of probability" (*JW* 31). But this "history," as Fielding makes clear, is not of a particular rogue, but of roguery in general (29)—in effect, an anatomy of it. His aims here thus appear very different from those in his novels, wherein we are encouraged to regard his protagonists as true-to-life individuals whose fortunes we follow with interest and, Fielding seems to hope, affection. His method in *Jonathan Wild* appears more akin to that of *caricatura,* as he defines it in the preface to *Joseph Andrews:* "Its Aim is to exhibit Monsters, not Men; and all Distortions and Exaggerations whatever are within its proper Province" (*JA* 6). Despite its similarities to Fielding's novels in tone, structure, and even outlook, *Jonathan Wild* appears more closely related to a satirical text such as Jonathan Swift's *Gulliver's Travels.*[4] As with many portions of Swift's text, its aim is explicitly political rather than aesthetic; at this point Fielding wrote unambiguously for the Whig Opposition and, as his revered Swift had done earlier, took aim at the corrupt practices of Robert Walpole. Although Fielding clearly feels he must justify certain features of *Jonathan Wild,* he sees no need to provide a generic justification as he does with *Joseph Andrews.*

It is difficult to determine precisely what prompted such a fervent admirer of the classical tradition to take on the task of inaugurating a purportedly new genre—the self-proclaimed "comic Epic-Poem in Prose" (*JA* 4). Many variables must surely have played a part: the 1737 Licensing Act, which effectually stifled Fielding the Opposition Playwright (as was its intent) and left him searching for new outlets for his creative energy and ambition; Fielding's admiration for *Don Quixote, Gil Blas,* and assorted other Continental narrative fictions; and his disgust with the "biographies" of Pamela and Colley Cibber.[5] As with all complex systems, however, the variables cannot be disentangled, and no one can be positively identified as more influential than another. Nonetheless, without Richardson, Fielding the novelist would not have existed as we know him.

Pamela, after all, led to Fielding's first venture into sustained narrative fiction in the form of *Shamela,* one of the funniest parodies ever written—a text that "marked a turning point in the development of the modern novel."[6] And the importance of *Pamela/Shamela* in Fielding's own development as a novelist certainly cannot be underestimated. Good parody requires an intimate acquaintance with the original, for it is only thereby that one can achieve the subtle (and sometimes not so subtle) shifts in language, structure, and characterization that can transform the serious into the ribald, the lofty into the low—as we see, for example, in Fielding's spoof of the near rape in *Pamela.* After his failed attempt Mr. B. tells Richardson's virtuous heroine, "I know not, I declare, beyond this lovely bosom, your sex" (*Pam* 235). Fielding varies the passage only slightly: "Pamela, cryed he, can you forgive me my injured maid? by Heaven, I know not whether you are a man or a woman, unless by your swelling breasts" (*Sham* 544). Yet through that slight variation of phrasing, Fielding manages to transform Mr. B.'s impassioned apology into a disparagement of Pamela/Shamela's vaunted femininity. By studying Richardson's text and then subverting it, Fielding came to understand what could be done in narrative fiction—and what should not.

Satirically exposing the specious morality of Pamela is, of course, Fielding's main motive.[7] Pamela's concern with material goods, her ambivalent feelings toward her master, her continuance at Mr. B.'s estate (motifs that continue to spark debate among critics of the novel) are reread/rewritten in *Shamela* as the unchaste Shamela's calculated plot to entrap a booby squire into marriage. At the end of Fielding's text, Parson Oliver's gloss on *Pamela*, wherein he lists its immoral tendencies, wickedly mimics Richardson's pious summary of those features in *Pamela* that he hoped would prompt "a laudable emulation in the minds of any worthy persons" (*Pam* 520). According to Parson Oliver, rather than teaching that emulating Pamela's virtues may bring about "the rewards, the praises, and the blessings, by which PAMELA was so deservedly distinguished" (520), *Pamela* instead recommends greed and hypocrisy: "all chambermaids are strictly enjoined to look out after their masters; they are taught to use little arts to that purpose: And lastly, are countenanced in impertinence to their superiours, and in betraying the secrets of families" (*Sham* 568). Indeed, in some respects, *Shamela* tells us more about the mode of satire than the genre of the novel.

Nevertheless, as he exposes the moral deficiencies of *Pamela*, Fielding also brings to light its deficiencies as narrative fiction, intertwining the moral and aesthetic issues. Oliver tells his correspondent Tickletext that he is concerned with the way Shamela has "endeavoured by perverting and misrepresenting facts to be thought to deserve what she now enjoys" (*Sham* 537–38). This misrepresentation of "facts" can be linked to the limited perspective allowed by the epistolary format—at least, Richardson's use of it in this instance. The lack of sustained alternative perspective in *Pamela* allows for the heroine to impose her version of her motives and deeds upon the credulous reader. Our modern dictum that *all* narrators are unreliable may cause us to regard as naive Fielding's concern with subjective perspective. But the reactions of Fielding's contemporaries—from the commoners of Slough to the preachers in their pulpits—showed him that Pamela's professions of purity and piety were taken at face value; there was little questioning of the discrepancy between what Pamela said and what Pamela did.[8] In order to work against the specious sincerity of the first-person narrator, Fielding provides an alternative explanation of Pamela's behavior that accords with her actions as readily, or even more readily, than the explanation she gives in Richardson's novel. Richardson himself experimented with alternative perspectives in his next novel, *Clarissa*, bringing about a far more sophisticated work of fiction and no small amount of distress to the writer, who found his control of reader response thereby weakened.

The narrow perspective of the epistolary form also disallows the sort of narrative distancing that Fielding finds essential for certain kinds of material. By rewriting several of the most crucial scenes in *Pamela*, Fielding brings to the fore the prurient tendencies of Richardson's text. When Shamela, in a passage that does not significantly alter the original, describes Mr. Booby "kissing one of my breasts as if he would have devoured it" (*Sham* 554), we have a far different experience than we do, say, reading the famous seduction scene at Upton in *Tom Jones*. Without an obtrusive external narrator mediating between us and the scene, we are apt to be caught up too directly in the experience, and we can understand why Oliver advises that a text such as *Pamela* should "not be put into the hands of his daughter by any wise man" (*Sham* 538).

Moreover, through its very attempt to achieve authenticity, the epistolary structure paradoxically works against its own aims. *Pamela* relies on a narration presupposed as occurring between the moments of the action, a narration that is virtually to-the-moment. In perhaps one of the most well-known passages from *Shamela*, Fielding makes clear that the convention of interpolated narrative risks falling into absurdity as narrative and narrating instance converge: "Well, he is in bed between us, we both shamming a sleep, he steals his hand into my bosom" (*Sham* 543). A subsequent narrative, mediated by an omniscient narrator, may actually seem less artificial than one that suggests the letter writer does nothing *but* write.

Through *Shamela* Fielding also attacks the democratizing tendencies of epistolary fiction writing. In his Preface to *Familiar Letters on David Simple*, he worries that the "epistolary Style" is "so easy that any Man may write it, and which, one would imagine, it must be very difficult to procure any Person to read."[9] In *Shamela*, after having Oliver speak ironically about the "Ciceronian eloquence, with which the work *[Pamela]* abounds" (*Sham* 538), Fielding proceeds to bring Richardson's admittedly middle style down a few notches, giving Shamela the vocabulary of a fishwife and her supposedly aristocratic lover that of a churl. Booby's imprecations to Shamela ("you are a d—d, impudent, stinking, cursed, confounded jade, and I have a great mind to kick your a—") are close enough to the original to make Fielding's fastidiousness about authorial qualifications seem valid (542).

Although *Shamela* succeeds as a clever satire of both Richardson's theme and his form, it offers no meaningful alternative to the novel genre except by implication. *Joseph Andrews*, on the other hand, offers that alternative, although its inability to integrate its diverse materials indicates that Fielding has not yet established a clear direction for where he wants to take the novel—both his own and the genre. Fielding cannot quite relinquish his conviction that his work can legitimately aspire to literary fame only if it conforms to traditional generic categories. In the preface to *Joseph Andrews*, he asserts that his text is an example of the venerable comic epic, whose pattern was put forward in Homer's lost text the *Margites*. Lest we not have marked closely his prefatory remarks on the subject, Fielding even has Parson Abraham Adams, in an otherwise extraneous discussion of Homer, remind us: "He was the Father of the Drama, as well as the Epic: Not of Tragedy only, but of Comedy also; for his *Margites*, which is deplorably lost, bore, says *Aristotle*, the same Analogy to Comedy, as his Odyssey and Iliad to Tragedy" (*JA* 197–98).

Homer Goldberg argues that the designation of epic must be taken broadly: "epic carries no more specific or qualitative meaning than 'extended narrative.'"[10] Ian Watt is downright skeptical of Fielding's epic claims: "Fielding's Homerican style itself suggests a somewhat ambiguous attitude to the epic model: were it not for the Preface we would surely be justified in taking *Joseph Andrew* as a parody of epic procedures rather than as the work of a writer who planned to use them as a basis for the new genre."[11] But Fielding's phrase "comic Epic-Poem in Prose" (*JA* 4) is a deliberate attempt to show that his new species of writing derives from a venerable lineage. Although Fielding often parodies epic procedures, he intends that we take seriously his claim that his work exemplifies the lost generic pattern; the novel may be new, but it is sanctioned by antiquity. His literary authority derives from his profession that he follows his venerable ancestor Homer. In making such a claim, Fielding implicitly makes a case as well for the masculinization of the novel genre. After all, Homer the putative originator of the masculine epic form has in some sense fathered Fielding's text as well.[12]

By drawing upon traditional generic categories Fielding can also make a distinction between his text and "the Productions of Romance Writers on the one hand, and Burlesque Writers on the other" (*JA* 10). Thus, even while opening up the possibility for a new species of writing, Fielding sets up exclusionary principles based on aesthetic criteria sanctioned by tradition. He effectually de-authorizes competing texts.

But the piling-up of diverse, even contradictory, terms as he attempts to categorize his text bespeaks Fielding's struggle to reconcile his allegiance to the classical genres with his desire for the new. Fielding conceives that his narrative will unsettle the generic expectations of "the mere English Reader" (*JA* 3).[13] Although in the preface he provides only "some few very short Hints (for I intended no more) of this Species of writing," he thereby alerts us to marking differences (10). When he adds that he will "leave to my good-natur'd Reader to apply my piece to my Observations," he implies that it is not according to any generic expectations but to his critical commentary that we must judge the text (10). His "observations" about what he is doing are not restricted to the preface but occur throughout *Joseph Andrews*. The text will prove itself according to the rules he provides; the rules will themselves be validated by the text that demonstrates their soundness, Fielding thereby putting forward a notion of a literary meritocracy.

In the remainder of the text Fielding attempts to make *Joseph Andrews* stand apart from contemporary fictional narrative and also to provide a rationale for its distinctiveness. He makes clear that, although there are no contemporary models for what he is doing, there is literary precedent—Cervantes's *Don Quixote*. *Joseph Andrews* may be structured according to the "lost" generic pattern, but it is, as Fielding asserts on the title page, "Written in Imitation of The *Manner* of Cervantes" (*JA* 1), a claim he will also make with regard to *Tom Jones*. We can trace similarities in incidents, settings, and characters, particularly in the gullible Abraham Adams.[14] Equally important, Fielding, like Cervantes, chooses an intrusive author/narrator to mediate the story he tells, a strategy that enables him both to distinguish his novel from others and to provide an aesthetic validation of it.

For the most part, *Joseph Andrews* sets itself apart from contemporary fictional narratives that we would now designate as novels. Early novelists such as Aphra Behn and Daniel Defoe insisted upon the truth of the texts they brought forward. The narrator in Behn's texts—whom we are encouraged to imagine as Behn herself—tells us, for example, that she knew Oroonoko and that she had the story of "the fair jilt" (in the novel of the same name) from several of her victims. Defoe disavows the role of author, choosing instead to style himself the editor of his tales of rogues and castaways. In his preface to *Robinson Crusoe*, he solemnly avers that "The Editor believes the thing to be a just History of Fact; neither is there any Appearance of Fiction in it."[15] Only a few years before the appearance of *Joseph Andrews*, Richardson had cast himself as the editor of those weighty bundles of letters that comprised *Pamela*, initially even pretending that his virtuous heroine actually lived. The fictions of Behn, Defoe, and Richardson conform fairly readily to the sorts of novels that, as Michael McKeon argues, predominated through the mid–eighteenth century, wherein the writer denied or effaced his or her own role and claimed that the text was based on historical fact.[16]

Joseph Andrews, on the other hand, assertively draws our attention to the artifice that brought it into being, insisting that it has been *authored*. Fielding creates a characterized author figure to serve as the ostensible overseer of the plot of authorship, a textual construct presented as if he were the creator of the fiction. My use of the male pronoun is intentional, for the characterized author figure is assertively masculine, presenting authoring itself as a masculine prerogative.[17] With regard to narrational strategy perhaps the closest precedent for his text in England is Swift's *Tale of a Tub*. Swift's author/narrator, like Fielding's, comments on his compositional processes, presents himself as a learned wit, draws upon scholarly tradition in order to enforce his points, and intersperses his story with essays. Yet Swift's exacerbation of the technique of narrative intrusiveness, his undercutting of any epistemological certainties, and the overtly allegorical nature of his story have precluded the *Tale of a Tub* from being called a novel. Most important, Swift himself did not insist on the generic novelty of his enterprise. Fielding's author figure, however, explicitly serves to authorize his notion of what the novel genre should be and do and to demonstrate that *Joseph Andrews* fits the bill.[18]

Through the commentary itself Fielding validates its presence in the text. Such commentary appears throughout the novel but is especially prominent in the initial chapters at the outset of the first three books—chapters that contain matter we have difficulty classifying as purely "literary" in a post-Romantic and pre-postmodern sense.[19] This extra-literary element accounts in part for the importance of *Joseph Andrews* in literary history, for it serves as a gesture toward self-canonization, a somewhat sporadic but nevertheless considered effort to establish a new line. Here Fielding comments upon compositional problems, draws our attention to his stylistic audacities, and cavils with the critics.

Although offering a more sketchy theory of the novel than we find in the later *Tom Jones*, the authorial commentary in the initial chapters or prefaces attempts to establish the epistemological validity for the sort of fiction Fielding is writing. In the first two prefaces, however, Fielding has not yet hit his stride. The preface to book 1 serves primarily as yet another occasion for Fielding to take aim at Colley Cibber and Samuel Richardson. Moreover, it confuses the issue, seeming to suggest that Joseph Andrews will turn out to be a pious hypocrite à la Pamela. In the preface to book 2, Fielding attempts to justify the division of the text into books and chapters, citing classical precedent: "These Divisions have the Sanction of great Antiquity" (*JA* 90). Characteristically, Fielding playfully undercuts his own pretensions. When he points out that Virgil modestly divided the *Aeneid* into twelve books, half that of Homer's epics, and thus assumed "No more than half the Merit of the Greek," he leaves himself open to the charge that, by giving us only four books, he assumes not more than a third the merit of Virgil (92). Furthermore, he follows the argument of literary precedent with the homely observation "That it becomes an Author generally to divide a Book, as it doth a Butcher to joint his Meat" (92). Fielding may lay claim to a distinguished lineage, but he simultaneously deflates his own pomposity, as if he followed no method at all. Although these first two prefatory chapters begin to distinguish *Joseph Andrews* from inferior productions and to validate its structure, they offer no sustained poetics of the novel genre.

In the prefatory chapter to book 3, Fielding puts forward his most considered discussion of what his new species of writing might entail: a species that asserts its truth-value while acknowledging its own artifice. The preface is noteworthy for its confusion of fictional and nonfictional genres—some of which may be deliberate on Fielding's part, some of which may be indicative of his own confusion as he struggles to give a name to what he is doing, and some of which may have to do with the more permeable boundary in the eighteenth-century between what, for us, have up until recently been fairly rigid categories. Indeed, the epistemological discussions in texts such as *Joseph Andrews* lay the groundwork for the subsequent crystallization of such categories. The key terms that appear in the preface are "history" and "biography" (which we traditionally categorize as nonfictional genres) and "romance" (which we traditionally categorize as a fictional one). From the outset, however, Fielding calls such categories into question. Actual historians—Clarendon, Whitlock, Echard, and Rapin—are "Romance Writers," whose differing views of "facts" undermine the epistemological validity of their works: "Facts being set forth in a different Light, every reader believes as he pleases, and indeed the more judicious and suspicious very justly esteem the whole as no other than a Romance, in which the Writer hath indulged a happy and fertile Invention" (*JA* 185–86). From these histories, the only truth to be gained is "the Scene where the Fact is supposed to have happened" (186); the rest is, in effect, fiction. But Fielding also attacks the epistemological validity of actual romance writers, contemptuously describing them as "those Persons of surprising Genius, the Authors of immense Romances, or the modern Novel and *Atalantis* Writers; who without any Assistance from Nature or History, record Persons who never were, or will be, and Facts which never did nor possibly can happen" (187). The historian writes about people he cannot know, the romancer writes about people who cannot be, and neither accurately conveys the truth of experience.

Fielding, on the other hand, intends to present a fiction based on another sort of fact—the fact not of place but of "the Actions and Characters of Men" (*JA* 185)—and to this truthful fiction he appends the name "biography." Unlike Defoe, Fielding does not need to assert that the events of his story actually took place; he need only assert the probability of such events in light of human behavior, as he explains in a passage that recalls Aristotle's notion of impossible probabilities and anticipates Johnson's well-known literary dictum in *Rasselas* on numbering the streaks of the tulip:

> I declare here once for all, I describe not Men, but Manners; not an Individual, but a Species. Perhaps it will be answered, Are not the Characters then taken from Life? To which I answer in the Affirmative; nay, I believe I might aver, that I have writ little more than I have seen. The Lawyer is not only alive, but has been so these 4000 Years. (*JA* 189)

And it is to the reader's own experience that Fielding appeals for proof of his veracity: "I question not but several of my Readers will know the Lawyer in the Stage-coach, the Moment they hear his Voice" (189). By the end of the preface, Fielding can assert that *Joseph Andrews* is a "true History" (191)—history itself now redefined not as a truthful account of what happened (impossible to obtain) but as an account of what can happen according to the enduring truth of human nature.[20]

In spite of, or perhaps because of, the slipperiness of the terms appearing in the prefatory chapter to book 3, Fielding therein makes his most valiant effort to set out a theory of the novel. That he does not yet have his bearings is clear, however. He vacillates between whether his literary authority has been passed down through a distinguished lineage or whether it must be substantiated through the unfolding of the story. In the narrative plot itself, Fielding struggles to find the proper direction for *Joseph Andrews*—and consequently for Joseph Andrews—as he discards parody and attempts to originate a viable form for fictional narrative. But, as with the prefatory poetics, he is only partially successful.

Initially, *Joseph Andrews* appears to be a parody à la *Shamela*, offering an obverse instead of an opposing view of the events in Richardson's text. The ironic commendation of Pamela in the opening chapter, Joseph's ostensible relationship to Richardson's heroine, and the motif of besieged virtue—all set us up for a text that will parallel the events in *Pamela* from the male point of view, offering, as does *Shamela*, insights into Richardson's deficiencies as a moralist and writer. It has been argued that *Joseph Andrews* is a parody that gets out of hand, leading Fielding serendipitously into his real subject. But more accurately it is a parody that does not work, leading Fielding to struggle throughout to figure out what his real subject is.

Quite frankly, Fielding does not really know what to do with the issue of male chastity, which is seemingly the central focus of the text. Battestin has argued persuasively that the issue is integral to the latitudinarian Christian ethos of *Joseph Andrews*:

> Joseph Andrews' chastity, however, has wider implications than merely the preservation of his virginity. Like their biblical prototypes, Abraham and Joseph, Fielding's good men exemplify the sum of the individual's duty to God, society, and himself. Adams' personification of true faith expressed through chastity comprehends the first two and Joseph's charity the last.[21]

But such a formulation reduces Joseph Andrews and Abraham Adams to allegorical figures, and, although allegorical elements certainly appear in Fielding's texts, the nature of his enterprise requires that they be subsumed to the exigencies of a realistic plot. Joseph's chastity may indeed be integral to Fielding's moral purpose, but it serves little purpose with regard to the text's overall narrative design.

Granted, the preservation of his chastity serves as the ostensible impetus for Joseph's journey, just as the quest for wisdom may be said to serve as the impetus for Tom Jones's. However, unlike Tom's quest, which masterfully combines the allegorical and the causal, Joseph's journey (except for the brief struggle with Betty in the inn) has nothing to do with the situation that triggered it—his resistance to Lady Booby's wiles.[22] Once Joseph has left Lady Booby's house, where he claims he is in some danger of forgetting "every word Parson Adams had ever said to me" (JA 47), there is no actual suspense about whether he will retain his chastity. Traveling with his mentor, Adams, and the chaste heroine, Fanny, he has no incentive to go against his own principles, and Fielding makes clear that the external threat is nil: "How ought Man to rejoice, that his Chastity is always in his own power, that if he hath sufficient Strength of Mind, he hath always a competent Strength of Body to defend himself: and cannot, like a poor weak Woman, be ravished against his Will" (87). As Jill Campbell argues in her ambitious study of Fielding and gender, the very fact that male chastity is in a man's own power mitigates against its significance: "the relative invulnerability of male chastity to coercion makes it less valued, less available as a privileged symbol of self-determination—the symbol on which Pamela's story centered."[23] Indeed, in the last three books of the text Fanny's attempts to preserve her chastity (rather than Joseph's attempts to preserve his) generate the greater suspense, Fielding demonstrating again that "a poor weak Woman" does not have her chastity in her own power. Fanny thus serves as a more interesting counter to Pamela than Joseph, a sobering reminder that against her desires a woman can be ravished and that male protection may be her only remedy. Because Fielding focuses only intermittently on Fanny, however, her function as an anti-Pamela is negligible.

In *Pamela* the heroine's chastity is integral to the resolution of the plot, for Richardson makes clear that Pamela's preservation of her virtue leads to her reward. In *Joseph Andrews* Fielding drops any sort of causal connection; Joseph's preservation of his virtue has nothing to do with his final outcome. In book 4, although Lady Booby spitefully but ineffectually attempts to thwart Joseph's marriage plans, her role as a threat to his chastity disappears entirely; the two are never even alone together. By straining we might say it is Joseph's virtue that leads to his eventual reward, but Fielding makes no explicit connection between Joseph's effort to preserve his chastity and his elevation. In the road scenes we focus more on Joseph's other virtues, such as bravery, generosity, and humility, Fielding thereby suggesting that, if reward is to be had, it should not be because of one virtue's being touted above all others.[24]

Unlike Pamela, as well, Fielding's hero serves little in the way of an exemplary function with regard to his chastity.[25] He masters his own sexual urges certainly, resisting the seductive charms of Lady Booby and waiting until his wedding night to enjoy the lovely Fanny. But although Joseph thus exemplifies the good man, as Battestin argues, Fielding presents his behavior in a manner far more likely to elicit snickers than to inspire emulation. In the preface to book 1, Fielding sets us up to see Joseph's chastity as a joke, telling us that the "actual history" we are about to read "is an Instance of the great Good that Book *[Pamela]* is likely to do . . . since it will appear that it was by keeping the excellent Pattern of his Sister's Virtues before his Eyes that Mr. *Joseph Andrews* was chiefly enabled to preserve his Purity in the midst of such great Temptations" (*JA* 19–20). Fielding's scorn of Pamela's exemplary function makes us think that Joseph will be a pious hypocrite in imitating her and that we would be so in imitating him. We remember not Joseph's sound sentiments as he defends male chastity to Lady Booby, but Fielding's piling up of various comical analogies as he attempts—professedly in vain—to describe the look on Lady Booby's face as she listens to the defense. Too, considering that Joseph bases his defense on sentiments he has garnered from the letters of Pamela, we have a hard time taking his professions seriously, especially in that they are so sententiously expressed.

Certainly Joseph is no exemplar to the other characters in the text either. According to the argument of *Pamela* the heroine's chaste behavior brings about the reform of the rakish Mr. B. and prompts the neighboring gentry to take stock of their own moral lapses. Joseph's determination to preserve his chastity has no similar effect on Lady Booby, who is, on the contrary, disgusted. No one lauds him, as people do Pamela, for the shining example of virtue he presents. Joseph clearly is neither a Pamela nor a Grandison, to invoke a later Richardsonian avatar of chastity.

As readers we are probably far more likely to be impressed by Joseph's sexuality than his ability to keep it in check. From the outset Fielding draws our attention to Joseph's "great Endowments" (*JA* 20), ensuring we keep in mind the titillating possibilities of the phrase by likening Joseph's early occupation at the Booby estate to that of "the god Priapus" (21). Fielding dwells on Joseph's physicality: the "Legs and Thighs . . . formed in the exactest Proportion," the "broad and brawny" shoulders, the "wanton Ringlets" of his "nut-brown" hair, the dark eyes "as full of Sweetness as of Fire," the "Cheeks, in which his Blood glowed" (38). Bursting with virility Joseph makes an incongruous figure in a sustained argument for male chastity.

The chastity motif is actually more interesting for what it undesignedly illuminates about gender and class issues than for the purpose it fulfills in moving the narrative along.[26] To a certain extent Joseph's chastity serves as a foil against which Fielding can display—and disparage—female sexual voraciousness. Lady Booby, Mrs. Slipslop, and Betty all are subject to various degrees of ridicule for their aggressive sexuality. Indeed Slipslop's pimply face, piggy eyes, cowlike breasts, and uneven gait make her passion for the pretty Joseph appear unnatural and monstrous, and the epic simile with which Fielding describes the scene renders her comic and bestial:

> As when a hungry Tigress, who long had traversed the Woods in fruitless search, sees within the Reach of her Claws a Lamb, she prepares to leap on her Prey; or a voracious Pike, of immense Size, surveys through the liquid Element a Roach or Gudgeon which cannot escape her Jaws, opens them wide to swallow the little Fish: so did Mrs. *Slipslop* prepare to lay her violent amorous Hands on the poor *Joseph*. (*JA* 33–34)

Although Fielding's descriptions of the failed seductions may make us laugh, he makes clear that we should find female aggressiveness no laughing matter. Unharnessed female sexuality sets a snare for the innocent hero. The motif occurs throughout Fielding's novels, wherein it is the women who seduce (or try to seduce) the heroes, not the other way around. In fact Fielding implies that, if left to themselves, Tom Jones and Billy Booth would be sexually circumspect. Even the exemplary Joseph is tempted at one point, a sign of the threat posed by female sexuality.

There is never any question that Joseph's preservation of chastity will lead to the same type of reward—hypergamy—granted to his illustrious "sister." Although Lady Booby at one point actually contemplates marriage with Joseph, she is well aware that it will lead to her fall rather than to his rise: "Marry a Footman! Distraction! Can I afterwards bear the Eyes of my Acquaintance?" (*JA* 327). Hypergamy can elevate women, but not men. Only when Joseph is revealed as the son of the gentleman Wilson does he become an eligible marriage partner for Lady Booby, but as this revelation also clears up the incest threat that had renewed her hopes, the issue becomes moot. Although a woman cannot engineer Joseph's rise, a man can; upon arriving at the Booby estate, Joseph's supposed brother-in-law, Mr. Booby, dresses him like a gentleman and resolves that he shall hereafter be regarded as such. More important, the revelation that Joseph's true father is the gentleman Wilson rather than Gaffar Andrews enables his change in status, marking yet another shift from the *Pamela* model.

By centering the chastity issue on a male protagonist the text highlights the asymmetrical situation of men and women in Fielding's society, but that very asymmetry works against any clear parodic aim.[27] Although Joseph's status as the chaste male hero leads to some of the funniest scenes in the text and some of the most interesting insights on gender and class, it functions as a joke with no clear purpose. The parodic underpinnings confuse rather than enlighten us as to Fielding's aim in putting forward his new species.

The text is somewhat more successful in its employment of the picaresque elements borrowed from Cervantes. The extensive view of the English countryside, the many English types that Joseph and Adams encounter on their journey, the wonderfully comic set pieces, and the interpolated stories that allow Fielding to play with other styles and genres not only bespeak his indebtedness to his Spanish forebear but also demonstrate his ability to render his borrowings uniquely his own. Too, the deluded wanderings of Fielding's secondary protagonist, the lovable innocent Abraham Adams, are deliberately meant to recall those of Don Quixote. Fielding ensures that we make the connection, particularly during Adams's farcical rescue of the effeminate Beau Didapper from the "witch" Mrs. Slipslop.

Whereas Cervantes uses Quixote to criticize the romance genre, Fielding is not quite sure what to do with Adams. Later writers, such as Charlotte Lennox and Jane Austen, employ quixotic protagonists to fulfill a purpose similar to Cervantes's. In *The Female Quixote* Lennox pokes fun at the Continental romances that lead Arabella into a series of misadventures, while in *Northanger Abbey* Austen ridicules the gothic fictions that delude Catherine Morland into regarding General Tilney as another Montoni. A Quixote-like figure might well serve Fielding's purpose, enabling him to condemn the sorts of fiction against which his text will stand as a corrective. But the only text we see Adams reading is his hand-copied edition of Aeschylus, certainly no target for Fielding's satire.

Adams's problem is not that he reads the wrong materials but that he substitutes reading for experience, as we see during his debate with the cynical worldly-wise innkeeper at the end of book 2. Adams has less in common with Quixote than with those figures of deluded goodness—such as Squire Allworthy, Amelia, and Dr. Harrison—that we find in Fielding's subsequent novels. Through such figures Fielding points toward the paradox of true goodness: lacking the worldly experience to discern evil, true goodness often unknowingly facilitates evil's cause. Adams, Fielding suggests, would do better to get his nose out of a book and acquire some worldly wisdom. In all, rather than serving to expose the falsity of contemporary fiction, Adams's Quixote-like behavior serves to expose the chicanery and venality of contemporary types. Fielding, however, runs into difficulties as he tries to align Adams's behavior with his moral stature, for the ridiculous situations in which Adams finds himself threaten to divest him entirely of our respect; we have a hard time taking seriously the moral pronouncements of the man who tangles in bed with the bearded Mrs. Slipslop.[28]

Although Adams's adventures afford a source of humor, ultimately the true picaresque does not suit Fielding's purpose, for a journey that leads to fighting with windmills covers no new ground. The meandering, quasi-random structure of the picaresque leaves Fielding with little to do but show the snares laid for innocence. Fielding's main hero, Joseph Andrews, cannot simply wander. Through his journey Fielding must establish the legitimate basis for moral, and by extension literary, authority. At the time Fielding is writing, such authority can no longer be assumed as intrinsic to traditional forms—whether they be the upper classes or the established genres—although Fielding is reluctant to abandon entirely his allegiance to them. Authority must be substantiated through action. Joseph Andrews must prove himself as he journeys toward a definite destination, just as *Joseph Andrews* must demonstrate the soundness of the critical principles on which it is based. Fielding thus takes on the difficult task of turning the casual progress of the picaresque into the causal development of the bildungsroman.

Fielding draws upon both the bildungsroman structure and the birth-mystery plot as a way of establishing the authority of Joseph Andrews/*Joseph Andrews*. Like Tom Jones, Joseph is in effect a foundling, bearing a borrowed name as he journeys toward an identity that he will substantiate along the way. By withholding the true origins of his hero Fielding compels us to evaluate him according to his merit rather than his birth. But by putting forward a traditionally romantic solution to the mystery of Joseph's birth Fielding also favors tradition.

Although the overall plot of *Joseph Andrews* bears striking similarities to that of *Tom Jones*, the uneven structure of it shows that Fielding had not yet learned to exploit the possibilities of his materials effectively. Tom Jones's need for self-discovery takes on real urgency, and his journey toward knowledge constitutes both an understanding of his own character and a discovery of his origins, the argument of the text progressing with structural inevitability. In *Joseph Andrews*, on the other hand, Joseph has little to learn except his origins, and the downplaying of the hermeneutic code makes the eventual revelation seem improvised.

It has been argued that Joseph grows and develops during his journey, but such arguments are strained.[29] He certainly has increasing occasion to manifest his bravery and demonstrate his adherence to principles of right, but overall he ends as he begins—a good-hearted, heroic young man, although a bit of a dullard. He lacks the "lack" that would provide his story with narrative drive. In many ways his situation is akin to that of such heroines of eighteenth-century novels as Evelina, Miss Sidney Biddulph, and Fielding's own Amelia, whose perfections entail that the narrative interest must derive from startling incidents and events, from external rather than internal crises. The narrative interest in *Joseph Andrews* is deflected from the good behavior of its hero, which is a given, to the bad or faulty behavior of those around him. Even when Joseph chastises Adams for recommending stoicism while giving way to passion himself, the scene is less a demonstration of his having surpassed his mentor, as J. Paul Hunter argues, than an opportunity for Fielding affectionately to poke fun at Adams's foibles.[30]

A greater potential for narrative drive occurs in the embedded tale of Mr. Wilson. Battestin calls the apparently irrelevant digression "the philosophic, as well as structural, center of *Joseph Andrews*."[31] I would add that it provides Fielding with the model for a bildungsroman structure that he would use to advantage in his subsequent two novels. Although intrinsically good-hearted, Wilson lacks the discretion or (to use a term that Fielding invokes in his next novel) prudence to escape the snares of corrupt London society, and it is only after he has reached the nadir of what Battestin terms his "rake's progress" in the London prison that he presumably comes to a self-recognition that will enable him to lead the exemplary life in which Adams and Joseph find him. Although the tale suffers from being told as a retrospective summary in the first person, it nonetheless sets up an integral connection between the events that occur and the hero's development, a connection that Fielding later employs with varying success in the stories of Tom Jones and Billy Booth.

Because Joseph, on the other hand, has little to learn on his journey, the incidents that occur often appear random, and it seems they could just as easily follow a different order. Granted, the birth-mystery motif mitigates against an entirely casual plot structure. After all, the encounters with the generous peddler and with Mr. Wilson bring about the eventual resolution—the discovery that Joseph is Wilson's son. Until the final few chapters, however, we have no idea that there is indeed a mystery, unless we are canny enough to catch the ambiguous phrasing of the false genealogy Fielding gives us at the outset of the novel: "Mr. Joseph Andrews, the Hero of our ensuing History, was esteemed to be the only Son of Gaffar and Gammer Andrews" (*JA* 20). If so, we might suspect that Wilson's story of his kidnapped child has some bearing on Joseph's fate, although we would be at a loss as to exactly what that might be.

The downplaying—or even elision—of the mystery does manage to bring the meritocracy issue to the forefront. For most of the text, we must regard our hero as a true member of the servant class, Fielding seemingly making the Richardsonian suggestion that the lower classes have as much claim to moral authority and literary representation as their "betters." Fielding explicitly argues throughout for merit over birth. After providing the false genealogy for Joseph, which links his hero to "an excellent Cudgel-player" (*JA* 20), he argues that honor should be determined by virtue, not station:

> But suppose for Argument's sake we should admit that he had no Ancestors at all, but had sprung up, according to the modern Phrase, out of a Dunghill, as the *Athenians* pretended they themselves did from the Earth, would not this *Autokopros* have been justly entitled to all the Praise arising from his own Virtues? Would it not be hard, that a Man who hath no Ancestors should therefore be render'd incapable of acquiring Honour, when we see so many who have no Virtues, enjoying the Honour of their Forefathers? (21)

According to these sentiments, origin is immaterial; issue is all. Joseph himself is presented as an original of heroism, in a passage wherein Fielding explains his inability to come up with an appropriate simile for Joseph's courage: "Let those therefore that describe Lions and Tigers, and Heroes fiercer than both, raise their Poems or Plays with the Simile of *Joseph Andrews*, who is himself above the reach of any Simile" (241). Joseph Andrews/*Joseph Andrews* is the pattern to which others shall refer, and one may discover the merit and authority of each without needing the validation of an illustrious ancestry.

The actions of various characters support the argument that true merit is not class-based. The lowly postilion clothes Joseph when the well-born passengers will not. The peddler pays the travelers' reckoning after the preacher Trulliber has refused to help them. The most egregious villain in the piece—the roasting squire—is one of the wealthiest. No class has a lease on villainy or virtue, and the poorer members of society often come across as the purer.

Even Lady Booby would seem to place higher value on merit than birth. When justifying to Slipslop her inclination for Joseph, she expresses sentiments that echo those of the Fielding author figure:

> Is he not more worthy of Affection than a dirty Country Clown, tho' born of a Family as old as the Flood, or an idle worthless Rake, or little puisny Beau of Quality? And yet these we must condemn ourselves to, in order to avoid the Censure of the World; to shun the Contempt of others, we must ally ourselves to those we despise; we must prefer Birth, Title and Fortune to real Merit. (*JA* 296)

Yet by putting such sentiments in the mouth of Lady Booby, Fielding problematizes them; she is, after all, concerned with other endowments than Joseph's merit, and she attempts to explain away her desire to bed her servant as attraction to his worth.

More important, whether such sentiments are voiced by the all-knowing author/narrator or by the self-deluded Lady Booby, they are to a certain extent problematized by the solution to the mystery. The plot culminates in both an anagnorisis and a peripeteia, although in a much more limited sense than those that occur in *Tom Jones*. Just as the form of *Joseph Andrews*, "discovered" by the author figure, revives the missing genre of the *Margites*, Joseph is the lost "pattern," finally discovered by his "author," Mr. Wilson. Once he has been recognized for who he is, Joseph can marry Fanny and escape the schemes of Lady Booby, although his position as Mr. Booby's supposed brother-in-law has already enabled him to do so in part. Perhaps even more important, he can take his place as Mr. Wilson's heir, shedding the trappings of servitude that have disallowed recognition of his moral authority. Although Wilson is no Allworthy, he nonetheless appears at the end of the novel as the most fitting representative of the upper classes. As he embraces his heir he provides Joseph with the material worth that confirms and reinforces his spiritual worth—a worth he has actually inherited from his other "father," Abraham Adams. Because Joseph is a gentleman-born, his noble actions demonstrate not only that merit can occur no matter what the rank, but also that merit can persist no matter what the demotion. Ultimately, Joseph's meaning—his moral authority—derives from his relationship with his father; he is what he is because he is who he is—a man of property.[32] The text may seem to argue for a meritocracy, but it retreats from this position at the end by giving Joseph a genteel heritage.[33]

Nevertheless, we are left with a double image of the protagonist—Joseph the footman, Joseph the gentleman's son. At the sudden revelation of his true parentage we cannot suddenly rid ourselves of our notion that he is somehow good simply because he is good, and not because he comes of noble forebears. Fielding tries to have it both ways; his ostensibly progressive argument may circle back to the regressive romantic motif that genteel birth will out, but before it does so it covers new ground, leaving a space open for the new.

Fielding's ambivalent feelings about the link between birth and worth appear also in the figure of Fanny, another foundling whose origins finally come to light. Like Joseph, Fanny is presented as someone whose station appears incommensurate with her breeding, according to traditional ways of thinking: "she had a natural Gentility, superior to the Acquisition of Art, and which surprized all who beheld her" (*JA* 153). Like Joseph, too, the discovery of her true birth elevates her, although not as high as Joseph; she simply goes from being the nameless child for whom Sir Thomas Booby paid three guineas to being the child of Gaffar and Gammer Andrews—the position previously occupied by Joseph. While she is yet a foundling Mr. Booby attempts to talk Joseph out of marrying her, arguing that Joseph lacks the wherewithal to elevate Fanny as he did Pamela: "And besides, Sir, as you civilly throw my Marriage with your Sister in my Teeth, I must teach you the wide Difference between us; my Fortune enabled me to please myself; and it would have been as overgrown a Folly in me to have omitted it, as in you to do it" (302). Joseph's impassioned rejoinder that he will choose Fanny over the social elevation promised by Mr. Booby puts us on the side of merit over birth, and we are struck not with the soundness of Mr. Booby's argument but with the blatant hypocrisy with which he makes it. Fielding also uses the occasion to take yet another swipe at Richardson's paragon, exposing Pamela's humility as a sham as she, too, tries to talk Joseph out of his marriage: "I am no longer Pamela Andrews, I am now this Gentleman's Lady, and as such am above her" (302).

Although continuing to deride Richardson's upwardly mobile character, Fielding ends up in ostensible agreement with his argument for upward mobility. After initially feeling some "Reluctance," Mr. Wilson agrees to his son's marriage with the humble Fanny, determining that "the Disadvantages of Birth and Fortune might be compensated" (*JA* 340). Yet Fielding finesses the issue once again. By the time of her marriage Fanny is no longer a nameless foundling but the sister-in-law of Mr. Booby, bringing to the union a dowry of two thousand pounds. Certainly, Fielding demonstrates that worth resides in the lower classes and that, in Abraham Adams's unwittingly felicitous phrase, "there are several Boobys who are Squires" (325), but he cannot quite relinquish his conviction that worth and birth are indeed interrelated.

The shifting class affiliations of the characters highlight Fielding's struggle to mediate between, in McKeon's terms, conservative and progressive forces—to demonstrate that true worth must be proved but that traditional forms have not lost their meaning. Like its improperly named hero, *Joseph Andrews* similarly is marked by contradictions as Fielding struggles to come up with a viable aesthetic for the kind of fiction he is writing. He simultaneously claims to bring forward a new "species" and provides the text with a venerable ancestry, but he never quite aligns these competing claims. He is still uncertain about the nature of his literary inheritance.

In many ways *Joseph Andrews* is a raw text, for Fielding had not yet learned how to wrest authority from the apparent reconciliation of conflicting forces. It lacks the consistent self-consciousness as to intention and effect that renders *Tom Jones* a virtual novel of the novel.[34] Whereas the plot of the author in *Tom Jones* is sustained and developed, leading to a complex thematic intertwining with Tom's story, in *Joseph Andrews* it is sketchy and tentative, lacking the thematic resonance we find in the subsequent text. Although both texts feature a journey toward nomination, only in *Tom Jones* does the final revelation follow inevitably from what has come before, the seemingly casual transformed into the causal. *Joseph Andrews* is ultimately a novel in search of a character—in its most saturated sense—aiming toward a culmination that it never quite realizes. However, although *Joseph Andrews* may lack the rigor and consistency of *Tom Jones*, its very flaws provide us with insight into the development of the novel form and make us conscious of the generic expectations we now bring to a text that itself attempted to bring such expectations into being.

CHAPTER TWO

Written by "A Lady"

Sir Edward was surprized; he had perhaps little expected to meet with so spirited an opposition to his will. "Where Edward in the name of wonder (said he) did you pick up this unmeaning Gibberish? You have been studying Novels I suspect."
—Jane Austen, "Love and Freindship"

If a woman writer replicates an ideology that suspects women as public voices, contradictions will bloody her. The status of her text will resemble that of a bastard. Its mere existence challenges hegemonic notions of appropriate birth, but its acceptance of the label of bastard, if done without the ironic self-consciousness of Lear's Edmund, will simultaneously endorse those notions. —Catherine Stimpson, "Ad/d Feminam"

NORTHANGER ABBEY has the dubious distinction of being the first of Jane Austen's novels to be accepted for publication and the last, along with *Persuasion*, to be actually published. It is tempting to regard this posthumous volume as felicitously marking both the starting point and the end point of Austen's literary career. The volume's inapt but revealing designations of "romance" and "novel" for, respectively, the earlier and later text simultaneously sum up Austen's literary maturation and encapsulate an entire history of changing literary fashions. The later work returns to several concerns treated in the earlier one—the fallible autocratic patriarch, the forbidden engagement, the foibles that take place in a fashionable watering place, the spirited defense of women's ways of knowing—as if Austen wants to return to where she began but also to provide a deeper, more complex vision. Yet the aesthetic satisfaction we may derive from the posthumous volume is imposed from without; Austen herself had no control over the disposition of her first and final novels.

Whether we should even regard *Northanger Abbey* as Austen's "first" novel is open to question. Cassandra Austen's note on the dates of the novels' composition indicates that *Elinor and Marianne*, its revision as *Sense and Sensibility*, and *First Impressions* (the early version of *Pride and Prejudice*) predate *Northanger Abbey*.[1] Critics have traditionally assumed, however, that *Pride and Prejudice*, at least, was substantially revised before its publication date of 1813 and that, despite the change in the name of the heroine and the title, the *Northanger Abbey* of 1818 is substantially the same as the draft of 1803, when it was first submitted for publication under the title *Susan*.[2]

Certainly, *Northanger Abbey* is the only one of the fictions that Austen submitted for publication to address directly the question of what the novel should be and do. We can thus make a case that it serves as a bridge between the juvenilia, which explicitly satirize contemporary generic conventions, and *Sense and Sensibility* and *Pride and Prejudice*, which implicitly take for granted the soundness of the generic conventions that they assume. The satire in *Sense and Sensibility* is, after all, directed at a mode—the Romantic—rather than a genre. Like *Joseph Andrews*, *Northanger Abbey* serves as a counterfiction, self-consciously putting itself forward as an alternative to the prevailing narrative fictions of the time—the sentimental novel of a young woman's entry into society, the gothic novel, and the Wollstonecraftian novel of female oppression.[3]

Similarly, in presenting themselves as counterfictions, both *Joseph Andrews* and *Northanger Abbey* address contemporary conflicts over epistemological and moral authority. Only Austen, however, acknowledges that such conflicts may have a gender bias. Fielding's text foregrounds the contest between meritocracy and aristocracy, but the contest occurs in a masculine realm. Female characters are there to foster or impede the hero's aims, not to put forward a competing point of view. For Fielding a masculine perspective is the norm, a feminine perspective beside the point. As he "originates" a genre he simply bypasses the feminine (or even excludes it) through linking his production to the traditionally masculine epic form.

Austen, on the other hand, attempts not to originate a genre but to establish the legitimacy of the feminocentric novel. *Northanger Abbey* puts itself forward as an alternative not only to contemporary fiction but to a system of representation linked with patriarchal privilege—a system that can both include and exclude the novel genre depending on how well it accommodates itself to the master narrative of the culture, which defines women and their concerns as secondary or negligible. Indeed, by the time

Austen begins writing, the novel has for the most part become gendered feminine in a world encoded masculine. Austen must both criticize the contemporary novel for inadequately representing reality and assert its suitability for aptly representing women's experience. She must make the case that women's experience deserves representation—that Catherine Morland's concern over whether Henry Tilney will dance with her deserves our attention as much as Joseph Andrews's worries about saving Fanny from her abductors. Austen simultaneously defends and deplores female fictions and the male critique of them, performing an audacious juggling act that takes our breath away even as the colored balls fall from formation and roll off into corners. Like *Joseph Andrews*, *Northanger Abbey* ultimately fails to subsume its conflicting impulses to the overarching plot, in its failings testifying to the difficulties besetting Austen and her sister novelists.

By the late eighteenth century the genre of the novel was well on its way to being established.[4] Writers no longer made recourse to explicit metacommentary on the generic status of their texts, such as occurs during the authorial intrusions in *Joseph Andrews* and *Tom Jones*. Nevertheless, the generic legitimacy of the novel was still being called into question, particularly when the genre was perceived as feminine. Although women took to novel writing in unprecedented numbers during the eighteenth century, such quantitative output did not guarantee critical acceptance—and probably even worked against it.[5] Checklists of prose fiction during the period show a fairly even distribution of texts by men and women, with women writers predominating as the century drew to a close. But the overall number of texts tended to be published anonymously. Whether we should, as Virginia Woolf suggests, regard that appellation as a sign of a woman writer is not ultimately answerable. Certainly, however, toward the end of the century, the titles of the "Anonymous" texts increasingly betray a "feminine" sensibility, for example, *Edward and Sophia. A Novel of Incident. By a Lady* or the similarly titled *The History of Miss Pittborough. In a Series of Letters. By a Lady*.[6] That the majority of eighteenth-century writers refused to provide their "offspring" with the name of its author suggests that the taint of illegitimacy still clung to novels written by women or addressing women's concerns. The negative portrait of the inveterate letter writer "Scrivonia," appearing in a 1775 edition of *The London Magazine*, indicates the sort of contempt meted out to a woman who wrote merely letters: "her pen is avoided as a kind of common prostitute, that retails its favours without partiality to every stranger who may chance to fall in their way."[7] It is little wonder that the woman novelist, granting her "favors" to a wider public, often chose to withhold her name.

Just as legitimizing offspring traditionally depends on a father's acknowledgment, the novel's legitimation depended upon masculine intervention. When Fielding, who proudly affixed his name to his novels, asserts his authority against "the Authors of immense Romances or the modern Novels and Atalantis Writers" (*JA* 187), his singling out of the works of Mrs. Delarivière Manley counterposes the implicitly masculine epistemological validity of his text to the implicitly feminine falsifications of hers. In *Tom Jones* the criteria Fielding prescribes for the would-be novelist—an extensive familiarity with the classics and an acquaintance with all walks of life—precludes the majority of eighteenth-century women. From its putative inception the legitimate, "literary" novel was gendered masculine.

However, although women writers could not meet Fielding's criteria, they could write about that realm of life with which they were acquainted—the domestic. The domestic or, more broadly, feminocentric novel could be praised for its capacity to inculcate proper feminine values. Jane Spencer points out that "Eighteenth-century commentators were full of praise for women's didactic writing, their sentiments, their knowledge of the heart, their knowledge of their own sex."[8] As Nancy Armstrong maintains, the domestic novel itself functioned as a sort of conduct book, constructing a feminine domestic ideal.[9] Yet, as Laura Runge argues, the gender hierarchy underlying eighteenth-century literary criticism both limited the subject matter that female writers could address and belittled them for that limitation: "Criticism placed female authors in a specific and confined critical sphere while it located male authors in another, more respected field. Female novelists conformed to the standards of modestly written, pleasing tales of domestic harmony, while male authors strove for original plots and intellectual challenges."[10] The female writer thus found herself caught in a double bind: she was forced to restrict herself to certain subjects, but in doing so she precluded her work from being taken seriously. Paradoxically, she employed her talents in a demonstration calculated to undermine them.

Despite the qualified critical approval accorded the feminocentric novel for its apparent inculcation of proper feminine values, its epistemological and moral authority continued to be called into question. Conduct books, including those written by women, denigrated the genre that supposedly complemented them. Hannah More regarded the novel as a threat to proper female education: "Will it not be ascribed to a captious singularity if I venture to remark that real knowledge and real piety, though they have gained in many instances, have suffered in others from that profusion of little, amusing, sentimental books with which the youthful library overflows?" Rather than inculcating virtues, such books tended to inspire "a self-complacency, a self-gratulation," causing readers to assume "a mere political piety."[11] In effect, in modeling themselves according to the conduct-book heroines populating the novels, young women would acquire the form—not the spirit—of virtue. In a passage that Austen's Fanny Price might have found baffling, More rails against "the hot-bed of a circulating library" on the grounds that it encourages superficial intellectual skills.[12]

More's attack on the novel extends to what she considers its self-generating tendencies. More paints a satirical portrait of the female novel reader, foolishly venturing from reading to writing:

> Who are those ever multiplying authors, that with unparalleled fecundity are overstocking the world with their quick succeeding progeny? They are novel writers; the easiness of whose productions is at once the cause of their own fruitfulness, and of the almost infinitely numerous race of imitators to whom they give birth. Such is the frightful facility of this species of composition, that every raw girl while she reads is tempted to fancy that she can also write. . . . [A] thorough paced novel reading Miss, at the close of every tissue of hackney'd adventures, feels within herself the stirring impulse of corresponding genius, and triumphantly exclaims, "And I too am an author!"[13]

Thus, not only do novels inspire young women to develop superficial charms, but they also prompt them to display their superficiality in literary productions of their own, giving them the temerity to lay claim to the masculine prerogative of authorship. More describes the self-generating tendencies of the novel in terms of a fertility gone wild, giving way to seemingly monstrous growth. If a woman writes a story, it is not because it is meaningful in itself but only because "writing a novel suggests itself as the best soother of her sorrows!" More disregards the fact that novel writing might enable a display of female artistry, professionalism, or ingenuity. Moreover, she ignores (perhaps not surprisingly) the way such an endeavor might constitute one of the few means for economic independence among middle-class women of the time. For More, novel writing serves as "the only resource which the idle and the illiterate have always in their power."[14] As a remedy to women's novel reading, she offers the following list: "Watt's or Duncan's little book of Logic, some parts of Mr. Locke's Essay on the Human Understanding, and Bishop Butler's Analogy"—significantly, a list that is insistently gendered masculine.[15]

It was not only the conservative More who attacked the novel genre. Her political opposite Mary Wollstonecraft similarly regarded the novel as a threat to female improvement.[16] Like More, Wollstonecraft blames the novel for fostering superficial, even corrupt, values in women: "These are the women who are amused by the reveries of the stupid novelists, who, knowing little of human nature, work up stale tales, and describe meretricious scenes, all retained in a sentimental jargon, which equally tend to corrupt the taste, and draw the heart aside from its daily duties."[17] Wollstonecraft's own novel *Maria, or The Wrongs of Woman* suggests that Maria's reading gives a "romantic turn" to her thoughts, which leads to her disastrous attraction to Venables: "[my uncle] brought me books, for which I had a passion, and they conspired with his conversation to make me form an ideal picture of life."[18] Unlike More, Wollstonecraft does temper her criticism of the novel, regarding "any kind of reading . . . better than leaving a blank still a blank." Furthermore, she suggests, such reading might provide "some foundation to work upon," inducing women to graduate to works of a higher moral and intellectual stamp. Nevertheless, Wollstonecraft's discussion of novels makes clear that they are lesser productions, generally to be put forward as bad examples: "if a judicious person, with some turn for humour, would read several to a young girl, and point out both by tones and apt comparisons with pathetic incidents and heroic characters in history, how foolishly and ridiculously they caricatured human nature, just opinions might be substituted instead of romantic sentiments."[19] For Wollstonecraft, the novel is ultimately more deserving of ridicule than praise.

Writing at the outset of the nineteenth century, Austen could not have helped but be aware of the consistent, insistent cultural message that the novel in its most popular manifestation was an inferior genre. And it was inferior precisely because of its connection with the feminine realm—the "raw girl" writers of limited knowledge, churning out "meretricious scenes" of sentiment that corrupt the intellect and sensibilities of female readers. Austen's oft-cited letter to James Stanier Clarke—written after she had three successful novels published and after he had asked her to dedicate a future work to the Prince Regent—displays an awareness of the limitations constraining the female writer and the feminocentric text. Replying to Clarke's self-serving suggestion that she "delineate in some future Work the Habits of Life and Character and enthusiasm of a Clergyman" (Letter 113a, *LSC* 430), Austen self-consciously addresses her literary inadequacies with regard to "serious" subjects:

> I am quite honoured by your thinking me capable of drawing such a clergyman as you gave the sketch of in your note of Nov. 16th. But I assure you I am *not*. The comic part of the character I might be equal to, but not the good, the enthusiastic, the literary. Such a man's conversation must at times be on subjects of science and philosophy, of which I know nothing; or at least be occasionally abundant in quotations and allusions which a woman

> who, like me, knows only her own mother tongue, and has read very little in that, would be totally without the power of giving. A classical education, or at any rate a very extensive acquaintance with English literature, ancient and modern, appears to me quite indispensable for the person who would do any justice to your clergyman. (Letter 120, *LSC* 443)

Although, as Susan Lanser suggests, the passage can be read ironically, its surface meaning could very well be echoing the magisterial Fielding of *Tom Jones*, who argues that the skillful novelist needs a wide acquaintance with life.[20] But, whereas a writer/critic such as Fielding would disqualify anyone who lacks a classical education and an extensive knowledge of literature from writing novels at all, Austen simply disqualifies herself (and by extension her sister writers) from a certain kind of subject.

However, the sort of disqualification that Austen makes is value-laden. Austen herself sets up a distinction between a talent for the "comic" and a talent for rendering "the good, the enthusiastic, the literary" that Clarke's subject would require—a distinction very much in keeping with the eighteenth-century marginalization of the feminocentric text. Austen does, of course, implicitly connect her inability to tackle such an ostensibly weighty subject with the lack of educational opportunities available to women, but the criticism is muted—indicative of the ticklish situation in which Austen found herself as she framed a reply to the influential, self-important Clarke. Austen's concluding "boast" in the letter to Clarke—that she is "the most unlearned and uninformed female who ever dared to be an authoress"—may be merely a conventional disclaimer; in the mature works, we have no indication that Austen herself deplored the "limitations" of the subject matter that she did address. But it nevertheless reinforces the notion of female incompetence.[21]

In many of the juvenilia Austen advances the notion that the novel genre is trifling, silly, even harmful. She parodies the sentimental excesses of her sister novelists in such works as "Frederic and Elfrida" and "Edgar and Emma," stories that appear in the early *Volume the First* and that are predicated upon the nonsensical complications besetting the eponymous lovers. The 1790 epistolary "Love and Freindship" mounts a sustained attack against both the mode of sensibility and the literary conventions of the sentimental novel. The self-centered heroine, Laura, considers that her exquisitely heightened sensibilities excuse all manner of improprieties, even going so far as to justify stealing on these grounds: "and having agreed together that it would be a proper treatment of so vile a Wretch as Macdonald to deprive him of money, perhaps dishonestly gained, it was determined that the next time we should either of us happen to go that way, we would take one or more of the Bank notes from the drawer" (*MW*

96). Just as Fielding reduces Pamela's "vartue" to flagrant gold digging, so does Austen reduce Laura's sensibility and, by extension, that of the sentimental heroine in general to sheer selfishness, a position strikingly akin to More's. Whereas the later *Sense and Sensibility* frames its attack on sensibility in a context that reclaims the novel genre and even makes a qualified case for sensibility's charms, "Love and Freindship" so links the literary devices of the sentimental novel with the vitiating exaltation of sensibility that the genre itself must be regarded as aesthetically and morally deficient.

Like *Shamela,* "Love and Freindship" and various other examples of the juvenilia deplore both the form and the content of contemporary fictional narrative. Sandra Gilbert and Susan Gubar have persuasively demonstrated that the object of Austen's satire is not simply the fictions themselves but the social conditions that make such fictions a viable model for female behavior: "Far from being the usual appeal for female sobriety and submission to domestic restraints so common in anti-romantic eighteenth-century literature, *Love and Freindship* attacks a society that trivializes female assertion by channeling it into the most ridiculous and unproductive forms of behavior."[22] Although many of these early works implicitly point to the limited realm to which the eighteenth-century heroine/writer/woman is relegated, they nevertheless openly mock the literary conventions primarily employed by Austen's sister writers. Mockery serves, after all, as another way of keeping women in their place, and the juvenilia explicitly undermine the feminocentric text. With hindsight we can see Austen's anger at woman's confined lot. However, by poking fun at the sentimental effusions, surprising coincidences, contrived dilemmas, and exotic locales of her sister authors, Austen ends up reinforcing the trivialization of woman's writing, adding her voice to the patriarchal chorus. As Alison Sulloway points out, although Austen satirizes "the very patriarchal systems that granted men absolute legal and social power over [women]," her "satirical purposes may have been so oblique that they have not been recognized for close to two centuries."[23] Austen's intention may be salutary, but as she provides no viable alternative, she risks injuring the profession to which she aspires.

Austen's mockery is not confined merely to women writers. She applies it as well to what we might call men's ways of knowing. Coming into its own during the eighteenth century, historical narrative was a province of male authority, predicated upon the notions of historical progress and definitive events engineered primarily by men. Austen's 1791 "History of England"—"By a partial, prejudiced, and ignorant Historian" (MW 138)—draws our attention to the way historical narrative has been shaped to advance a particular political agenda. She certainly makes no bones about advancing hers, asserting that she rides roughshod over facts in pursuit of her political purpose: "indeed the recital of any Events (except what I make myself) is uninteresting to me; my principal reason for undertaking the History of England being to prove the innocence of the Queen of Scotland" (149). It is significant that a great woman is the primary focus of Austen's history. To vindicate Charles I "from the Reproach of Arbitrary and tyrannical Government with which he has often been charged," Austen offers a telling non sequitur: "with one argument I am certain of satisfying every sensible and well disposed person whose opinions have been properly guided by a good Education—and this Argument is that he was a Stuart" (149). As Fielding does in *Joseph Andrews*, she undermines the veracity of historical representation, in this case by actually writing the falsified history and calling attention to its falsifications. If the novel presents a specious view of reality so too, Austen implies, do those weightier, more respectable tomes.

In some of the later juvenilia Austen begins to blunt her satirical edge, making a qualified case for the novel genre. The 1792 *Catharine, or The Bower* begins in seeming parody, with Catharine having "the misfortune, as many heroines have had before her, of losing her Parents when she was very young" (*MW* 192). But Austen soon drops the parodic tone, and with its story of false friends and domestic dissatisfactions the unfinished novel has more in common with the mature works than with the other juvenilia. *Catharine* even contains an incipient defense of the novel genre, although it is qualified by a comparison with historical narrative: "though She was well read in Modern history herself, she chose rather to speak first of Books of a lighter kind, of Books universally read and Admired, [and that have given rise perhaps to more frequent Arguments than any other of the same sort]" (199). The phrase in brackets, as R. W. Chapman notes, was originally canceled by Austen. Her cancellation here suggests she was unwilling to acknowledge that the novel's claim for literary merit was debatable. In the passage that follows, wherein Catharine/Kitty extols the merits of Charlotte Smith's *Emmeline* and *Ethelinde*, we are encouraged to align ourselves with the heroine's perspective, as opposed to that of the shallow Miss Stanley, who has skipped the "Descriptions of Grasmere" in *Ethelinde* because she "was in such a hurry to know the end of it" and devalues the novel because it is "so long" (199). The defense of the novel, the mockery of undiscerning novel readers, and the positive assessment of a sister novelist are anticipatory of the more extended metacommentary that Austen supplies in *Northanger Abbey*. In *Catharine* Austen moves beyond a potentially misogynistic satirical mode and begins to make a claim for the legitimacy of the feminocentric novel.

Although *Northanger Abbey* returns to the belittling mode of satire, it attempts at the same time to serve as a countersatire, belittling the belittlement. Austen wishes to ridicule the fantastic conventions of the feminocentric novel and simultaneously demonstrate/defend its ability to represent the reality of woman's experience. The novel appears like one of those gestalt-shift trick pictures, which can represent either a vase or a pair of lovers but never both at once. Drawing on the work of Carol Gilligan, Ismay Barwell sees such a gestalt-shift occurring as we attempt to locate a feminine point of view within a male-dominated society:

> a moral perspective is a set of organizing concepts and terms which provide the framework by means of which moral decisions and judgments are reached. These operate on the underlying nonmoral "facts" in an analogous way to that in which two sets of organizing concepts guide the interpretation of the black-and-white shapes to yield a rabbit picture or a duck picture. These two points of view are exclusive in that while one is looking at the shapes from the duck-picture perspective, one cannot also be looking at them from the rabbit-picture perspective, and vice versa.[24]

Throughout *Northanger Abbey* Austen maintains a dual moral perspective, at times inviting us to join in a patriarchal critique of the novel, at times encouraging us to embrace its feminocentric possibilities, and throughout keeping us unsettled with regard to the stance we should adopt.[25]

To pull off this delicate balancing act Austen resorts to a Fieldingesque metacommentary, relying on a characterized author figure to provide a legitimating gesture that otherwise might be disregarded in the surrounding satire. The well-known defense of the novel in chapter 5 is unique in Austen's mature work. In all her texts, we have, in varying degrees, the sense of an authorial presence; but only here do we have the author figure herself step forward, intruding into the fictional universe to comment upon it directly. Just as Fielding's author figure is insistently masculine Austen's is insistently feminine, championing women's concerns and ways of knowing. Fielding's metacommentaries, although aesthetically displeasing to Jamesian advocates of authorial unobtrusiveness, are integrated into the scheme of *Joseph Andrews*, and even more so into that of *Tom Jones*. The effect of the authorial intrusion in *Northanger Abbey*, however, is singularly jarring. Yet what we might see as Austen's uncharacteristic disregard of aesthetic concerns is testimony to her anxiety lest her satire of feminocentric novels be regarded merely as yet another condemnation of "the stupid novelists."

After all, Austen's defense of the novel is framed by a context that to a certain extent contradicts it. When Austen claims she "will not adopt that ungenerous and impolitic custom so common with novel writers, of degrading with their contemptuous censure the very performances, to the number of which they are themselves adding" (*NA* 37), she makes her assertion in the face of her own censure—mild, yet pointed—of the sentimental and gothic novels of her sister novelists. Too, the defense itself springs from a situation that undermines it—Catherine and Isabella shutting "themselves up to read novels together" (37). Their reading provides Isabella with the heroine-like language with which she can disguise her selfishness and sparks Catherine's gothic-induced delusions at the Abbey, motifs that argue against the novel's being a positive force.

Despite the contradictory context that frames it, Austen's defense makes a strong case for the importance of the feminocentric novel. Significantly, although Austen pleads for novels in general she cites only those written by women: "It is only Cecilia, or Camilla, or Belinda" (*NA* 38). It is as if she regards the battle of the books as being drawn up along gender lines; she opposes these texts against those of "the nine-hundredth abridger of the History of England, or of the man who collects and publishes in a volume some dozen lines of Milton, Pope, and Prior, with a paper from the Spectator, and a chapter from Sterne" (37)—a list that like More's is gendered masculine. The heroine of one novel may turn over the "insipid pages" of another "with disgust" (37), but according to Austen it is the *Spectator* that is calculated to "disgust a young person of taste," with its "improbable circumstances, unnatural characters, and topics of conversation," couched in language "frequently so coarse as to give no very favourable idea of the age that could endure it" (38). She here questions the reputed ease and familiarity of Addison's and Steele's styles and thus both puts forward a female-based canon and denigrates the supposed superiority of the male-based one. Yet she is aware, too, that the feminocentric novel must cease undermining its own aims and, with a fervent plea, makes clear the need for a female community: "Let us not desert one another; we are an injured body" (37). Her reproach of characters that do not champion the medium that gives them life applies equally to the women who invent those characters: "Alas! if the heroine of one novel be not patronized by the heroine of another, from whom can she expect protection and regard" (37). Heroines—both characters and writers—need to stick together, for they cannot expect protection and regard from the arbiters of contemporary culture.[26]

Elsewhere in the text Austen characteristically relies on the characters rather than the author figure to affirm her support of the novel. She proceeds at first by contraries, putting the condemnation of the novel genre in the mouth of a fool, the boorish John Thorpe: "I never read novels," he proclaims, adding by way of explanation that they "are all so full of nonsense and stuff" (*NA* 48). The questionable—and gender-based—literary judgments that follow, wherein Thorpe extols the racy *Tom Jones* and sensationalistic *The Monk* and condemns the feminocentric *Camilla*, confirm his ignorance, and by extension that of other "literary critics" who facilely dismiss the novel genre or judge it according to suspect standards.

Whereas the condemnation of the novel genre comes from a male character, so too, however, does the defense. Catherine herself may eagerly read novels, but when discussing them with Henry Tilney she proceeds very much along the lines of the "heroine" deplored by the author figure, who exclaims, "'Oh! it is only a novel!'" and "lays down her book with affected indifference, or momentary shame" (*NA* 38). Like her prim sister heroines, Catherine takes the inferiority of novels for granted, telling Henry: "they are not clever enough for you—gentlemen read better books" (106). We must assume that her assumptions about gentlemen's reading matter derive from her earlier encounter with Thorpe; their literary discussion had left her "humbled and ashamed" (48), and her words to Henry attempt to atone for her prior "ignorance," in keeping with her efforts at self-correction throughout the novel. Henry's reply, however, echoes not the pronouncements of Thorpe but those of the author figure: "The person, be it gentleman or lady, who has not pleasure in a good novel, must be intolerably stupid" (106.) He adds that young men "read nearly as many as women," citing his own reading of "hundreds and hundreds" (107). The passage is Austen's sly rejoinder to the common criticism that novel reading is a female vice, for the Oxford-educated Henry makes clear that not only do men do it but they enjoy doing it. The passage also suggests that Austen's authorial defense cannot in itself be relied upon to elevate the novel critically; she needs the voice of the wise "male" critic to validate her own.

Like Fielding, Austen is aware that the metacommentary in itself will not make a case for the value of the novel. The rest of the text must still demonstrate that the novel genre can indeed display "the greatest powers of the mind" (*NA* 38)—not simply by parodying what has gone before but by providing a viable alternative to prior novelistic conventions. Just as *Joseph Andrews* opposes itself to *Pamela* in order to evolve a "new" conception of the novel, *Northanger Abbey* opposes itself to popular subgenres in order to demonstrate what the feminocentric novel should and should not do.

From the outset Austen takes aim at the improbable incidents and idealized heroines found in the Burneyesque novels of the era. She indeed at times seems to be following Wollstonecraft's method for turning young women away from novels, ridiculing novelistic excesses in order to direct the readers toward something better. Whereas an early work like "Love and Freindship" satirizes such sentimental novels by exaggerating their dominant motifs, *Northanger Abbey* instead works by contraries, with

Austen pointedly violating expectations about heroines and their experiences, expectations that readers have picked up from prior reading. To a certain extent Austen's procedure recalls that of Charlotte Lennox in *The Female Quixote*, wherein Lennox invokes the term "heroine" in order to set up and then deflate her quixotic Arabella. Notably, however, Lennox gives Arabella great beauty and charm, thus fulfilling readers' expectations about the ideal nature of the heroine. Austen, on the other hand, emphasizes Catherine Morland's ordinariness. How can we regard Catherine as a heroine when she has "a thin awkward figure, a sallow skin without colour, dark lank hair, and strong features" (*NA* 13) and can "never learn or understand anything before she was taught" (14)? As Austen makes clear, these are unlikely qualities to readers who have been exposed to the physical and mental perfections of a Miss Sidney Biddulph, a Cecilia Beverly, a Lady Matilda Elmwood, an Emily St. Aubert. Yet how much more likely it is that the novel readers would find Catherine's sentiments in the following passage an accurate reflection of their own: "To look almost pretty, is an acquisition of higher delight to a girl who has been looking plain the first fifteen years of her life, than a beauty from the cradle can ever receive" (15). Rather than being an exalted person that few can aspire to imitate, the heroine as Austen portrays her is someone with whom the (female) reader can identify. She is unique in her very ordinariness.

Such ordinariness extends to Catherine's actions as well. Many of the plot complications of the feminocentric novel derive not from the heroine's flaws but from her improbably high-minded behavior. One need only think of the misunderstandings that occur between Evelina and Lord Orville or between Cecilia and Delvile simply because the heroine could not bring herself to deal frankly with the hero. In her charming naïveté Evelina is somewhat of a prototype for Catherine, but she is much more circumspect than Austen's heroine, courting misunderstanding as a result. Austen allows her own heroine to have feelings that are "rather natural than heroic" (*NA* 93), the implication being that prior conceptions of heroic behavior are themselves rather unnatural. When Henry Tilney gives Catherine a cold bow in response to her supposed slight, she behaves in a manner contrary to that of her sister heroines:

> instead of considering her own dignity injured by this ready condemnation—instead of proudly resolving, in conscious innocence, to shew her resentment towards him who could harbour a doubt of it, to leave to him all the trouble of seeking an explanation, and to enlighten him on the past only by avoiding his sight, or flirting with someone else, she took to herself all the shame of misconduct, or at least of its appearance, and was only eager for an opportunity of explaining its cause. (93)

The new heroine values frankness over the artificial dignity to which her older sisters clung. Catherine may cast herself in the role of the conventional heroine, but she consistently allows her "natural" instincts to triumph over proper heroine-like behavior.

To reinforce the criticism of the feminocentric sentimental novels, Austen puts the conventional cant in the mouth of the false Isabella. In a gush of Cecilia-like sentiment, she declaims, "Had I the command of millions, were I mistress of the whole world, your brother would be my only choice" (*NA* 119). She bamboozles Catherine at the time, giving her "a most pleasing remembrance of all the heroines of her acquaintance" (119), but subsequent events make clear that Isabella has assumed merely the language, not the feelings, of the true heroine. As she does in many of the juvenilia, Austen takes to task a formulaic sentimental language that facilitates the assumption of superficial virtues.

Austen's other main satirical target is, of course, the gothic novel, and against it she levels her most forceful broadsides—or perhaps, most *broad* broadsides. As Alan D. McKillop has noted, the antigothic segment of the novel "takes us back to the earlier mode of crude burlesque in which heroines were made to behave outrageously in order to reduce romance to absurdity."[27] Much of the burlesque occurs in the narrative commentary, the characterized author figure playing against apparent reader expectations as she does when she takes aim at the conventions of the sentimental novel. She introduces Captain Tilney by telling us that he will not fulfill our expectations as to his villainy:

> whatever might be our heroine's opinion of him, his admiration of her was not of a very dangerous kind; not likely to produce animosities between the brothers not persecutions to the lady. *He* cannot be the instigator of the three villains in horsemen's great coats, by whom she will hereafter be forced into a travelling-chaise and four, which will drive off with incredible speed. (*NA* 131)

At this point, Catherine is "undisturbed by the presentiment of such an evil" (131), a marked contrast to her later tendency to see gothic horrors in the most ordinary of circumstances.

During the "gothic" episodes at the Abbey, Catherine ostensibly serves as a new "female quixote," her delusions, like Arabella's, exposing the falsity of the genre that has inspired them. Catherine's assessment of the world through the lens of gothic conventions, followed by the deflation of her expectations, leads to some of the sillier episodes in the text—her fearful examination of the mysterious cedar chest, which yields only a counterpane; the anxious night she spends after discovering the hidden manuscript, which turns out to be merely a laundry list; the improper search of the "forbidden" chamber (Mrs. Tilney's), which is a cheerful apartment rather than the quasi-dungeon Catherine had been envisioning. Catherine here functions as the surrogate for an implied reader envisioned by Austen, one whose judgment is so clouded by the gothic novels she has read that the most mundane of circumstances become invested with dreadful significance. As such, Catherine serves an admonitory purpose, Austen thereby demonstrating the pitfalls that can occur should one regard gothic novels as representing reality. The problem here is that we find it hard to take seriously such an implied reader in the first place; Catherine's credulousness itself appears a false representation of the reality Austen appears to be aiming for throughout most of the novel, and the gothic sections of the novel indeed seem to return to the belittling tendencies of the juvenilia.

Unlike Lennox's satire of Continental romances, however, Austen's satire of the gothic does not simply poke fun at a feminocentric subgenre. Lennox's Arabella is simply ridiculous, her absurd behavior signifying the false notions of reality promulgated by the texts she reads.[28] Although she handles her material somewhat clumsily, Austen complicates the issue by demonstrating how the gothic novel is simultaneously a response to the societal constraints placed upon women, an attempt to mask those constraints, and consequently a means for reinforcing patriarchal imperatives.

Women's immersion in the fantastic realm of gothic literature seems a response to a lack of power and self-determination. Catherine and Isabella, those inveterate readers of gothics, are to some extent defined by their powerlessness; both have limited economic and social resources, and while in Bath, both (whether wittingly or not) must draw upon the little they have to make the best bargain in the marriage market. Forced to dance attendance upon the indolent Mrs. Allen, Catherine is initially limited to shopping excursions and visits to the Pump Room, "where they paraded up and down for an hour, looking at everybody and speaking to no one" (*NA* 25). In the early scenes in Bath, Austen emphasizes the stultifying boredom of Catherine's existence. It is no wonder that Catherine and Isabella, because they are dependent on the whims of others for their limited pleasures, turn to novels that despite their representations of female victimization nonetheless present heroines who court adventure and thus provide readers with vicarious thrills. It is significant that Catherine and Isabella's discussion of their reading alternates with a discussion of clothes and conquests, moving from gothic terrors such as the black veil in *The Mysteries of Udolpho* to mundane yet crucial concerns such as Miss Andrews's cloak and Mr. Tilney's good looks. During her long-desired walk with the Tilneys, Catherine, silenced when the conversation turns to politics, breaks into the conversation with the solemn pronouncement "that something very shocking indeed, will soon come out of London" (112). The confusion that ensues—with Eleanor's mistaking Catherine's discussion of a forthcoming gothic novel for an account of a riot—underscores how the imaginary adventures found in gothic novels substitute for the realm of political events, from which women are traditionally excluded.[29]

Not only do gothic thrills substitute for actual ones, but they also displace women's victimization to an imaginary realm. Gilbert and Gubar have persuasively argued that Austen's burlesque of gothic conventions enables her to reveal the "real threat to women's happiness," which is not gothic terrors but domestic constraints.[30] An evil Montoni, confining his unwilling victim to a house of horrors, cannot perhaps exist in the "neighbourhood of voluntary spies" (*NA* 198) that Henry Tilney envisions constitutes English society. Yet if women are led to believe that real evil occurs in such a lurid form, they may be less able to discern the more subtle evils with which they are daily beset, as Gilbert and Gubar suggest: "Austen rewrites the gothic not because she disagrees with her sister novelists about the confinement of women, but because she believes women have been imprisoned more effectively by miseducation than by walls and more by financial dependency, which is the authentic ancestral curse, than by any verbal oath or warning."[31] Northanger may not be the Udolpho of Catherine's dreams, but it is the site of her nightmares of confinement, dependency, and humiliation.

Austen drives home this point in a passage that brilliantly parodies, reverses, and redefines gothic suspense and terror:

> the sound of footsteps, she could hardly tell where, made her pause and tremble. To be found there, even by a servant, would be unpleasant; but by the General . . . much worse! . . . At that instant a door underneath was hastily opened; some one seemed with swift steps to ascend the stairs, by the head of which she had yet to pass before she could gain the gallery. She had no power to move. With a feeling of terror not very definable, she fixed her eyes on the staircase, and in a few moments it gave Henry to her view. (*NA* 194)

Being discovered behaving improperly by the man upon whom her future happiness depends is as terrifying as being discovered by a villainous Montoni after a clandestine visit to his wife's prison. Yet, although Catherine may tremble with horror, she cannot pinpoint the evils of Northanger because they do not appear in the gothic trappings to which her reading has accustomed her.

Henry Tilney "authors" the gothic tale within the text itself, and the consequences of his narrative underscore how gothic conventions can keep women in their place. Again, Catherine does not initially invest her circumstances with gothic trappings. Certainly, she is eager for the Abbey to be "a fine old place, just like what one reads about" (*NA* 157), but it is Henry who supplies her with the requisite narrative. Rather than disabusing her of mistaken notions, he creates a fiction in which he casts her as the heroine, providing the lens through which she will subsequently view Northanger and its inhabitants. When Henry cuts off the story at the most exciting part, Catherine grows "ashamed of her eagerness" (160). When, acting on hints from Henry, she eagerly investigates the old chest and the "ebony cabinet" only to discover their mundane contents, she deplores her own folly. Although Henry does not actively abet her in her most egregious folly—imagining that the General has imprisoned his wife—he has to some extent planted the seeds by encouraging her to evaluate the Abbey in gothic terms. Henry's fiction ensures that Catherine will maintain a sense of her own inability to read her world properly. The female reader is given gothic adventures to keep her entertained and is then derided for succumbing to the fantasy.

By reworking sentimental and gothic conventions Austen demonstrates that she finds them inadequate for representing female experience. But she wants us to avoid thinking that inadequate representations are the province of feminocentric genres. As in the juvenilia she also takes aim at a male-centered province—historical narrative. Catherine's ingenuous comments function as a sly critique of this genre:

> The quarrels of popes and kings, with wars or pestilences, in every page; the men all so good for nothing, and hardly any women at all—it is very tiresome: and yet I often think it odd that it should be so dull, for a great deal of it must be invention. The speeches that are put in the heroes' mouths, their thoughts and designs—the chief of all this must be invention, and invention is what delights me in other books. (*NA* 108)

The more educated Tilneys defend history, but even Eleanor admits that, when reading it, one must "take the false with the true" (109). Catherine's point about the fictional nature of historical narrative recalls the similar point in *Joseph Andrews*, and Austen intends thereby, like Fielding, to make a case for the truth-value of the novel. Unlike Fielding, however, she also asserts that the fictions of history are gendered masculine, a situation that may account for their greater respectability—and their dullness to a reader like Catherine who senses, albeit imperfectly, that historical narrative represents neither her experience nor that of other women readers.

Through the metacommentary of the characterized author figure, the parodies of various genres, and the discussion of texts by the characters, *Northanger Abbey* makes a sustained argument about how textual representations always mediate our experiences. As in the best of postmodern metafiction *Northanger Abbey* focuses upon the way we read texts (including the text of our lives) according to conventions that we have naturalized. We laugh at Catherine's folly in reading the Abbey according to gothic conventions; but is her act of reading any different from Henry's "reading" of the landscape according to eighteenth-century notions of the picturesque? As Austen makes clear, nature itself is assessed through a particular cultural frame, one that supplants alternative perspectives: "It seemed as if a good view were no longer to be taken from the top of an high hill, and that a clear blue sky was no longer proof of a fine day" (*NA* 110). As he does during the later discussion of the Abbey, Henry teaches Catherine the "proper" way to read: "a lecture on the picturesque immediately followed, in which his instructions were so clear that she soon began to see a beauty in everything admired by him" (111). When Austen tells us that Henry becomes "perfectly satisfied of [Catherine's] having a great deal of *natural* taste" (111; emphasis mine), she ironizes the notion of an unmediated response, suggesting that taste itself is subject to coercion.[32]

Austen forces us to confront the fact that we are reading her text according to the conventions we have absorbed from our prior reading. Austen deflates many of our expectations, yet we know that when we are confronted with a "heroine" such as Catherine, "Something must and will happen to throw a hero in her way" (*NA* 17). Critics have often deplored Austen's apparent capitulation to the conventional happy ending at the close of *Northanger Abbey*. Gilbert and Gubar, for example, point out that "Austen is writing a romance as conventional in its ways as those she criticizes."[33] Austen does succumb to convention, granted, but while doing so she makes clear the deliberate nature of what she is doing. With a joking self-awareness she gives her expectant readers what "naturally" must occur: "Henry and Catherine were married, the bells rang and every body smiled" (252). The conventional romantic ending, interestingly, is undercut by the fact that Henry to some extent takes Catherine by default; his romantic attachment to her is downplayed. Gilbert and Gubar's statement that "Austen presents herself as a 'mere' interpreter and critic of prior fictions," who "quite modestly demonstrates her willingness to inhabit a house of fiction not of her own making," does not fully account for the complex argument she puts forward about the naturalized conventions we have absorbed.[34]

In simultaneously criticizing the feminocentric novel and making a case for it, Austen runs into difficulties. Nowhere is this more apparent than in her presentation of the heroine. Like Joseph Andrews before her, Catherine Morland has too much of a burden to bear. She is the counter-heroine, according to contemporary standards of heroine-ism, who must nonetheless conform to heroine-like behavior. She is, in Marvin Mudrick's words, a "functional" character, but one who must also develop according to the standard of representational realism.[35] Alternately conceived as heroine, counter-heroine, and alternative heroine, Catherine—like Joseph—has no clear role.

We find, for example, that Catherine's naïveté must be assessed in different lights according to the competing satiric points Austen wants to make. At times, her ingenuous responses constitute a sort of perceptive wisdom, as when she criticizes the exclusion of women from history or demurs at Henry's sweeping generalization that "Every body allows that the talent of writing agreeable letters is peculiarly female" (*NA* 27). In several scenes Catherine functions as Henry's complement; each goes against the received opinion—she because she has not been fed it, and he because he sees through it. Yet in other parts of the novel, her naïveté makes her appear downright silly, as benighted a parody heroine as Lennox's female Quixote. This motif serves as a cultural critique in that Austen makes it clear Catherine is usually socialized into her faulty perceptions. Nevertheless, we are disconcerted by a Catherine with whom we identify at certain times and at whom we laugh at others, in part because our experience of the novel genre has prepared us for a consistent moral stance on the part of the character.

The protagonist's development, another feature we have come to expect from the so-called realistic novel, is intermittent and only weakly connected to the plot. In the later novels Austen makes a connection between the protagonist's insights about herself and the accomplishment of the plot, newfound understanding causally linked with the reward of a happy ending. In *Northanger Abbey* the requisite elements appear to be in place—Catherine has her moment of éclaircissement, presumably learns her lesson, and ultimately lands the man she loves. But just as in *Joseph Andrews*, wherein Joseph's attainment of family and fortune has no strong connection to his own actions, no strong causal connection exists between Catherine's actions and Catherine's reward.

Reading back through the tradition of the bildungsroman, we expect that Catherine's folly will somehow account for her estrangement from Henry and that her new self-awareness, stimulated in part by him, will lead to their reconciliation. (We need only think of Austen's own *Pride and Prejudice* and *Emma* for the model.) Although her suspicions of the General and her search of his wife's room are grave social breaches, they have a negligible effect on her fortunes. Certainly, Henry's remarks after he has discovered her in Mrs. Tilney's room shame and humble her, making her aware of "the extravagance of her late fancies" (*NA* 199). She makes the resolution "of always judging and acting in future with the greatest good sense" and apparently begins to carry it out: she realizes that "even in Henry and Eleanor Tilney, some slight imperfection might hereafter appear"; she understands that, though her suspicions of the General were unjust, she is right in regarding him as "not perfectly amiable"; and she can now see the "inconsistencies, contradictions, and falsehood" of Isabella's letter (200–201, 218). But neither Catherine's folly nor her burgeoning self-awareness appears to have any real impact on Henry's feelings for her. Indeed, after Henry surprises her in her improper search, "the only difference in his behaviour to her, was that he paid her rather more attention than usual" (199)—yet another proof perhaps of Austen's cynical maxim that "imbecility in females is a great enhancement of their personal charms" (111). Although it could be argued that, by witnessing Catherine's folly and contrition, Henry becomes aware of her teachability, no scene exists wherein Catherine reveals to Henry her newfound understanding, as Elizabeth does to Darcy.

When Catherine is expelled from Northanger Abbey, she worries momentarily that the General has learned of her "shocking suspicions" (*NA* 230): "If aware of her having viewed him as a murderer, she could not wonder at his even turning her from his house" (231). We might expect that Catherine's delusions, like those of the female Quixote before her, would have serious repercussions. It is not her folly that results in her expulsion from the Abbey, however; the General's anger stems rather from John Thorpe's false representation of her—a motif that reinforces Austen's satire on society at the expense of the bildungsroman structure. Catherine risks being little more than the conventional heroine of sentimental fiction, whose fate is determined by flaws in society rather than by flaws in herself. By making the solitary journey home from the Abbey, Catherine may prove that she is no longer the "sad little shatter-brained creature" (234) that her mother thought her. In the final episode of the novel, however, she exerts little of her newfound strength: "Henry returned to what was now his only home, to watch over his young plantations, and extend his improvements for her sake, to whose share in them he looked anxiously forward; and Catherine remained at Fullerton to cry" (250). She may as well be Cecilia Beverly, driven mad by the consequences of her secret marriage, or Matilda Elmwood, pensively weeping when she is expelled from the paternal mansion—or Austen's own Laura and Sophia from "Love and Freindship," who respond to all calamities by weeping, sighing, or fainting.

Like the protagonists of Austen's mature fiction Catherine is somewhat of a Cinderella figure. With neither great accomplishments, striking looks, nor large fortune to recommend her, she marries a man who possesses intelligence, "a pleasing countenance," and "a very considerable fortune" (*NA* 25, 249)—even if he is only a second son. Yet, unlike Catherine, Austen's later protagonists such as Elizabeth Bennet and even Fanny Price rescue their Prince Charmings as well as are rescued by them. By reaffirming the tradition of the passive heroine, *Northanger Abbey* ultimately shies away from giving us a viable alternative to the conventions of sentimental fiction. Catherine may be an atypical heroine in many respects, but she winds up as no role model.

Austen's characterization of Henry Tilney also epitomizes the complicated nature of Austen's response to the novel genre and to the gender issues it raises. With his ironic comments upon society and his perceptiveness about other characters, Henry has traditionally been regarded as an author surrogate. Mudrick claims, for example, that "Henry Tilney is the willfully ironic and detached spectator as no one except the author herself is in any other of Jane Austen's novels."[36] Again, Henry's defense of the novel confirms and validates Austen's, and his parodying of novelistic conventions is in keeping with hers. Yet contemporary critics have also pointed out his misogyny.[37] He chastises Catherine for her mistaken notions about her father, but he also helps inspire those notions initially. He is thus both mentor and tormentor, and his ironic observation on Catherine's notions of education is unwittingly at his own expense rather than hers: "I use the verb 'to torment,' as I observed to be your own method, instead of 'to instruct,' supposing them to be now admitted as synonimous" (*NA* 109). Eleanor Tilney hastens to assure Catherine (and the readers) that Henry "must be entirely misunderstood, if he can ever appear to say an unjust thing of any woman at all, or an unkind one of me" (114). Yet her excuses occur after we have heard him speak of the faultiness of women's letters, call his sister "stupid" (113), and observe that nature has given women "so much" understanding "that they never find it necessary to use more than half" (114). Henry's satirical comments may be playful, but they sting nonetheless. And, unlike Austen's later heroes, Henry does not have an epiphany that would cause him to temper his criticism or to alter his behavior, as do Fitzwilliam Darcy, Edmund Bertram, George Knightley, and Frederick Wentworth. Catherine may be humbled, but the "author" of her shame is not.

If Henry is indeed an author surrogate, what does that tell us about Austen's notions of herself as an author? In satirizing the feminocentric novel Austen has, as in the juvenilia, joined the patriarchal chorus. Yet she implicitly allows the satire to rebound on the male critic as well. In all, the problematic presentation of Henry, like so many other aspects of

Northanger Abbey, is indicative of the problems Austen encounters as she attempts simultaneously to criticize and to defend a genre linked with feminine values.

Like *Joseph Andrews* before it, *Northanger Abbey* testifies to the crisis of representation out of which the novel is born. Austen, however, emphasizes that the crisis is due in part to the differences between men's and women's ways of knowing. The text engages this issue not only through discussions among the characters but also through its disconcerting shifts between the masculine condemnation and the feminine championing of the feminocentric novel. Seemingly realizing, in Carol Gilligan's terms, "how accustomed we have become to seeing life through men's eyes," Austen turns the lens upon female concerns and values, although she never quite escapes the masculine vision that sees them as inconsequential or negligible.[38]

The irresolvable conflicts in the text reflect the irresolvable conflicts faced by Austen as she attempted authorship. She is uncertain about what to make of her authorial inheritance, simultaneously embracing and faulting the matrilineal literary tradition. Susan Lanser deplores the fact that, in the novels following *Northanger Abbey*, we lose "that bold young narrator who openly claimed a place in literature in a voice as daring as Fielding's but written insistently in the 'mother tongue,'" implying that the diminishment of "overt authoriality" in the subsequent texts is a regressive move.[39] Certainly, the characterized author figure disappears in the subsequent texts, and the direct authorial engagement with issues of gender and genre disappears. By the time that *Pride and Prejudice* is published, Austen takes for granted the legitimacy of the feminocentric novel and its capacity for accurately representing the experience of women like herself, yet she mutes her social and aesthetic critique, containing her work within a patriarchal master narrative. With *Northanger Abbey* Austen may escape the confines of that master narrative, but she is not able successfully to create a woman's version.

Part Two

Mastering the Novel

CHAPTER THREE

Tom Jones

The Plot of the Author

"Now I believe that the author of my story is no sage but an ignorant chatterer," said Don Quixote, "and that he set himself to write it down blindly and without any method, and let it turn out anyhow, like Orbaneja, the painter of Ubeda, who, when they asked him what he was painting, used to answer 'Whatever it turns out.' Sometimes he would paint a cock, in such a fashion and so unlike one that he had to write in gothic characters beside it: *This is a cock*. And so it must be with my history, which will need a commentary to be understood."
—Cervantes, *Don Quixote*

But does a preface exist? —Jacques Derrida, "Outwork"

IN THEIR MASTERPIECE NOVELS both Fielding and Austen assume authority through reconciling conflicting forces under an overarching plot. But the more satisfying resolutions of each text are made at the expense of an openness to change and consideration of alternative possibilities that make their initial efforts so provocative. In Fielding's case, we may feel that it is but a small price to pay. After all, the best-known and best-loved bastards of eighteenth-century literature are Tom Jones and the text that tells his story. Throughout *Tom Jones* Fielding sets up thematic reverberations between the fate of his bastard hero and that of his bastard text.[1] In *Joseph Andrews*—the older, less refined "brother" text to *Tom Jones*—Fielding had begun to make a tentative connection between the fate of his hero and that of his text. Like the changeling Joseph Andrews, who exchanges his servant's livery for the "neat, but plain Suit" of a gentleman (*JA* 342), the text too is a changeling: apparently the male version of the *Pamela* story, it reveals itself (so Fielding suggests) as the true heir to a venerable literary tradition. But *Joseph Andrews* does not resonate with us as does *Tom Jones*.[2] The problem does not lie simply with the difference between the respectable but dull Joseph and the raffish but appealing Tom. With *Joseph Andrews* Fielding challenges our assumptions about gentility and genre, but he has no clear sense of purpose. With *Tom Jones* Fielding takes greater risks, placing both hero and text outside the bounds of legitimacy so that he can explore at length questions of moral and textual authority. Yet this more audacious undertaking goes hand in hand with a more definite aim and a firmer effort at control, Fielding thereby mastering what threatens to undo him.

Putting forward a veritable plot of the author, *Tom Jones* is a self-canonizing text, establishing the importance of the "novel."[3] Both the plot of Tom Jones and the prefaces by the ostensible author of that plot deal with the question of identity, the threat of misrepresentation and usurpation, and the establishment of authenticity and authority.[4] Tom Jones runs the risk of being mistaken for someone else—"a Monster" (*Tom* 1:308)—rather than Squire Allworthy's proper heir. *Tom Jones* runs the risk of being mistaken for "the foolish Novels and monstrous Romances" (1:487) that swarm out of Grub Street. Both the workings of the plot and the poetics advanced in the prefaces attempt to provide solutions to these dilemmas. Both, too, attempt to defuse the conflict between competing ideologies by demonstrating that traditional forms can remain viable only by incorporating something outside their boundaries, although, as with *Joseph Andrews*, Fielding ultimately implies that what is outside has belonged inside all along. By the end of *Tom Jones* the illegitimate hero paradoxically has proved himself as the legitimate heir of Allworthy's moral authority. And the text, so Fielding implies, has proved itself as the legitimate heir of literary authority—has demonstrated that the novel itself is the proper descendent of venerable genres.

THE CRISIS OF IDENTITY

Joseph Andrews had set a precedent for Fielding's method in *Tom Jones*. Like its more illustrious brother text, *Joseph Andrews* featured a prefatory chapter to nearly each book, wherein a characterized author figure advanced a poetics about the type of writing he was doing. Yet the poetics in Fielding's first novel is a fairly sketchy one, Fielding apparently still feeling his way as he played with and against traditional genres to achieve something "novel." However, in the prefaces to *Tom Jones*—variously termed "essays," "prologues," and "introductory writing"—the sketchy poetics of *Joseph Andrews* is developed, refined, and validated, making Fielding's second novel stand out as a unique meld of theory and practice. Although as we have seen there were precedents for Fielding's practice, the "prolegemenous" theorizing in which he engaged certainly did not play a significant part in the continuing development of the novel genre.[5] Granted, there were a few texts that continued the practice. *The History of Charlotte Summers, the Fortunate Parish Girl*, includes a discussion of literary matters in the preface to each book. The anonymous author styles himself "a Natural Brat of that facetious Gentleman" Fielding, thus extending the connections Fielding makes between genealogy and authorship in his text. Later, Richard Cumberland appended Fieldingesque prefatory chapters to his adulatory *Henry*.[6] These works were short-lived, however, and they are remembered now mainly for their connection to Fielding's novel. Entangling the story with an ongoing discussion of the writing process, *Tristram Shandy* has been regarded as the reductio ad absurdum of Fielding's method. But rather than advancing a poetics of the novel Sterne's text explores how the mind shapes experience through narrative; it is concerned with demonstrating mental processes, not with establishing a genre.[7]

It is impossible to draw up a sharp distinction between the prefaces and the passages in the story that include commentary; there is a permeable boundary between the two. Yet the prefaces call attention to themselves as prefaces, and it is as such that I find them significant. Unlike the prefaces in *Joseph Andrews*, which have not generally been subject to detailed analyses, those in *Tom Jones* have consistently provoked discussion about their meaning in the text.[8] Fielding's contemporaries regarded them as separable from the story—either delightful or deplorable but invariably superfluous. Fielding's initial French translator found them "obstacles to the pleasure" and excised them, as well as other reflective matter, from the text. In his *Of the Origin and Progress of Language*, for example, Lord Monboddo cited a "fault" that he found in the novel, "namely, the author's appearing too much in it himself, who had nothing to do in it at all. By this the reader will understand that I mean his reflections with which he begins his books, and sometimes his chapters."[9] Throughout the twentieth century critics have tended to grant the prefaces increasing aesthetic value: for Ian Watt, the prefaces provide the autonomous intellectual structure that enables Fielding to enforce the points he wants to get across; for Wayne Booth and Michael Bliss, they work in conjunction with the rest of the commentary to establish the value-universe of the story; for Patricia Meyer Spacks, they present the "shadow autobiography" of an author; for Robert Alter, they constitute an intrinsic element of the "lesser tradition" of the self-conscious novel, foregrounding the status of the text as a made thing that pits itself against the existential condition of uncontrollable reality.[10] Inevitably, because of our not-so-distant drive to discover aesthetic closure in all texts, the prefaces were eventually considered integrally related to what occurs in the main text. Fred Kaplan discovers a point-to-point relationship between the individual prefaces and the books they introduce, claiming that they are the key without which the novel cannot be understood.[11]

If we regard the prefatory chapters as a key, we must regard the narrative itself as a cipher, which that key unlocks. In so doing, however, we must question why we need a key to decipher the text in the first place. To answer this question we need to approach the prefatory chapters from a different perspective—indeed, to reverse direction and examine them for a moment not as components of the novel but as prefaces—as "attending discourse," the validation by the father/author.[12] We must look less at how each preface is tied to the matter of the individual books than at how they thematically echo Tom's story, a story of establishing authority and founding a line. The answer lies in Fielding's conception that he is originating something in the world of letters and thus must ensure that it is received properly—a conception that he only half-realized in *Joseph Andrews*. If we examine the prefaces in light of contemporary theory on the nature of the preface and the nature of authorship, we can regard them not merely as the key that unlocks the meaning of Tom's story but as the key that unlocks the door to an institution—that of the novel. The prefaces advance a plot of authorship, the legitimation of the text, and this plot is overseen by the characterized author figure Fielding.[13]

Tom's bastardy foregrounds questions of identity and meaning with which Fielding must contend as he "originates" a genre. Tom Jones arrives in the world—or, more accurately, in Allworthy's bed—as an unknown quantity. Although village gossip, Deborah Wilkins's sycophancy, and Jenny Jones's self-serving lies name Jenny and Partridge as his mother and father, these spurious parents disappear from the district during Tom's infancy, not to be heard from again until the time is right for their crucial revelations. Thus, to all intents and purposes Tom has no clear origins, no father to confer meaning on him by granting him a proper name and linking him to an established line. Even if matrilineage were meaningful in Fielding's society (which it was not), Tom's link with the mother, signified by the surname Jones, is itself a false one.

Bastardy cannot confer essential meaning upon Tom, for it tends to be an uncertain signifier in his world.[14] In an earlier age it signified moral depravity. The bastard, offspring of a union occurring outside God's ordered plan of marriage, exemplified the sinfulness and disorder inherent in such an unsanctioned coupling; he was a child of fallen nature, beyond the pale of God's civilizing covenant with humanity. Shakespeare's Edmund, that "natural" child who pledges himself to fallen nature rather than to God-ordained law, epitomizes the evil bastard of the pre-Enlightenment. But Fielding wrote in an age that increasingly questioned the notion that God's providential design was reflected in a person's placement within a hierarchical social structure, and his latitudinarian beliefs went against the doctrine that the sins of the fathers were visited on their children.[15]

Some of the characters in Tom Jones do subscribe to the antibastard cant of earlier times. While Allworthy pities the sweetly slumbering infant, Deborah Wilkins declares that "It doth not smell like a Christian" (*Tom* 1:41). And later, angered by Allworthy's supposed slight of her in his will, she mutters, "It would have become him better to have repented of his Sins on his Death-bed, than to glory in them, and give away his Estate out of his own Family to a mis-begotten Child" (1:246). Like Deborah, Captain Blifil claims that the bastard is a creature of sin. In an effort to persuade Allworthy to cast off the infant Tom, he quotes several biblical texts (an instance of the Devil/Blifil quoting Scripture) and argues for "the Legality of punishing the Crime of the Parent on the Bastard" (1:79). Yet both Deborah and the Captain are motivated by self-interest rather than righteousness; their antibastard cant is thus only lip service paid to the old beliefs.

For other characters the moral stain of bastardy can be erased by money. Although the maid Honour huffily asserts that her legitimate birth makes her superior to Tom, she nevertheless understands that wealth whitewashes (quite literally) the stain of illegitimacy:

> as for abusing Squire Jones, I can call all the Servants in the House to witness, that whenever any Talk hath been about Bastards, I have always taken his Part: "For which of you," says I to the Footmen, "would not be a Bastard, if he could, to be made a Gentleman of? and," says I, "I am sure he is a very fine Gentleman; and he hath one of the whitest Hands in the World." (*Tom* 1:206)

Squire Western's treatment of Tom hinges upon the state of Tom's fortunes; he is eager to promote a marriage between Sophia and the formerly scorned Tom once Tom has been named Allworthy's heir. For worldly characters such as Honour and Western, signs of material worth thus serve as a means for determining the bastard's inner worth.

For Fielding's exemplary characters it is the connection with virtue, not wealth, that renders negligible the stain of illegitimacy. After extolling

Tom's "Perfections" to her aunt, Sophia asks, "What signifies his being base born, when compared with such Qualifications as these?" (*Tom* 1:288). From the outset Allworthy maintains that the foundling came into this world in innocence; Tom's actions in life, rather than the facts of his birth, influence Allworthy's perceptions of him. Despite Tom's base birth Allworthy can, by the end of his story, embrace him as his heir.

In the world of the novel Tom's illegitimacy thus serves as no sure indicator of his character; it does not allow us to place him. Fielding further reinforces the fact that "illegitimate" is an ambiguous designation with the connection he draws between Tom's genesis and Blifil's. Like Tom, Blifil was conceived out of wedlock, as Fielding indirectly and wittily makes clear through his description of Bridget's "conversations" with the Captain and his ironic comments in regard to Blifil's premature birth.[16] In fact, the circumstances of Blifil's conception bear a striking similarity to those of Tom's. In each case a guest in Allworthy's house seduces his supposedly disinterested but actually eager sister, while Allworthy sees no evil. Because of Fielding's uncharacteristic reticence about Summer we have no way of knowing whether Summer, like Captain Blifil, would have wed his pregnant mistress and was prevented from doing so only by his untimely demise. Although Bridget's singular charmlessness makes such an act seem somewhat surprising, we must take into account Summer's acknowledged gentility and good breeding. In any case such a marriage is no more unlikely than the fact that this apparent paragon would engage in an irregular liaison with the unprepossessing Bridget, plausible behavior on the part of these secondary characters perhaps subordinated to the exigencies of the plot.[17] Thus Tom is a bastard because of an untimely case of smallpox; Blifil is not because of a hurried-up wedding. The tenuous nature of this distinction between legitimate and illegitimate is made clear in the following exchange between Molly and Goody Seagrim:

> "She's the vurst of the Vamily that ever was a Whore." "You need not upbraid me with that, Mother," cries Molly, "you yourself was brought to-bed of Sister there within a Week after you was married." "Yes, Hussy," answered the enraged Mother, "so I was, and what was the mighty Matter of that? I was made an honest Woman then; and if you was to be made an honest Woman, I should not be angry; but you must have to be doing with a Gentleman, you nasty Slut, you will have a Bastard, Hussy, you will; and that I defy any one to say of me." (*Tom* 1:184–85)

Even the child of a nine-month-pregnant bride is legitimate.[18] Whereas Bridget can acknowledge the child conceived out of wedlock but born within it, she must disown her bastard—at least until death removes her from gossip's sting.

By making Tom a literal bastard (and Blifil a figurative one), Fielding draws our attention to his era's anxiety about the problematic relationship between outer signs and inner meaning—an anxiety integral to questions of authority. Just as bastardy as a sign of sin no longer points unambiguously to the sinfulness of the bastard, traditional signs for assessing virtue and moral authority (and their opposites) are no longer precise indicators. Formerly Tom would have had a clear place in—or rather, perhaps, outside of—the cosmic order; now he has none. He signifies an undermining of signification, representing through his ambiguous status the crisis of authority with which neoclassical thinkers still contended.

During the early seventeenth century, as J. G. A. Pocock points out, people conceived that "authority and magistracy were part of a natural and cosmic order." Yet the English Revolution had undermined this comforting belief, and the burden fell upon the individual to discover a new source for authority. According to Pocock, the issue prompted the "greatest radicalism" among contemporary thinkers: "since authority had disintegrated, and God had withheld his word as to where it was now lodged, the individual must rediscover in the depths of his own being the means of reconstituting and obeying it."[19] This reconstitution of authority characterizes an essential element of Tom's purpose and experience.

But how is authority to be reconstituted? During the late seventeenth and early eighteenth centuries, as the belief that noble lineage was a guarantee of inner nobility was increasingly called into question, individual merit began to replace noble lineage as a sign of virtue. Nevertheless, individual achievement, like the sign that it replaced, soon became disconnected from what it was supposed to represent. As Michael McKeon points out, there is a "tendency to transform the outward signifiers of merit into self-validating and self-sufficient signifieds."[20] Fielding's worldly Mrs. Fitzpatrick astutely sums up this circular validation through her comments to the unworldly Sophia: "by whatever Means you get into the Polite Circle, when you are once there, it is sufficient Merit for you that you are there" (*Tom* 2:582). Tom's bastard status highlights the difficulty in ascertaining the grounds for legitimate moral authority. Himself an ambiguous sign, he points to the ambiguity inherent in all signs.

Although it questions both traditional and progressive signs of virtue, *Tom Jones* nevertheless features a character who ostensibly exemplifies moral authority. Squire Allworthy is not an empty sign. In possession "of one of the largest Estates in the County" (*Tom* 1:34), vested with the legal authority of both squire and magistrate, he validates with his inner goodness both his outer signs of worth and his authoritative position in the social order. In many ways Allworthy recalls an idealized past wherein property served as a guarantee of virtue. In the late seventeenth century, as Pocock suggests, "the function of property remained the assurance of virtue," in that property gave the individual "independence of any relation which might render him corrupt."[21] Allworthy's actions (as well as his name) bespeak the virtue of this man of property: he takes in the foundling, regulates the morals of the community, and adheres to the true meaning of charity. Fielding proclaims him "the one Object alone in this lower Creation . . . more glorious than the Sun" (1:43). Through overblown prose, the passage strikes us as quasi-parodic, an impression later confirmed by Fielding's subsequent acknowledgment that he has no idea how to rescue his readers from the rhetorical heights to which he has led them. The sun analogy nevertheless reinforces Allworthy's figurative function as father, god, origin.

Granted, the paragon himself has flaws, as critics have often noted. Allworthy makes several significant blunders in judgment: he determines Partridge's guilt upon the flimsy evidence of the jealous Mrs. Partridge; he proposes to send Molly Seagrim to Bridewell, where she will only become more hardened in her sins; he can discern neither Blifil's intrinsic evil nor Tom's intrinsic good. Fielding attempts to explain away these lapses as proceeding from Allworthy's disinterested desire to do right, as we see in the following passage on Allworthy's harsh-seeming decision to commit Molly to Bridewell:

> A Lawyer may, perhaps, think that Mr. *Allworthy* exceeded his Authority a little in this Instance. And, to say the Truth, I question, as here was no regular Information before him, whether his Conduct was strictly regular. However, as his Intention was truly upright, he ought to be excused in *Foro Conscientiae*, since so many arbitrary Acts are daily committed by Magistrates, who have not this Excuse to plead for themselves. (*Tom* 1:192)

But Fielding doth protest too much; rather than exonerating the squire, the above passage and others like it ironize the claim for his "allworthiness."[22] Allworthy himself cannot be a self-presenting sign of goodness but requires the commentary of his ostensible creator to validate him. However well-intentioned, the agent of authority is fallible, a demonstration of the difficulty of acting well in an all too imperfect world.

Despite the faint tarnish on his gilding, Allworthy nonetheless serves as the ideal to which Tom must aspire. Allworthy is an influential force for good because he joins external signs of virtue to noble behavior. In order to take his place as the heir of Paradise Hall, Tom must match inner goodness to an appearance that would validate it.[23] According to the explicit argument of the text, Tom, although illegitimate, indeed has the true virtue that shows him to be the proper successor to Allworthy. His generosity to Black George, his resolution not to forsake Molly (before he discovers that she has forsaken *him*), his heroic rescues of both the Man of the Hill and Mrs. Waters, his generosity to the beggar who finds Sophia's pocketbook—all incidents bespeak Tom's intrinsic goodness. We may raise our eyebrows at Tom's sententious lecture to Nightingale about shouldering responsibilities in light of his questionable capacity to do so himself. Yet the lecture has the desired effect, bringing about Nightingale's marriage to Nancy (a female version of Tom's generous but imprudent self) and consequently averting the ruin of the Miller family. The episode indicates that Tom has begun to assume the status of an Allworthy-like moral arbiter, regulating sexual behavior for the good of society. Tom's merciful treatment of Enderson, which preserves the Enderson family, is yet another demonstration of his assumption of patriarchal—even paternalistic—responsibility.

Tom does not need to develop virtue but to join his intrinsic goodness with an appropriate outer sign—to become a self-presenting sign of goodness in a world wherein exists an ever-widening gap between signs and what they stand for. Tom shows such a gap in himself, being "deficient in outward Tokens of Respect" and lacking that prudence that would give him moral credibility (*Tom* 1:133). As Fielding didactically expounds, virtue requires the proper form or sign in order to shine forth:

> Prudence and Circumspection are necessary even to the best of Men. They are indeed as it were a Guard to Virtue, without which she can never be safe. It is not enough that your Designs, nay that your Actions are intrinsically good, you must take Care that they shall appear so. If your Inside be never so beautiful, you must preserve a fair Outside also. This must be constantly looked to, or Malice and Envy will take Care to blacken it so, that the Sagacity and Goodness of an *Allworthy* will not be able to see through it, and to discern the Beauties within. (1:141)

By disregarding appearance Tom does not allow his intrinsic goodness to be discerned.

Although Fielding professes his "Shame and Sorrow" at having to report Tom's sexual peccadilloes (*Tom* 2:529), these are presented as not so much signs of Tom's lack of virtue as signs of his lack of control and restraint. Indeed, Tom's sexual generosity—even to Lady Bellaston, a more subtle version of Lady Booby—is meant to stand in healthy contrast to Blifil's implied onanism. Fielding observes that Blifil's "Appetites were, by Nature, so moderate, that he was able by Philosophy or by Study, or by some other Method, easily to subdue them" (1:284). Blifil's onanism signifies the self-love that causes him to harm others to benefit himself. Tom's lapses are forgivable because he errs on the side of too much love (particularly of the carnal kind) for others rather than too little, as Allworthy makes clear during the reconciliation scene:

> there is this great Difference between those Faults which Candour may construe into Imprudence, and those which can be deduced from Villainy only. The former, perhaps, are even more apt to subject a Man to ruin; but if he reform, his Character will, at length, be totally retrieved; the World, though not immediately, will, in Time, be reconciled to him; and he may reflect, not without some Mixture of Pleasure, on the Dangers he hath escaped: But Villainy, my Boy, when once discovered, is irretrievable; the Stains which this leaves behind, no Time will wash away. (2:960)

Tom lacks not intrinsic goodness but the form of virtue, and once he has assumed that form his character can be retrieved.

Although Tom learns to be more circumspect, we see little in him of what we might call modern character development, as more than a few critics have noted and deplored. This fixedness of character, common in the eighteenth-century novel, is in keeping with Fielding's belief that one's disposition is determined at birth.[24] In "An Essay on the Knowledge of the Characters of Men," Fielding argues that, because even people educated in the same manner display "so manifest and extreme a Difference of Inclination or Character," we must "acknowledge some unacquired, original Distinction, in the Nature of Soul of one Man, from that of another" (*Misc* 1:154). Education cannot teach a person virtue but only the concealment of vices. I hardly need add that Tom and Blifil, subject from birth to the same environment and education, exemplify Fielding's theory of character. Yet despite his lack of psychological development, Tom is a more interesting character than Joseph Andrews simply because there is a gap between who he appears to be and who he is; his unformed quality gives the text narrative drive.

As the novel demonstrates, the disjunction between sign and referent is rife in society, and the appearance or forms of virtue can often substitute for the fact of virtue, in effect usurping the rightful position of a legitimate moral authority. Because Tom lacks the appearance of virtue, he risks being unrecognized as Allworthy's most worthy successor. Blifil is an empty sign, the imitation heir who supplants the true one for most of the novel. Blifil gives the appearance of Allworthy-like virtue, preserving that prudence which, when taken to extremes, comes to stand for a rigid adherence to virtue's forms but not its essence.[25] In his speeches to Allworthy he pays lip service to the virtuous precepts that Allworthy not only expresses but lives by. But no true virtue lies behind Blifil's appearance of it. When he buys Tom's Bible, the "prudent Lad" does so not because of his friendship for Tom but because of his unwillingness "that the Bible should be sold out of the Family at half the Price" (*Tom* 1:144). When he continually reads it, he does it not out of piety but out of a desire to get Tom in trouble. His concern that the news of Bridget's death not be withheld from Allworthy masks a hope that such information will finish off his uncle. He withholds information of Tom's transgressions not because he is forgiving, as he professes, but because he wants to use it when it will do the most damage. Yet such false coin passes for true currency in the world of *Tom Jones*. Appearance without essence seems to be praised more highly than essence without appearance, as Fielding observes: "The most formal Appearance of Virtue, when it is only an Appearance, may perhaps, in very abstracted Considerations, seem to be rather less commendable than Virtue itself without this Formality; but it will however be always more commended" (2:615). Despite the increasing skepticism toward traditional signs, the appearance of virtue is often sufficient unto itself, just as the fact of legitimacy is regarded as the guarantee for proper succession.

Although the designations *legitimate* and *illegitimate* may be empty of meaning, they nevertheless exert a powerful legal force. Although both boys are Allworthy's nephews, their claims to Allworthy's estate according to contemporary law are quite different. Legally, as Homer Brown has pointed out, Tom as a bastard probably cannot inherit the Allworthy estate but only receive it in trust.[26] Conceived outside the formal bonds of matrimony Tom cannot be an actual heir. On the other hand, Blifil's legal right to Allworthy's estate before Allworthy disinherits him derives from a legal formality. We find an interesting gloss on this subject in Samuel Richardson's nearly contemporaneous *Clarissa*. Writing to discourage the libertine Lovelace from seducing Clarissa, John Belford points out the problems a man may encounter once he has fathered illegitimate children:

> If he has children, and has reason to think them his, and if his lewd courses have left him any estate, he will have cause to regret the restraint his boasted liberty has laid him under, and the valuable privilege it has deprived him of; when he finds that it must descend to some relation, for whom, whether near or distant, he cares not one farthing; and who perhaps [for] his dissolute life, if a man of virtue, has held him in the utmost contempt.[27]

Even after Tom has been acknowledged as Allworthy's nephew (and the elder one at that), the law would require that Blifil inherit if Allworthy died intestate or without making a formal provision. The law would, in effect, serve as a form empty of meaning, enabling the perpetuation of evil in Paradise Hall. In legend and history, the bastard was traditionally a usurper. But Fielding turns the tradition on its head, for it is the legitimate Blifil who would usurp what we come to regard as the rightful place of the bastard Tom. He is Edmund to Tom's Edgar, even prone to the same manipulations by which Shakespeare's cunning villain turns Gloucester against his true son.

Just as the story of Tom's adventures serves as an attempted demonstration of his essential goodness, the prefaces attempt to argue for the text's qualifications as a deserving heir to literary authority, an argument for which the story itself must serve as evidence. Through the use of genealogical metaphors in the prefaces Fielding draws up an implicit connection between the status of the hero and the status of the text. He compares the relationship between an author and his book to that between a father and his son. In the preface to book 11 he explains that a book can be considered as "the Author's Offspring, and indeed as the Child of his Brain" (*Tom* 2:568). Half-seriously, half-parodically (in light of an earlier expulsion of the muses), he elaborates upon this conceit. In producing a book the writer gets his muse with child; she in turn undergoes a "painful Labor," and "the tender Father" subsequently "nourishes his Favourite, till it be brought to Maturity, and produced into the World" (2:569). The work of art is the author's issue.

Just as Bridget essentially disappears from Tom's life, the mother/muse disappears from this account. In both cases Fielding inverts the traditional bastard motif, wherein the child is mother-identified.[28] Throughout the text Tom calls Allworthy "father" and, by the end, demonstrates that he is a worthy "son." But Bridget serves as a mother in name only, and then only in the last few pages of the novel, having nothing to do with Tom's development. The muse may give birth to the book, but it is the father who nourishes it, assuming the female task of nursing. Here Fielding is playing with a traditional poetic conceit. Yet the motif of the father-identified bastard reinforces the notion of authorship as a masculine prerogative and confirms, rather than subverts, patriarchal law.[29] The text's "father" assertively lays claim to his "bastard" offspring, for Fielding (unlike many contemporary writers) affixes his name to the title page and oversees the text's development in the person of the author figure.

Fielding is concerned whether readers will dismiss the text at the outset as "Sad Stuff, horrid Nonsense" when there is a gap between what they expect from significant literature and what they find in this particular story. His text has no clear identity. Like its hero, the novel (as Homer Brown comments) "is a text with only a borrowed, not a proper name."[30] Fielding does not call the text "a novel" at all but instead resorts to "Heroic, Historical, Prosaic Poem" (*Tom* 1:152). Reminiscent of the designation Fielding comes up with in *Joseph Andrews*, this heaping-up of self-canceling terms confuses rather than enlightens us. The difficulties with terminology illustrate how Fielding attempts to fix identity for a form that inherently calls issues of identity into question. As Mikhail Bakhtin's studies of novelistic discourse demonstrate, the novel as a genre resists being defined in generic terms because its impetus is to absorb other genres; rather than manifesting a stable identity it tends to destabilize the identities of the genres it absorbs.[31] Just as Tom decenters notions of the aristocracy because he cannot be placed, the novel (I refer both to Fielding's and the group of works to which Fielding's belongs) decenters notions of aristocratic genres. We need only refer to Fielding's transmutation of epic, tragic, pastoral, and satiric conventions in order to observe this decentering force at work. Yet, against its destabilizing impetus the novel (again, both Fielding's and the group of works) strives to fix its own identity, to become namable. The author figure is thus integral to Fielding's project.

The novel's problems with fixing its identity go hand in hand with its murky epistemological status. Whereas, according to the movement of the plot, Tom can assume his true identity as Allworthy's heir only once he has established moral authority, the novel can be identified as a genre only once it has established its literary authority. Since Aristotle refuted Plato's attack on poetry, the traditional genres had justified their existence by claiming that they conveyed a certain poetic truth, thus preserving the formal requirements of epistemological and, by extension, literary authority. But by eschewing the conventions of the received genres, the novel cuts itself off from the authority of a priori poetic truths. Nor can it rely upon the "truth" of historical fact, although historical personages and events may appear in its pages. As in *Joseph Andrews*, such authority derives from the truth-value of what occurs in the text itself, as Fielding demonstrates.

According to the argument Fielding puts forth in the preface to book 9, the foundation for the truth of this text is a fixed, universally comprehensible nature (both human and otherwise)—that prior "text" that authorizes all others: "we have good Authority for all our Characters, no less indeed than the vast authentic Doomsday-Book of Nature" (*Tom* 1:489), which as Ernst Curtius points out is a more valuable form of knowledge than that to be found in actual books.[32] The book-of-nature commonplace thus becomes a means for validating the epistemological authority of Fielding's text and for undermining that of others. As Fielding makes clear, he has the knowledge others may lack; in the oft-discussed "theatrical" preface, for instance, he explains that he is "admitted behind the Scenes of this great Theatre of Nature" (1:327). We may dispute the claim that *Tom Jones* accurately reproduces nature (and with our current self-consciousness about the constructed nature of all representations, I do not see how we could not). Nevertheless, the claim serves as an attempt to assert the legitimacy of the novel according to the criteria that Fielding draws up.

Although most contemporary texts also do not themselves conform to the traditional genres, they still pose a threat. Just as Blifil threatens to usurp Tom's deserved place as Allworthy's heir, so do pernicious literary productions threaten to usurp the literary crown. If critics cannot easily determine the status of the novels they read, there is the risk that they may devalue a deserving heir. Furthermore, because so many potential "heirs"—bastards all, some Jonesian and some Blifilian—are vying for the literary crown, the critics may elevate an impostor (as they had done, in Fielding's view, with *Pamela*). According to Fielding much of the outpouring of prose fiction appearing in the mid–eighteenth century is specious, an opinion shared by many of the age's eminent men of letters.

Just as Blifil assumes the outward signs of virtue and so imposes upon the innocent characters, so does "a Swarm of foolish Novels, and monstrous Romances" impose upon the credulous reader, occasioning a "great Loss of Time, and Depravation of Morals" (*Tom* 1:487). Just as the narrative exposes Blifil, Fielding attempts to expose such romances as shams, dismissing them on the grounds that they do not speak truth, for they derive not from universal nature but from idiosyncratic, even hallucinatory, interior experience: "Truth distinguishes our Writings, from those idle Romances which are filled with Monsters, the Productions, not of Nature, but of distempered brains" (1:150). He herein draws upon a commonplace of high neoclassicism, that the mind's individual experience is not the stuff of art or truth—a commonplace succinctly allegorized in the fable of the spider and the bee in Swift's *Battle of the Books*.

Fielding must also contend with "factual fictions" (to borrow Lennard Davis's term), fictions that present themselves in the guise of actual documents, such as the seemingly historical narratives of Defoe or the discovered letters of Richardson.[33] After all, it could be argued that such texts adhere to nature more accurately than do Fielding's. Yet, according to Fielding, their very accuracy works against them: "Such Histories as these do, in reality, very much resemble a News-Paper, which consists of just the same Number of Words, whether there be any News in it or not" (*Tom* 1:75–76). The passage is perhaps an implicit jab at Richardson's painstaking account of each daily occurrence, whether anything of significance happens or not—a method that prompted even Samuel Johnson to exclaim, "Why, Sir, if you were to read Richardson for the story, your impatience would be so much fretted that you would hang yourself."[34] Such minutely detailed texts may derive from what actually occurred, or at least *seem* to do so, but their accumulation of particulars conveys nothing. Rather than "trouble the Public" with these "Blanks in the grand Lottery of Time," Fielding's text will inform us only "when a great Prize happens to be drawn" (1:76–77). Meaning is found not within events themselves but in how those events are given shape and emphasis by the narrator.

Fielding's position as literary heir is threatened not only by other texts but by critics as well. In the prefaces he thus rejects the received authority of the critics on the grounds that they have wrongfully assumed their power. The critic's job was originally only to enforce laws, not to make them:

> The Critic, rightly considered, is no more than the Clerk, whose Office it is to transcribe the Rules and Laws laid down by those great Judges, whose vast Strength of Genius hath placed them in the Light of Legislators in the several Sciences over which they presided. This Office was all which the Critics of old aspired to, nor did they ever dare to advance a Sentence, without supporting it by the Authority of the Judge from whence it was borrowed. (*Tom* 1:211)

But the critic eventually took on the prerogative of the writer: "the Clerk began to invade the Power and assume the Dignity of his Master" (1:211). Lacking the immanent authority of the writer—that "Strength of Genius" that enables him to convey truth—the critic now assumes an authority that is form only, just as the usurping heir Blifil assumes the form of virtue but lacks its essence. Unable to exercise the true judgment that his profession requires, the critic often elevates the accidental production of "a great Author" into "Essentials to be observed by all his Successors" (1:211). The rules the critic prescribes are necessarily empty of meaning—as hollow as the virtuous homilies mouthed by Blifil. The critic may thus aid a Blifilian text in supplanting *Tom Jones*. We should bear in mind that the epithet of slanderer accrues both to Blifil and to Fielding's critics.

Captious critics are like inflexible lawgivers: "For these Critics being Men of shallow Capacities, very easily mistook mere Form for Substance. They acted as a Judge would, who should adhere to the Lifeless Letter of Law, and reject the Spirit" (*Tom* 1:211). Rather than elevating the worthy *Tom Jones* to the important position it merits in the literary world, the critics would elevate an empty text that bears an apparently proper form. Similarly, rather than installing Allworthy's heir in spirit in Paradise Hall, the "lifeless Letter of Law" would grant the estate to that dead letter Blifil. The true heirs must find means for coming into their own.

LEGITIMATING TOM JONES AND *TOM JONES*

Without the anchoring force of what we might call metaphoric coincidence between sign and referent, both Tom and the text are subject to metonymic drift. The gap between what Tom is and what he appears to be causes Allworthy to expel him from Paradise Hall, and he subsequently embarks on a journey that seems to be directed by chance. Calling on fortune to direct his course, Tom finds this course determined by his accidental meetings with the company of soldiers, Mrs. Waters, and the beggar who finds Sophia's pocketbook. At each of the three main locales in the novel (country, road, and city), he discovers substitutes for his true love, Sophia, whom we do not do wrong in regarding at times as Battestin's emblem for the wisdom Tom seeks.[35] Until Tom can close the gap between sign and referent, essence and appearance, he dooms himself to wandering.

Within the gap that exists before Tom makes this discovery lies the space wherein the play of narrative can take place. Tom inspires a rash of storytelling, most of it unanchored in any sort of truth.[36] From the outset his foundling state, which renders him a virtual blank slate, provokes others to attempt to confer meaning on him, and his subsequent lack of fixed meaning provides further provocation. Of course, in the world of Tom Jones, characters habitually fashion fictions about one another, one of the most notable being the landlord's story that Sophia is Jenny Cameron; indeed, fiction making and storytelling appear throughout as vital mechanisms in the workings of society.[37] Tom, however, seems to exacerbate this storytelling proclivity. Everyone wants to tell his story.

Throughout the text Tom seems to infect those he meets with the storytelling disease. His very birth gives rise to all sorts of false tales: Jenny Jones claims him as her own, Partridge's wife ascribes him to Partridge, and the parish confers him on Allworthy. Once Tom sets out on his travels his history is continually being rewritten. The neighborhood tells how Tom was turned away from Allworthy naked and penniless. The landlady in the inn where Tom lies wounded claims that he is an apprentice, turned away for making love to his young mistress. The "vile Petty-fogger" (*Tom* 1:431) at the Bell announces that Tom is the son of a horse thief, and he paints such a black picture of his villainy while under Allworthy's roof that the normally gracious Mrs. Whitefield (one of the "real" people Fielding inserts in his text) refuses Tom service. Determining that the history Tom has given of himself is "a Fiction" (1:427), Partridge decides that

Tom is running away from both his "father" Allworthy and the unwelcome attentions of Sophia. Although Partridge's fabrications have no grounding in fact, they nevertheless anticipate the outcome that actually occurs (Tom's reconciliation with Allworthy), Fielding thereby implying that alternative versions of stories may have a certain validity all their own.

Even Fielding plays with the notion of telling a different story of Tom than the "facts" he has claimed to uphold would warrant:

> In Regard to *Sophia* it is more than probable, that we shall somewhere or other provide a good Husband for her in the End, either *Blifil*, or my Lord, or Somebody else; but as to poor *Jones*, such are the Calamities in which he is at present involved, owing to his Imprudence, by which if a Man doth not become a Felon to the World, he is at least a *Felo de se*; so destitute is he now of Friends, and so persecuted by Enemies, that we almost despair of bringing him to any good; and if our Reader delight in seeing Executions, I think he ought not to lose any Time in taking a first Row at *Tyburn*. (*Tom* 2:875)

Because Tom has not yet clarified his rightful identity, such an outcome is possible. For purposes of plot, the most significant tales about Tom come from Blifil, who constructs the fiction of Tom as a monster of ingratitude by cunningly blending in enough fact to make such self-serving fiction appear as truth. But most stories about Tom have only a marginal relation to the movement of the plot. They thus serve as reinforcement to the notion that the bastard Tom—that text without a verifiable author—is vulnerable to being rewritten by another.

Without the restraining form of prudence Tom risks being charged with other men's bastards, as indeed happens in the case of Molly Seagrim. Moreover, by scattering his seed wastefully Tom risks dissociating it from any soil, any estate, any line. Wandering, authorless, lacking fixed identity, Tom has the potential to impose this fate on his own issue. Tom runs what I shall call (borrowing a suggestive phrase from Derrida) "the risk of dissemination," the risk of having his issue beyond his authorial control, as he himself has been disconnected from the paternal line.[38] In fact, as a bastard himself, Tom epitomizes this risk, although according to the explicit argument of the text he also comes to eliminate it.

Just as Tom may be misrepresented and charged with other men's bastards, so may Fielding. He deplores the fact that the works of scurrilous writers have often been ascribed to him: "And what is a very severe Fate, I have had some of the abusive Writings of those very Men fathered upon me, who in other of their Works have abused me with the utmost Virulence" (*Tom* 2:914). In his earlier preface to his sister Sarah's *David Simple*, Fielding had made a similar complaint:

> For my own part, I can aver, that there are few Crimes, of which I should have been more ashamed, than of some Writings laid to my charge. I am as well assured of the Injuries I have suffered from such unjust Imputations, not only in general Character, but as they have, I conceive, frequently raised me inveterate Enemies, in Persons to whose Disadvantage I have never entertained a single Thought.[39]

At the same time he expressed his wish for a law that would require writers to set their names to their publications. Clearly Fielding's anxiety over false "paternity suits" weighed heavily on him, and his insistent claims of authorship in *Tom Jones* serve as an attempt to combat the situation.

Like Tom, Fielding's "issue" risks being misinterpreted and misunderstood, as the following instance of anxious explanation makes clear: "It is in reality for my own Sake, that while I am discovering the Rocks on which Innocence and Goodness often split, I may not be misunderstood to recommend the very Means to my worthy Readers, by which I intend to shew them they will be undone" (*Tom* 1:142). But even such attempts at authorial control may not do the trick, as Samuel Richardson's censure of *Tom Jones* makes clear:

> I have taken the Liberty to account, elsewhere, for the good Reception the Character of the weak, the insipid, the Run-away, the Inn-frequenting Sophia has met with. In that, as in the Character of her illegitimate Tom, there is nothing that very Common Persons may not attain to; Nothing that will reproach the Conduct of Actions of very ordinary Capacities, and very free Livers.

Like Richardson, other readers may regard *Tom Jones* as "a dissolute book."[40]

Fielding is only too aware that once the fond "father" consigns his literary issue to the public, he risks its being brought "to an untimely End" by the "poisonous Breath" of the slander-mongering critics (*Tom* 2:569). Fielding likens such slander to calling into question a person's legitimacy:

> as no one can call another Bastard, without calling the Mother a Whore, so neither can any one give the Names of Sad Stuff, horrid Nonsense, *&c.* to a Book, without calling the Author a Blockhead; which tho' in a Moral Sense it is a preferable Appellation to that of Villain, is perhaps rather more injurious to his worldly Interest. (2:569)

If the legitimacy of the text is questioned, it may wander aimlessly, never coming into its literary estate.

In order to come into their inheritance, both Tom and the text must progress toward nomination and legitimation—in Tom's case a figurative rather than actual legitimation. Tom's foundling status and wandering state would seem to align him with the heroes of the picaresque.[41] But Tom's journey from Paradise Hall to London proves not to be the errant one of the picaro. The seeming picaresque gets gathered into a quest for identity. In *Joseph Andrews* Joseph discovers his true father about the same time we begin to understand that his birth might be an issue; the quest for identity is essentially a buried motif. In *Tom Jones*, however, we see from the outset that identity is an issue, and that who Tom is and what he is (Allworthy's rightful heir) are inextricably conjoined. His seemingly random encounters during his journey concurrently provide the clues that will reveal his father in fact and provide the opportunities for noble action that will reveal his father in spirit. When Tom discovers his identity, the accidental is transformed into the causal. In parallel fashion, by their apparently digressive nature the prefatory chapters may seem like wanderings within the text. Yet, just as Tom's seemingly random encounters get gathered up into his quest for identity, so do the prefaces get gathered up into Fielding's quest to legitimate his novel, and by the end of the text, Fielding intends us to find that he has indeed substantiated his claims.

Tom gains the moral authority that qualifies him as Allworthy's heir by moving toward the place where what he is and what he appears to be coincide. Only by being anchored in self-presence—in an identity of essence and appearance—can Tom put an end to metonymic drift and the proliferation of stories about himself. During his journey Tom comes to recognize what form he must assume so that his goodness can be named. Granted, Tom's appearance actually deteriorates during his journey toward this identity, as he becomes Lady Bellaston's kept man and is charged with the crimes of murder and incest. But the apparent deviation from his movement toward nomination is in fact part of that movement. Tom's entanglement with Lady Bellaston drives home the realization of what he has to lose—Sophia's love. The possibility that he has committed incest enables Tom to recognize himself and understand the consequences of straying from proper behavior, as the following passage indicates: "'Sure,' cries *Jones*, 'Fortune will never have done with me, 'till she hath driven me to Distraction. But why do I blame Fortune? I am myself the Cause of all my Misery. All the dreadful Mischiefs which have befallen me, are the Consequences only of my own Folly and Vice'" (*Tom* 2:915–16). Tom finally takes responsibility for his own actions.

An obvious parody of the recognition scene in *Oedipus*, the scene yet maintains a comedic difference: although the incest issue teaches Tom what he is, it still holds back who he is. But it nevertheless leads to Allworthy's meeting with Mrs. Waters/Jenny Jones and the true solution to the mystery of Tom's birth. As Homer Brown remarks, the supposed incest leads to the fixing of Tom's identity: "In *Tom Jones* the transgression is purportedly actual, though just as quickly disproved, but it also marks a fold in which disorder of identity is stabilized. . . . transgression of the incest taboo at once marks a limit of possible narrative drift and serves as a threshold to the revelation of a proper name."[42] Thus Tom is ready to take on his rightful name once he understands that he must present himself in the proper form, that he must restrain his impulse to sow his seed unreservedly.

That Tom has conjoined essence and outward appearance comes clear during his reunion with Sophia. Attempting to put himself back into Sophia's good graces Tom differentiates between the love he feels for Sophia and that which he felt for his mistresses. Yet, as Sophia's following demur and Tom's rejoinder make clear, outward action must reflect inward feeling:

> "I will never marry a Man," replied *Sophia*, very gravely, "who shall not learn Refinement enough to be as incapable as myself of making such a Distinction." "I will learn it," said *Jones* "I have learnt it already. The first Moment of Hope that my *Sophia* might be my Wife, taught it me at once; and all the rest of her Sex from that Moment became as little the Objects of Desire to my Sense, as of Passion to my Heart." (*Tom* 2:973)

Tom's use of the future followed by the present prefect tense suggests an instantaneous conversion, appropriate to the elimination of the distinction, in the sense of division, within himself. He has seemingly closed the gap.

The argument of the text is that there are indeed no further gaps: Tom has attained self-knowledge. Like Sophia, who repeals her yearlong trial of his constancy, we must take Tom's reformation on trust. Although in the penultimate paragraph of the novel Fielding tells us that Tom's vices have been corrected, he gives us no postconversion examples of Tom's virtuous actions. The final proof of Tom's moral stature thus lies outside the bounds of the text. Of course, the apparent perfection that Tom has attained is not the stuff of narrative, as Fielding comes to realize with *Amelia*. The movement through metonyms is the impetus of narrative; the conjunction in metaphor ends it. As with all narratives, the "final coherence" of this plot occurs as "that metaphor that may be reached through the chain of metonymies," in Peter Brooks's terms.[43] The meeting with Partridge, the rescue of Mrs. Waters, the mercy shown toward Enderson, all can now be seen as parts of the process that culminate in Tom's nomination. Once Tom becomes self-presenting, he attains Paradise (Hall) and is fixed in his state of goodness; the temporal is erased.

By moving through that chain of metonyms to a metaphoric conjunction, it seems Tom achieves an immanent moral authority. Fielding complicates this issue, however, by inserting in the text the report of Bridget Allworthy's confessional letter. The letter serves a crucial plot function. It indirectly contributes to Tom's expulsion from Paradise Hall by alerting Blifil that he is not Allworthy's only kin and thus inflaming his desire to discredit Tom. Remember that Blifil's nastiest jibe—that he knows who his own parents are and Tom does not—occurs after he also knows who Tom's parents are, and it is shrewdly calculated to provoke Tom. Blifil's concealment of the letter and Dowling's subsequent slippery testimony to that effect impel Allworthy to put an end to Blifil's hopes of inheritance. We cannot know if the plot would have followed a different path had Allworthy received the letter as Bridget intended he should. Yet, presumably, Allworthy's sickbed tolerance, desire to heed Bridget's dying wishes, and original affection for Tom would have occasioned a different outcome. In other words, the concealed letter marks a possible bifurcation point in the plot—one fork leading to Tom's wanderings, the other leading to the narrative dead end of Tom's immediate assumption of his true identity.

What the letter says about Tom and what Tom proves about himself have a curiously dependent relationship. This letter serves as a supplement in its most saturated sense, both repeating and augmenting other information in the text.[44] The letter must be deferred in order for Tom to wander the path that will lead him to a conjunction of appearance and essence, but at the same time it must be presented in order for Tom truly to achieve identity—to be named. It seconds what Tom has already proved—his qualifications as Allworthy's heir—yet provides the vital information that will compel Allworthy to make him so in his will. It is interesting that both letter and wisdom, emblematized by Sophia, are discovered in London, a meshing of the two forms of legitimation.

Speaking from beyond the grave, bearing the signature of its author, the letter provides the truth about Tom's origins. Its author connects Tom to both maternal and paternal forebears. As Allworthy's quibble indicates, an oral report of the circumstances of Tom's birth is inadequate: "Yet sure it was a most unjustifiable Conduct in my Sister to carry this Secret with her out of the World" (*Tom* 2:942). Allworthy takes on trust the letter's contents, however, just as we must take on trust the claim for Tom's assumption of virtue.[45] Thus Allworthy embraces Tom as his nephew on the basis of a report of a report. The circumstance reinforces an implicit motif of continual deferral: Tom's realization of identity is always somewhat beyond reach. Bridget's letter nevertheless is intended to fix Tom's identity and confirm what he has already proved. Although it is apparently outside the text of Tom's experiences, it reinforces their meaning. Like the prefaces, the letter serves as an "attending discourse," the validation by the father—or, in Tom's case, the father speaking through the mother.

Bridget's letter is written before Tom's fall into narrative history actually commences but is not "read" until that history has almost reached its end. Because deferred revelation enables storytelling—that attempt to fill in the gap—the letter must wait until the plot is ready to be wound up. Tom can prove himself in the meantime. But if the text that tells Tom's story is slandered, it may have no opportunity to prove itself. The attending discourse of the prefaces provides that opportunity.

The prefaces attempt to legitimate and validate the text of which they are an integral part. In "Outwork," the self-deconstructing "preface" to *Dissemination*, Jacques Derrida deconstructs the classical notion of the preface as anterior and exterior to the text and brings to our attention the contradiction inherent in this type of discourse. Written "in view of their own self-effacement," prefaces nevertheless are inextricably part of the texts they introduce.[46] Written (presumably) after the text they attend, they sum up beforehand what will reveal itself hereafter. As ostensible doubles of what follows they should be able to fall away from the main text without affecting its meaning or indeed even replace the main text. Yet the very gesture of doubling, of supplementing, reveals that the text cannot stand by itself. Nor, of course, can the preface. Derrida regards the preface as an attempt at controlling the meaning of the text it precedes: "As the preface to a book, it is the word of a father assisting and admiring his work, answering for his son, losing his breath in sustaining, retaining, idealizing, reinternalizing, and mastering his seed."[47] In effect, the preface functions as the word of the father answering for his son.

Characteristically, Fielding ironizes the importance of the prefaces, suggesting that they are dispensable. He grants the reader permission to skip them and "begin the following Books, at the second Chapter" (*Tom* 1:215) or to opt for "the Advantage of beginning to read at the fourth or fifth Page instead of the first" (2:833). He claims that the prefaces "may as properly be prefixed to any other Book in this History as to that which they introduce, or indeed to any other History as to this" (2:832); seemingly, they may fall away from the main text without disturbing its meaning or their own. He calls their very meaning into question with the self-deconstructing titles he provides for them: "Containing little or nothing," "Containing five pages of Paper," "Too short to need a Preface," and "Containing a Portion of introductory Writing." He explains that he intends the prefaces to serve as contrast to the main narrative: "To say the Truth, these soporific parts are so many Scenes of Serious artfully interwoven, in order to contrast and set off the rest; and this is the true meaning of a late facetious Writer, who told the Public, that whenever he was dull, they might be assured there was a Design in it" (1:215). The prefaces are seemingly the deadweight that makes the rest of the text more buoyant.

But we must be dull readers indeed to find the prefaces dull or to believe Fielding really wishes us to find them so. Claims for the dispensability, the generality, of these chapters are at odds with Fielding's contention that they "have given the Author the greatest Pains in composing" (*Tom* 1:209). Fielding may playfully undercut his work, but he intends us to take it seriously.

The prefaces, after all, enable Fielding to establish his paternal link to the text. Without the attending discourse *Tom Jones* might be confused with its imitators: "Among the other good Uses for which I have thought proper to institute these several introductory Chapters, I have considered them as a Kind of Mark or Stamp, which may hereafter enable a very indifferent Reader to distinguish what is true and genuine in this historic Kind of Writing, from what is false and counterfeit" (*Tom* 1:487). Because the prefaces enable Fielding to display his talent and erudition, they secure him "from the Imitation of those who are utterly incapable of any Degree of Reflection, and whose Learning is not equal to an Essay" (1:488). We should not take the overblown claim too seriously, of course; Fielding's statements are subject to some of the same ironic undercutting as those of other characters in the text. Nevertheless, the passage reinforces the paternal claims he makes throughout, for it establishes that the prefaces function as a signature, proving authorship and ensuring against forgery.[48]

As we have seen, the prefaces assist and legitimate Fielding's "issue" by establishing the text's truth-value and undermining that of others, deflecting the hostility of critics, and clarifying meaning and purpose. Overall, legitimacy is based on a tautology: the text is a sound piece of literature because the attending discourse regards the way it is written as criteria for soundness; the criteria are sound because the demonstration shows them to be so. We cannot reject Fielding's poetics without rejecting the text, and vice versa.

Tom's legitimation may be similarly tautological: he can be absorbed into the Allworthy line because his actions show him to be deserving, but he may show he is deserving precisely because he is of the Allworthy line. In effect, both Tom Jones and *Tom Jones* are legitimated twice—once by what occurs throughout the narrative journey and once by the attending discourse. We question whether Tom could be embraced as Allworthy's heir without parental validation or without proving himself through his deeds. We question, too, whether the text could be meaningful without the prefatory poetics or whether the poetics would make sense without the demonstration provided by the narrative. In times when the sources of authority are thrown into question, when neither traditional nor progressive signs assuredly stand for their referents, such a double gesture of legitimation may be necessary—a hedging of bets, so to speak.

Tom's twofold legitimation in fact reflects Fielding's attempt to resolve the mounting tension between propertied and commercial interests. As Pocock points out, after the 1670s,

> there were two parallel and competing doctrines of propertied individualism: one which praised the gentleman's or yeoman's independence in land and arms as performing the functions of the *oikos* in an English or Virginian *polis*, and one which praised the mobility of the individual in an increasingly commercial society as teaching him the need for free deference to authority.[49]

Tom is both stable and mobile, linked to both the great estate and the road, to tradition and innovation.

Tom and the text that tells his story concurrently subvert and reinforce tradition, essentially enabling tradition to remain viable through an incorporation—or appropriation—of a nontraditional element that derives authority from the tradition it would seem to challenge. The situation is analogous to the way an appeal to a fundamental law located in a supposedly actual past had been used to support the Glorious Revolution.[50] This merging of the traditional and the nontraditional has subtle political ramifications in that an implicit Whig agenda was to demonstrate that the Hanoverian succession, although not in a direct line, was morally legitimate.[51]

Tom's bastard state is seemingly subversive in that it calls aristocratic notions into question. C. J. Rawson points out that Fielding could have made Tom "a legitimate foundling like Joseph Andrews," and he concludes that "Fielding must have known that it was in some ways bold and unorthodox to make his hero a bastard and keep him so."[52] The bastard state of the hero casts doubt on the traditional connection between moral worth and social position.

As a bastard Tom marks a rupture in the Allworthy line. Although the line has retained its moral integrity, it has come to a dead end, as Allworthy's childlessness indicates. Symbolically suggesting impotence, this childlessness reinforces Allworthy's impotence as a moral force.[53] However sound his principles and his advice, he cannot keep the Blifils out of Paradise Hall, and Blifil *fils*—the legitimate and hence traditionally acceptable successor—would ensure the destruction of all moral authority were he to inherit. As Tom journeys toward identity, he experiences instances of hypocrisy that will presumably provide him with the necessary wariness so lacking in the guileless Allworthy, and he undergoes trials that may give him the mercy sometimes wanting in the magisterial squire. Tom will thus presumably revitalize Paradise Hall. As Jenny Teichman makes clear in her study of bastardy, Tom cannot be considered as actually belonging to the Allworthy line, but he can found his own line: "the general rule was that a male bastard could found a lineage (i.e., pass on a name) but could not belong to one that already existed."[54] The foundling can found. And the end of the novel affirms that the line will continue, for Fielding tells us that "two fine Children"—one of them a boy—occupy the nursery (*Tom* 2:981). Moral authority is thus restored by the break in genealogical continuity, a break that enables the incorporation of the nontraditional.

But Bridget's letter complicates our perception of the novel's stance with regard to tradition. McKeon sees Tom's story as marking a shift in Fielding from a conservative to a progressive ideology: "Unlike Joseph Andrews [Fielding's 'aristocratic' hero], Tom, although of gentle lineage, is truly a bastard . . . . A rogue figure who makes good, Tom is much closer to the model of the progressive protagonist than anything Fielding had previously attempted."[55] As a progressive hero Tom proves his worth by his achievement, not by his birth. Yet what McKeon subordinates is the fact of Tom's "gentle lineage," attested to by Bridget's letter. If we, like Rawson, examine some alternative possibilities to Tom's heritage, we might wonder why Fielding did not keep Tom the son of Jenny and Partridge. Then Tom, climbing up from lowly origins to display his moral worth, could more accurately be called a modern, self-made man. But as the son of the well-born Bridget and the genteel Summer he, like Joseph Andrews before him, refers back to the romantic tradition that genteel birth will out.

With his genteel birth Tom bears the traces of a yearning for a golden age, free from the pull of history, when signs and their referents were joined by God in a timeless stasis of meaning and Paradise Hall could unproblematically stand for what it suggests. In his discussion of the act of beginning Edward Said notes that it "is basically an activity which ultimately implies return and repetition rather than simple linear accomplishment."[56] Tom begins as an unknown who must set out to prove himself, but he returns to become part of a prior tradition. In some sense we can see Tom as a repetition or double of Allworthy. Bearing Allworthy's first name at the outset Tom could conceivably bear his surname by the conclusion, in keeping with the practice of conferring the maternal grandfather's name on a bastard.[57] In effect, the name toward which he has moved throughout the text is Thomas Allworthy. The heir has circled back to become the father. Tom Jones as Thomas Allworthy thus represents a gesture toward stopping historical process, freezing time in a moment of moral perfection.

Such an age may be unrealizable, but change can still be kept within bounds. The world has fallen into history; the sign must move through time and space to its meaning, and there is no true return. Because of this gap between sign and referent, nothing can rest in a state of equilibrium. Even what would seem to be perfect is subject to change and thus requires continual renovation. The figure of Tom thus encapsulates both a desire for stasis and an acknowledgment of the need for change, for Tom finally both is and is not a double for Allworthy. Although he might legally become Thomas Allworthy, Tom Jones he remains, in the text's final passages and in his hold upon our imagination. The name Allworthy, as a type name, suggests an immanent connection between word and thing; on the other hand the name Jones, as a neutral appellation, suggests that the word gains meaning only through a discursive process. As his dual names indicate, Tom both renovates the status quo and preserves it. Although Tom's dual nature maintains a suggestive irresolution, the novel that bears his name ultimately presupposes a present that has built itself upon the sturdy foundations of the past. Tom resolves the conflict between competing ideologies: (1) he encompasses both aristocratic and progressive notions, (2) he represents both the stability of the man of property and the mobility of the man of commerce, and (3) he demonstrates that, despite his oblique relationship to the line of succession, he is the legitimate heir. He thus offers a consoling vision to an age beset with strife. The narrative journey begins and ends at Paradise Hall, and by the end it becomes a true paradise—the reptilian Blifil has been expelled and Allworthy's heir has proved his worth. The multiple marriages tie up all loose ends and provide a sense of completion and unity. Abraham Adams can even migrate from *Joseph Andrews* to join the happy band.

Tom is presented as a founder in the root sense—as someone who originates or makes grow. Fielding similarly styles himself as a founder, as one who initiates a new form of writing, yet his authority as an author comes from his ability not only to found but to continue. The words *author* and *authority* both derive from a word that can mean to originate or to augment. As Edward Said points out, the word *authority* itself functions as "a constellation of linked meanings," comprising notions of "beginning or inauguration, augmentation by extension, possession and continuity."[58] Such seemingly contradictory notions of beginning, continuing, and augmenting appear in Fielding's prefatory poetics.

At times, Fielding links his authority as a lawgiver to his capacity to originate; he thus attempts to prove himself a founder by purposefully cutting himself off from what has gone before. He imperiously declaims: "For as I am, in reality, the Founder of a new Province of Writing, so I am at liberty to make what laws I please therein" (*Tom* 1:77). As a founder he rejects the ancients' standard of the unities, their predilection for supernatural incident, their invocation of the muses. Received poetic forms have little place in this "new Province."

Although Fielding's claims that he is *originating* would seem to go hand in hand with a conception of his work as *original*, such is not the case. Despite his rejection of various prior forms, Fielding does not make a Wordsworthian argument that his text requires a shift in the readers' sensibilities and expectations. The same impulse that connects Tom, albeit nonlinearly, to an established line connects *Tom Jones* to literary tradition. Commencing with an epigraph from Homer that suggests the epic nature of its vision, *Tom Jones* depends throughout for its meaning upon prior texts and prior authority. It is dedicated to George Lyttleton in order that his virtuous character might serve as a guarantee of its own virtue, Lyttleton's authority thus validating the text's. Although Sophia's "sublime" introduction is semi-parodic, it is also semi-serious; we are meant both to laugh at the inflated diction and to form an elevated conception of Sophia. Attempting to ensure that we accept this technique, Fielding cites literary tradition: "And for this Method we plead many Precedents. First, this is an art well known to, and much practiced by, our Tragic Poets; who seldom fail to prepare their Audience for the Reception of their principal Characters" (*Tom* 1:152). The text throughout transmutes classical devices by the mock-heroic use it makes of them. Yet the mock-heroic flaunts its familial resemblance to its classical forebears just as Tom, although initially debased, displays the Allworthy character notwithstanding. The mock-heroic elements certainly announce the text's connection to the neoclassic tradition as practiced by Dryden, Pope, and Fielding's revered Swift. Furthermore, the mock-heroic depends for its meaning on the tradition it draws upon. Molly's battle in the churchyard, for example, draws much of its comic resonance from its connection to the *Iliad*. Fielding's multifarious quotations from classic and neoclassic sources serve as supporting evidence for the advancement of his particular arguments.

Thus, the "new Province" is in part carved out of an ancestral estate, and this reliance upon tradition is connected to an attempt to reinforce tradition. The figure of Tom is in a sense an ideological instrument in that it makes a claim for the viability of traditional modes of authority. The ruling classes can be revitalized without being rejected. In its own way the prefatory poetics put forth a similar argument. Prescribing both what may be written and who may write it, Fielding supports traditional hierarchies of class and gender, gentrifying and masculinizing the novel form. The necessary qualifications for the novel writer are "Genius," "Learning," the "Sort of Knowledge . . . to be had by Conversation," and "a good Heart."

Although genius and a good heart may cut through class boundaries (in fact, many of his good-hearted characters come from the lower classes), according to Fielding learning and conversation tend to be upper-class attributes. By "learning" Fielding means "A competent Knowledge of History and of the *Belles Lettres*" (*Tom* 1:492). Under this criterion, no "thresher-poet" could impose his wares upon a credulous public. Without the patina of learned allusion, such wares cannot be admitted into the literary institution. In a land lacking an egalitarian educational system, only an elite few (such as the Eton-trained Fielding) would have the requisite knowledge.

The class argument becomes even more apparent when we look at Fielding's fourth criterion for the writer. Knowledge garnered through conversation requires a broad range of experience: "Now this Conversation in our Historian must be universal, that is, with all Ranks and Degrees of Men: For the Knowledge of what is called High-Life, will not instruct him in low, nor *e converso*, will his being acquainted with the inferior Part of Mankind, teach him the Manners of the superior" (*Tom* 1:494). Such knowledge cannot be gathered from books; the only way a writer can gain the necessary acquaintance with both realms of experience is through direct contact. The lower classes, bent on catering to the whims of their "betters," apparently can be readily examined, whereas the "Higher Order of Mortals" is not generally displayed in ordinary walks of life. Thus, only people of higher rank can have acquaintance with its denizens: "In short, this is a Sight to which no Persons are admitted, without one or other of these Qualifications, viz. either Birth or Fortune; or what is equivalent to both, the honourable Profession of a Gamester" (2:742). Although the final qualification is a sly jab at the decadence of the upper classes, this passage nonetheless supports the notion that those in the lower ranks can have no adequate understanding of those in the higher. Fielding elides the fact that those higher beings who are so minutely observing their servants are just as likely to be themselves the objects of observation. Servants bent on elevating themselves indeed might have more reason to watch the masters than the masters would have to watch them. But such elision is necessary for Fielding to sustain his notion that the proper inheritors of literary authority come, like Tom Jones, from the upper ranks.

Women, needless to say, would in general lack the qualification of what Fielding considers "competent Knowledge," and the frequent sallies at learned women in Fielding's texts (for example, Mrs. Western in *Tom Jones* and Mrs. Atkinson in *Amelia*) suggest that the current state of woman's ignorance should be maintained. Mr. Allworthy's panegyric on Sophia—clearly Fielding's feminine ideal—makes explicit that the learned woman is anathema to Fielding:

> she hath one Quality which existed in a high Degree in that best of Women, who is now one of the first of Angels. . . . I never heard any thing of Pertness, or what is called Repartee out of her Mouth; no Pretence to Wit, much less to that Kind of Wisdom, which is the Result only of great Learning and Experience; the affectation of which, in a young Woman, is as absurd as any of the Affectations of an Ape. No dictatorial Sentiments, no judicial Opinions, no profound Criticisms. Whenever I have seen her in the Company of Men, she hath been all Attention, with the Modesty of a Learner, not the Forwardness of a Teacher. (*Tom* 2:882)

Fielding herein extols modest deference to male authority in women—clearly, a posture irreconcilable with the authorial vocation.[59] Under his criteria the traditionally dispossessed can—and should—have no voice.

The most vociferous claims for authorial control are self-subverting. Fielding conceives himself as a ruler whose "Laws, my readers, whom I consider my subjects, are bound to obey" (*Tom* 1:77). More audaciously, while cautioning readers against condemning seemingly irrelevant episodes in the text, he grandly proclaims: "This work may, indeed, be considered as a great Creation of our own; and for a little Reptile of a Critic to presume to find Fault with any of its Parts, without knowing the manner in which the Whole is connected, and before he comes to the final Catastrophe, is a most presumptuous Absurdity" (2:524–25). Although the deity passage has been taken at face value, most prominently by Battestin, its pomposity invites deflation.[60] Readers may pose a threat to Fielding's edenic creation, but he can hardly wish them to take seriously the statement that he considers them reptiles. Too, if Fielding is the god of his creation, he is an inadequate one: he bullies his readers and flaunts his superior knowledge, then undercuts his own omniscience, claiming not to know why the rug fell from Molly's cupboard or what goes on in the mind of a Blifil. The authorial stance is consistently ironized. Nevertheless, through the prefatory poetics Fielding both authors and authorizes the novel. He specifies who may speak and what may be spoken, providing, in Michel Foucault's terms, a "ritual" for novelistic discourse. This ritual

> defines the qualifications required of the speaker (of who in dialogue, interrogation or recitation, should occupy which position and formulate which type of utterance); it lays down gestures to be made, behaviour, circumstances and the whole range of signs that must accompany discourse; finally, it lays down the supposed or imposed significance of the words used, their effect upon those to whom they are addressed, the limitations of their constraining validity.[61]

Fielding's rejection of other texts, his establishment of rules, his qualifications for authorship, his validation of his own enterprise—all serve to set down the necessary ritual for the novel genre.

Ultimately, the very impulse that gives birth to the genre works against any and all totalizing claims. *Tom Jones* itself—with its wordplay, its recontextualization of other texts, its pastiche of genres and motifs, its persistent deflation of authorial pretensions—consistently calls authority into question. Yet the self-canonizing prefaces mark a significant moment in the establishment of the novel, charting a particular course for novelistic discourse with which we still contend. Discussing the scurrilous writings mistakenly fathered upon him, Fielding offers an optimistic prediction: "All these Works, however, I am well convinced, will be dead long before this Page shall offer itself to thy Perusal: For however short the Period may be of my own Performances, they will most probably outlive their own infirm Author, and the weakly Productions of his abusive Contemporaries" (*Tom* 2:914). Although other bastards die young, *Tom Jones* will live on, testimony to the control of its insistent author and the authority of the novel form—the legitimate heir of literary tradition.

CHAPTER FOUR

Pride and Prejudice

Jane Austen's Double Inheritance Plot

Single Women have a dreadful propensity for being poor—which is one very strong argument in favour of Matrimony.
—Jane Austen, *Letters* (483)

You tell me the plot of your novel in a nutshell. It sounds perfectly dreadful. But then so does *Pride and Prejudice* in a nutshell. —Fay Weldon, *Letters to Alice on First Reading Jane Austen*

IN HIS MASTERPIECE NOVEL *Tom Jones*, Henry Fielding more insistently and consistently assumed the overt authorial stance that he had taken in the rougher *Joseph Andrews*, thereby providing both a defense and a poetics of the novel genre. When Jane Austen published *Sense and Sensibility* and *Pride and Prejudice*, however, the narrator/author of *Northanger Abbey* had become narrator only—authoritative, to be sure, but no longer explicitly authorial. Although she drops the authorial role, she nevertheless continues implicitly to consider the nature of her authorial inheritance in *Pride and Prejudice*, revising Fielding so as to assert the importance of woman's role in the house of fiction.

Why Austen assumed and then dropped the stance of author is indeterminable. The earlier drafts *Elinor and Marianne* and *First Impressions* were reputedly epistolary, a mode that inherently bypasses the figure of the overseeing, omniscient author. As Austen transmuted them into their final versions she may have found that an overt authorial stance meshed awkwardly with what she already had. Too, in order to parody sentimental and gothic fiction Austen had needed to draw the reader's attention to writerly conventions. As she shifted from parody, however, she would have been more interested in naturalizing the conventions upon which she drew, rather than exposing their artificiality.

Certainly, the contemporary disparagement of the novel genre, which had prompted her spirited defense in *Northanger Abbey*, persisted. Even as late as 1815 Sir Walter Scott would begin his favorable review of *Emma* by discussing the morally suspect nature of novel reading:

> There are some vices in civilized society so common that they are hardly acknowledged as stains upon the moral character, the propensity to which is nevertheless carefully concealed, even by those who most frequently give way to them; since no man of pleasure would willingly assume the gross epithet of a debauchee or a drunkard. One would almost think that novel-reading fell under this class of frailties, since among the crowds who read little else, it is not common to find an individual of hardihood sufficient to avow his taste for these frivolous studies.[1]

Yet despite the fact that the novel continued to be regarded as an inferior literary genre, Austen may have felt that she had already said all she had to say in its defense in *Northanger Abbey*. Susan Lanser suggests that "the narrator's outspokenness" may have accounted in part for the publisher's failure to publish *Northanger* and that, "because an overt narrator risks the reader's dissent . . . Austen may be attempting to guarantee her narrators' authority by having them speak less openly" in her later texts.[2] But it may also be that, as she continued to write and revise, Austen developed greater confidence in the worth and merit of her enterprise, assuming that her subsequent texts could prove themselves without the validation of an "attending discourse." In any case, by dropping the authorial stance Austen redirects our focus from the plot of the author to the related plot of authority.

In eighteenth- and early nineteenth-century novels, the issue of inheritance customarily plays an important role in resolving conflicts over the grounds for moral and, by extension, literary authority. The landed estate maintains its representational significance as a traditional sign of moral authority.[3] But the question of who deserves to inherit it is foregrounded, as we see in *Tom Jones*. Fielding's text provides an archetypal inheritance plot. With the accession of the illegitimate but genteelly born Tom to the Allworthy estate, the text mediates between the notion that the grounds for moral authority reside in traditional hierarchical structures and the notion that the grounds for such authority must be demonstrated. Tom renovates Paradise Hall by restoring moral authority. Moreover, Tom's story resonates thematically with Fielding's explicit authorial commentary, which claims that the text simultaneously derives from traditional literary genres and renovates them.

The settlement of an estate is a key issue in Austen's texts as well, prompting more than a few sneers about her mercenary concerns. Like Fielding, Austen draws on this motif as a means for exploring issues of moral authority and authorship. But Austen delves into something that Fielding does not address at all in *Tom Jones* and only begins to glance at in *Amelia*—the question of woman's relation to an inherited tradition and the nature of woman's authority. Of all Austen's texts *Pride and Prejudice* most thoroughly draws on the traditional inheritance plot in an attempt to answer this question.

In *Northanger Abbey*, although the issue of property is important, the issue of inheritance is not. Granted, a deficient patriarch presides over the Abbey, and (based on what we know of Frederick Tilney's character) the inheritor will be as morally bankrupt as his father. But Austen does not focus on the renovation of the estate; Henry Tilney is a second son, and the question of how he or Catherine might reinvest the Abbey with moral authority is not adequately addressed. As Catherine serves little in the way of an exemplary function this all may be just as well. The Abbey itself functions not as a repository of values but as a means for Austen to effect her gothic parody. Like all of Austen's protagonists Catherine undergoes a Cinderella-like elevation to wealth and happiness, but her elevation has no significant impact upon her society.

Certainly, in *Sense and Sensibility*, the issue of inheritance has greater prominence than it does in *Northanger*. *Sense and Sensibility* begins with the Dashwood women being ejected from an entailed estate. Willoughby's cousin disinherits him when she learns of his sexual peccadilloes and then puts him back in her will when he marries "a woman of character" (*SS* 379). Edward Ferrars "forfeit[s] the right of eldest son" (377) because of his engagement to Lucy Steele, and Robert Ferrars assumes that right despite his marriage to her. Marianne Dashwood ends up married to the master of Delaford and becomes "the patroness of a village" (379). Yet, for all its emphasis on inheritance *Sense and Sensibility* puts forward no central inheritance plot and does not deal with the renovation of an estate.

Pride and Prejudice, however, draws heavily on the archetypal inheritance plot. It is Austen's revision of *Tom Jones* from a woman's perspective, with Elizabeth filling the Tom Jones role and Pemberley serving as Austen's version of Paradise Hall. Similar to Fielding's text in its fairy-tale components and comedic structure, it tells the story of a flawed but deserving person who, initially cut off from position in society by an unjust law, ultimately gains both self-knowledge and fortune, the latter a corollary of the former. Elizabeth Bennet, denied any share in her father's entailed estate and seemingly faced with a choice between material or intellectual want, ends up marrying the handsome prince, who can give her both ten thousand pounds and "judgment, information, and knowledge of the world" (*PP* 312).[4]

But the exchange is not merely one-sided. As in *Tom Jones* the protagonist not only is elevated to an estate, as in a fairy tale, but also is instrumental in renovating that estate. The owner of the Pemberley estate—that stronghold of traditional values—clearly lacks something at the outset of the novel. Darcy is, in fact, a little like a frog prince; Elizabeth's rebuff, rather than her kiss, prompts him to shed his cold reserve and achieve an integration of gentlemanly essence with gentlemanly appearance. The renovation of the most important estate in the novel thus comes not, as in *Tom Jones*, through the incorporation of a bastard but through the influence of a woman.

Although Elizabeth's function as a catalyst for social renewal makes a case for the importance of women's influence (a point complicated by a fairly slippery argument about class), essentially the novel supports rather than criticizes the traditional patriarchal institutions of society. Like *Tom Jones* the subversive elements are gathered up in a reinforcement of the status quo. *Pride and Prejudice* actually features not one but two inheritance plots, and this doubling enables Austen both to question traditional social structures and to validate them. Elizabeth links the two plots together: denied (what we might regard as) her birthright she ends up coming into a fortune by being incorporated into another line. While the first plot serves as a critique of patriarchal tradition, the second serves as a validation of it. The entail—that gesture toward perpetuation of the line through heirs male—may unfairly cut Elizabeth off from a share in the family estate, but the exemplar of aristocratic, patriarchal tradition confers another one upon her; she is rescued by Darcy, and only through his granting it to her does she have any power, a situation to which she willingly accedes. In effect, Elizabeth is circumscribed by the Pemberley estate—the repository of patriarchal values. The institutions of patriarchy may need female intervention to remain viable, but they are portrayed as intrinsically worthwhile; it is through them that the deserving (including women) get their rewards. The benevolent father may be in need of some correction, but he can finally put all things to rights. His ability to encompass criticism shows that the system has built into it a self-corrective "program." By undercutting the negative effects of the first plot, the second plot serves, if not as the last word on the subject, at least as a more insistent one. The ending of the novel is an attempt to defuse the tensions raised by the entailment issue.

We can regard the inheritance plot of *Pride and Prejudice* as reflecting not only the tension between competing value systems but also the plot of female authorship. Through her revision of an archetypal plot of self-discovery and social renewal, Austen makes clear the significance of woman's voice in the novel form. But by keeping her revision within the bounds of a patriarchal plot Austen ends up supporting, rather than subverting, the structures and conventions of her literary forefathers.

Elizabeth and the Entail

The first inheritance plot in *Pride and Prejudice* focuses on the settlement governing the Longbourn estate. The fact of the entail is a determinant of the heroine's insecure situation in society and a catalyst for much of the action in the novel. Just as the fact of his bastardy (coupled with the machinations of Blifil) deprives Tom Jones of any claim to Paradise Hall, so does the Longbourn entail cut Elizabeth off from what may seem to be her rightful inheritance. And Elizabeth's state of dispossession, like Tom's, causes her to embark on what becomes a quest for self-knowledge and position.[5]

Unlike Tom Jones, Elizabeth is not an actual foundling; nevertheless the romantic aura of that condition clings to her. As critics have often remarked, Austen heroines are often foundlings in spirit, if not in truth, and Elizabeth is no exception, with her improvident and often remote father and her silly and querulous mother.[6] With the exception of Jane, she finds herself in a nest full of cuckoos. The Gardiners seem more appropriate parental figures than her biological parents; Mrs. Gardiner in particular provides the advice and counsel that her own mother is incapable of giving. The Gardiners' adoption of Elizabeth as a member of their traveling party enables her partial reconciliation with Darcy at Pemberley. Indeed, when Elizabeth introduces the Gardiners to Darcy, she is able for the first time in his presence to feel pride in her family: "It was consoling, that he should know she had some relations for whom there was no need to blush" (*PP* 255). At this moment Elizabeth sheds the rags of familial impropriety before her prince and assumes her rightful position as the daughter of gentlefolk. In some sense, although it is subtilized almost beyond recognition, an archetypal story of the quest for true parents appears in *Pride and Prejudice*. The quasi-foundling motif enables Austen to reinforce a notion of women's essential marginality and dependence in the society she describes.

At the outset of the novel, Elizabeth does not live Cinderella-fashion in poverty and obscurity, but she will end up so unless she marries—and wisely. Along with her sisters she leads the leisured life of the lesser gentry, adequately if not lavishly supported by her father's two thousand pounds a year.[7] She is, however, dependent on others for any movement outside the family circle.[8] Mr. Bennet's death could abruptly plunge the Bennet daughters into straitened circumstances, for his estate is "entailed in default of heirs male, on a distant relation; and their mother's fortune, though ample for her situation in life, could but ill supply the deficiency of his" (*PP* 28). As the narrator later tells us, Mr. Bennet has neglected to set aside "an annual sum," and only five thousand pounds will come to his wife and daughters upon his death (308). Mrs. Bennet makes clear to Elizabeth that she considers the sum insufficient to the maintenance of both herself and her daughters: "But I tell you what, Miss Lizzy, if you take it into your head to go on refusing every offer of marriage in this way, you will never get a husband at all—and I am sure I do not know who is to maintain you when your father is dead.—I shall not be able to keep you—and so I warn you" (113). Mrs. Bennet's disappointment at Elizabeth's refusal of Mr. Collins may cause her to exaggerate the situation, but her outburst lets us know that if Elizabeth does not marry she will have little to support her.

The subject of finding employment is not even broached—as it is, say, in the case of Jane Fairfax in *Emma*—and thus appears to be no viable alternative for the Bennet daughters. Such a violation of class imperatives cannot be countenanced for the descendants of a gentleman, however it might alleviate their straitened conditions.[9] Indeed, for the Bennet daughters leisure is enforced; even household tasks are considered beneath them, as we discover when Mrs. Bennet "with some asperity" assures Mr. Collins "that they were very well able to keep a good cook, and that her daughters had nothing to do in the kitchen" (*PP* 65). Their lack of useful accomplishment may make them desirable, but it makes their situation all the more desperate. A good marriage holds out their only hope for the future. Mrs. Bennet's dire prediction of the family's being turned out by the Collinses before Mr. Bennet "is cold in his grave" no doubt exaggerates matters, even considering Mr. Collins's venal nature (287). But Mrs. Bennet is right in assuming that after her husband's death, she and her daughters will be dispossessed of any right to the estate. In *Sense and Sensibility*, Austen had already considered what could happen when an estate was entailed upon a man, John Dashwood, who had no affective ties to the women residing there: "No sooner was his father's funeral over, than Mrs. John Dashwood, without sending any notice of her intention to her mother-in-law, arrived with her child and their attendants" (5). Upon the death of their father the Bennet daughters, like Elinor and Marianne, will become unwanted guests in what used to be their home.[10]

Ironically, the very efforts taken by Mr. and Mrs. Bennet to avert this future catastrophe have served only to make their situation more desperate. As Barbara English and John Saville point out, an entail could only be broken by an alliance of father and son, or of the life tenant and the next in succession: "No part of the settlement could be broken (except by act of Parliament) until a person named in the entail as tenant in tail came of age; then, joining with his father or other life tenant (or acting alone if he was already in possession of the estates) the entail could be ended, by the legal processes of 'suffering a common recovery' or by 'levying a fine.'"[11] The Bennets had hoped to resettle the Longbourn estate by resorting to just such measures: "When first Mr. Bennet had married, economy was held to be perfectly useless; for, of course, they were to have a son. This son was to join in cutting off the entail, as soon as he should be of age, and the widow and younger children would by that means be provided for" (*PP* 308). But the very attempts to bring forth a male heir increased the need for him: Mrs. Bennet gave birth to five girls in a row, thus rendering the small sum Mr. Bennet's heirs would have at his death even more meager.

As little sympathy as Austen allows us to have for Mrs. Bennet, we cannot help but regard her as a very desperate baby-machine, frantically trying to produce the jackpot child who can save her and the girls from financial straits—and, of course, courting death with each successive childbirth. Lawrence Stone points out that during this time, "childbirth was a very dangerous experience," and Fay Weldon makes a persuasive case for the negative effect of so many lyings-in on Mrs. Bennet: "After sixteen pregnancies (which meant something like six babies brought to term and safely delivered) your chances of dying were . . . one in two. Mrs. Bennet, giving birth to Mary, must have been worried indeed."[12] Although Austen never touches on the risks of numerous pregnancies, we can assume that in her day such risks were understood, and Mrs. Bennet's plight thus casts subtextual shadows over the primarily sunny novel.[13] Mrs. Bennet's many efforts to produce a male heir and her continual worry that she get her daughters married off (comprising a sort of insistent chorus in the novel) make us aware of the desperateness of the situation into which the entail puts her. We can perhaps even begin to understand her rejoicing over the "patched-up business" of Lydia's marriage; why should she care for social forms when she no longer has to worry about keeping *one* daughter at least? As Weldon suggests, Mrs. Bennet is "the only one with the slightest notion of the sheer desperateness of the world."[14]

Mr. Collins's character reinforces our sense that the entail is harmful. Under the tenancy of Mr. Bennet, Longbourn is in the hands of a sensible man—although not a particularly responsible one. Under the tenancy of

Mr. Collins, however, it will be in the hands of an "oddity" (*PP* 64), as Elizabeth terms him—a man whose deficiency of sense "had been but little assisted by education or society" (70). Mr. Collins happily kowtows before the imperious Lady Catherine, derives his own self-importance from his ability to inflate hers, and falls in love with three different women in the course of eleven days.[15] The influence of the pragmatic Charlotte can but slightly temper his silliness, as Elizabeth's sojourn at Hunsford makes clear, and we must assume that his accession to the Longbourn estate will signal the beginnings of intellectual and moral decline.

By making Mr. Collins the heir of Longbourn, Austen implicitly indicts the principle of automatically settling an inheritance on the males rather than females in a line. As Lawrence Stone and Jeanne Fawtier Stone point out in *An Open Elite?* the so-called strict settlement, of which the entail was the cornerstone, enabled "the smooth passage of seat and main estate in the direct male line, relatively immune from dissipation or waste or sale by the owner for the time being."[16] English and Saville make clear that the settlement in tail male was a matter of custom, not law: "It was, of course, legally possible to name any person in a settlement; it was custom that kept it to near relatives, and custom that emphasized primogeniture." Settlements were often set up so as to "allow distant male relatives to succeed before much more closely related females," precisely the situation that occurs in *Pride and Prejudice*.[17] In effect, the entail was a means for both preserving property intact and providing a sense of genealogical continuity, represented by the endurance of the family name. Fixing the settlement on a male heir puts preserving the forms of family honor (the large estate and the family name) before preserving the fact of it. Throughout the eighteenth century, settlements, according to English and Saville, "became more common and more effective" and began "evolving towards the comprehensive strict settlements of the nineteenth century."[18] Because the equation of honorable name with honorable person was increasingly called into question during this period, we might regard the proliferation of the strict settlement as a sign of crisis, a legally binding assertion of the value of tradition in the face of an increasing questioning of it.

By having a Mr. *Collins* succeed to the Longbourn estate, Austen subtly reinforces the iniquity of settling estates on the nearest male heir. We must assume that, because he has a different surname from Mr. Bennet, Mr. Collins is connected to the estate through a female. Thus, although his connection with the family is through an apparently more remote distaff line, Mr. Collins has greater rights solely on the basis of his sex than the direct descendants who actually bear what we must suppose is the family name.[19] Austen never makes clear the actual details of the

Longbourn settlement (as she does, for example, the settlement in *Sense and Sensibility*); such ambiguity tends to give us a sense of the mystifications inherent in the very custom of entailment.

Conversations among the characters emphasize the arbitrariness and consequent unfairness of entailing in tail male. At one point Mrs. Bennet in a conciliatory mood ascribes the settlement on Mr. Collins to "chance" (*PP* 165); although it is true that powers beyond human intervention decreed that the Bennets should remain sonless, human intervention certainly loaded the dice against the Bennet daughters. Far more telling is Mrs. Bennet's query, "Why should he have it more than anybody else?" (130). Mr. Bennet can only respond, "I leave it to yourself to determine"—and we must assume that a satisfactory answer is ultimately indeterminable. Although Mr. Bennet is typically being ironic at his wife's expense when he avers that "nothing can clear Mr. Collins of the guilt of inheriting Longbourn" (62), the statement rightly points to the blameworthiness of the law that lets him do so. The system can no more be cleared than can one that would allow a Blifil to take over Paradise Hall.

Lady Catherine De Bourgh, in her usual high-handed fashion, makes the only direct pronouncement in the novel against settling the estate in tail male. That the statement comes from her complicates our reading of the argument against entails, for Lady Catherine appears throughout the novel as a specious authority, occupying a noble position but lacking the intrinsic worth that would validate it. To a certain extent she may be, as Sandra Gilbert and Susan Gubar suggest, one of Austen's "angry dowagers," who function not simply as objects of derision but as doubles for the protagonists, articulating the rage Austen cannot allow them to express.[20] Austen's plot of the entail, in any case, enables us to observe the plot of patrilineal descent in which the social order conspires. As Gilbert and Gubar note, Austen deals with "the specific ways in which patriarchal control of women depends on women being denied the right to earn or even inherit their own money."[21] In a very real sense, Elizabeth has more right to the inheritance than Mr. Collins, yet she can have a share of it only if she marries him—a very bad bargain indeed.

Just as Tom Jones appears, even with his flaws, as the moral heir to the Allworthy estate, Elizabeth appears the proper heir to Longbourn. In the first place, more than anyone else in the novel Elizabeth displays the Bennet "genes." She is quite clearly her father's daughter; like him, she "delight[s] in any thing ridiculous" (*PP* 12), the two of them, for example, sharing a laugh over Mr. Collins's foibles (until, for Elizabeth, such foibles begin to threaten her peace of mind). Although not the eldest child, Elizabeth is Mr. Bennet's favorite and the only one of his progeny that he singles out for praise: "they are all silly and ignorant like other girls; but Lizzy has something more of quickness than her sisters" (5). The statement is a troubling one in that it authorizes Lizzy at the expense of the rest of the female sex. Although it rebounds somewhat on Mr. Bennet, pointing to the shallowness of his judgments, it also implies that the qualities that make Elizabeth a worthy successor—her mental acuity and clear-sightedness—are male-identified.

In *Tom Jones*, Fielding implies that, for all his flaws, Tom will actually prove a better master of Paradise Hall than Allworthy had been because he has learned to recognize the face of evil. In a similar way Elizabeth appears to be a stronger moral force than her father and capable, if she were only allowed by law, of bringing about an "improvement of the estate" (to borrow Alistair Duckworth's apt phrase). We tend to find Mr. Bennet fairly likable because of his sharp intelligence and his sardonic outlook on the follies of others. But he is one of Austen's failed fathers—in Gilbert and Gubar's terms, a representative of "the emptiness of the patriarchal hierarchy."[22] I have already mentioned that he has made no material provision for his daughters in the event of his death. Nor has he made any moral provision. His principal amusement being to laugh at the follies of others, he refrains from any instruction that might curtail this amusement. As Ronald Paulson points out, he is "an ironist who lacks the moral fiber of a satirist."[23] His frequent retirement to his library, in itself a bastion of male tradition, is a mark of his abdication of the paternal role. Elizabeth herself deplores "that continual breach of conjugal obligation and decorum which, in exposing his wife to the contempt of her own children, was so highly reprehensible" (*PP* 236). He is the father who mocks but does not mend, and we might wonder if Austen, with her criticism of the derisive patriarch, takes a sly jab at a patriarchal satiric tradition, which depicts women in a manner that exposes them to the contempt of the reader.[24]

Mr. Bennet's most flagrant abdication of his duty as a father occurs when he refuses to forbid Lydia to go to Brighton. Rather than prevent his wild daughter from making a spectacle of herself, he actually ends up facilitating her, as we can see by the sooner-the-better argument he makes to Elizabeth: "Lydia will never be easy till she has exposed herself in some public place or other, and we can never expect her to do it with so little expense or inconvenience to her family as under the present circumstances" (*PP* 230). Elizabeth here becomes his instructor, reminding him that his duty as a father includes the regulation of his family: "If you, my dear father, will not take the trouble of checking her exuberant spirits, and of teaching her that her present pursuits are not to be the business of her life, she will soon be beyond the reach of amendment" (231). But her good advice is in vain, the sequel to this episode driving home the consequences of paternal irresponsibility. After Lydia does indeed "expose herself," Mr. Bennet acknowledges the accuracy of Elizabeth's early advice, blaming himself for Lydia's folly. But we do not actually see in this instance the kind of growth that might render him truly worthy of his estate. When Elizabeth admonishes him for being too severe upon himself, he replies: "let me once in my life feel how much I have been to blame. I am not afraid of being overpowered by the impression. It will pass away soon enough" (299). Thus, although Mr. Bennet can see his own faults, he cannot see his way to amending them; he is incapable of moral development.

Elizabeth, however, joins to her already existent admirable qualities the capacity to amend her faults. I need not go into all of Elizabeth's virtues; her admirers—and they are many—have more than adequately enumerated them. But let me just touch on what seems to make her stand out from the other characters in the novel. Elizabeth has the intelligence and clear-sighted moral vision both to recognize the importance of social forms and to reject those that are forms only. We might say that her behavior falls between those of Elinor and Marianne Dashwood, as Austen describes it in a well-known passage from *Sense and Sensibility*: "Marianne was silent; it was impossible for her to say what she did not feel, however trivial the occasion; and upon Elinor therefore the whole task of telling lies when politeness required it, always fell" (*SS* 122). Elizabeth serves as a happy medium between the two sisters in the earlier novel, for although she generally maintains the forms of courtesy, she refuses to give way to polite lies. Her walk to Netherfield to see the ailing Jane exemplifies what is most praiseworthy in her character. Affection for her sister wins out over an excessively scrupulous attention to propriety, and her act smacks of more true courtesy than all the insincere simperings of Miss Bingley and Mrs. Hurst. Elizabeth sees through pretense and affectation and stays true to a rigorous standard of personal integrity.

Elizabeth has flaws, of course, yet intelligence is not one of them. Marilyn Butler contends that Austen is critical "of Elizabeth's way of thinking" and that she regards her intelligence with "scepticism."[25] But the Austen narrator revels in the same sort of satiric observations she has her heroine make, the authority of the narrator's vision thus reinforcing that of the protagonist's and vice versa. Austen's epistolary commentary on her heroine supplies no evidence of a particular critical attitude to her: "I must confess I think her as delightful a creature as ever appeared in print, and how I shall be able to tolerate those who do not like her at least I do not know" (Letter 76, *LSC* 297). Granted, Elizabeth's satiric wit seemingly aligns her with her irresponsible father and can actually lead her into error, as when, with regard to Darcy, she decides she is being "uncommonly clever in taking so decided a dislike to him, without any reason" (*PP*

225). Unlike Mr. Bennet, however, Elizabeth (as Paulson points out) "intends improvement and instruction as the ends of her irony."[26] If such an intention is not with her throughout, it is certainly with her during the latter half of the novel, as we see by her attempts to bring the newlywed Lydia to an awareness of her folly and to shake Jane from the placidity that has previously made Bingley uncertain of her love for him.

It is not Elizabeth's intelligence but her misuse of it that Austen criticizes. Although I am stating the obvious and oft-noted, it is the overabundance of the title qualities that constitutes Elizabeth's greatest flaws. Her pride, hurt by Darcy and flattered by Wickham, causes her to make prejudicial, and potentially harmful, assessments of each.

Elizabeth's flaws do not cause her to be banished from her ancestral home, as happens with Tom Jones, but like him she must embark on a journey to improve herself. As in Fielding's text the casual, picaresque structure of the journey turns into the causal structure of the quest for self-knowledge and identity. At Rosings Darcy's letter makes Elizabeth aware of the pride and prejudice that have kept her from being truly wise. Her realization that her supposedly astute judgments are in fact just prejudices formed by self-interest and desire humbles her pride in her discernment. Later, the ostensible chance journey to Pemberley (resulting from the Gardiners' cancellation of their original travel plans and Elizabeth's belief that Darcy is not in residence) proves in itself to be part of the quest structure, for here Elizabeth receives further validation of Darcy's essential goodness and becomes aware of her love for him. Each of her journeys leads to an anagnorisis that brings about moral development, just as Tom Jones's seemingly random journey to Upton and London leads to recognitions that are integral to the discovery of his identity.

Divested of pride and alert to her propensity toward forming prejudices, her mental acuity ripened into wisdom, Elizabeth assumes the moral stature that would qualify her as the proper heir to Longbourn, indeed a potential matriarch. Tom Jones's journey to self-awareness coincides with a journey to his proper position in life at Paradise Hall. But the Longbourn estate cannot belong to Elizabeth; unlike Allworthy, Mr. Bennet cannot, with authorial fiat, circumvent the laws that deprive her of what appears to be her moral birthright. In some sense, as a woman Elizabeth has as little right to position as a bastard—and compared with the bastard Tom, even less so. Her quest is thus not, like Tom's, a circular return to her father's house. By accepting Mr. Collins, she could, of course, remain at Longbourn, but such an action would be a violation of all that she stands for and would show her to be as unqualified to inherit the estate as he. Dispossessed permanently of a share in the Bennet family estate, Elizabeth must attach herself to another line to find the social position that is congruent with her moral worth, Austen thus replacing an incipient vision of matriarchy with a revisioning of patriarchy.

To some extent Elizabeth's plight mirrors that of her author. Austen finds that the woman writer has no unentailed literary estate. As she pointed out in *Northanger Abbey,* the feminocentric novel had been devalued. Tellingly, her irony-laden postmortem of *Pride and Prejudice* betrays her fear of a dull reader, one who assumes that her novel lacks the seriousness of a male-authored text:

> The work is rather too light, and bright, and sparkling; it wants shade; it wants to be stretched out here and there with a long chapter of sense, if it could be had; if not, of solemn specious nonsense, about something unconnected with the story; an essay on writing, a critique on Walter Scott, or the history of Buonparté, or anything that would form a contrast, and bring the reader with increased delight to the playfulness and epigrammatism of the general style. (Letter 77, *LSC* 299–300)

Austen herein makes an implicit, somewhat sardonic reference to Fielding's *Tom Jones,* full of essays on writing and seemingly disconnected observations. Her point about contrast recalls one of Fielding's justifications for the prefatory chapters in his text. She understands only too well that a text like Fielding's, both despite and because of its "solemn specious nonsense," is regarded as a legitimate heir to literary tradition, whereas her own work risks being disinherited. Thus, just as Elizabeth attaches herself to Darcy's line Austen manages to attach herself, however obliquely, to Fielding's, revising yet concurrently reinforcing the plot of *Tom Jones.*

Pemberley and the Patriarch

The line into which Elizabeth is incorporated is Darcy's. The Pemberley estate constitutes the other important piece of inherited property in the novel. Rosings is significant only insofar as it represents what Pemberley could become—a spurious sign of moral authority—if Lady Catherine De Bourgh had her way about joining the two estates. Through the extended description of Pemberley, Austen makes clear that it stands for something beyond itself. She never really describes Longbourn, and what we learn of Rosings comes to us mainly through the skewed perspective of Mr. Collins. But Austen lingers over the description of Pemberley. Like Paradise Hall, which "owes less to Art than to Nature" (*Tom* 1:43), it meets the eighteenth-century ideal of a seamless blend between nature and art: "a stream of some natural importance was swelled into greater but without any artificial importance" (*PP* 245). At Pemberley nature and humanity seem to have worked in harmony, for Elizabeth "had never seen a place for which nature had done more, or where natural beauty had been so little counteracted by an awkward taste" (245). This notion of nature "doing" for Pemberley suggests that the estate is validated by nature, that it is part of some seemingly providential design. Its physical beauty renders Pemberley a fitting representation of its intended function as the repository of traditional authority.[27] It is not an empty sign. As Elizabeth discovers from the housekeeper, Pemberley's owner fulfills the duties of his office, being "the best landlord, and the best master . . . that ever lived" (*PP* 249). Austen's comments on Donwell Abbey—the moral center in *Emma*—could as easily be applied to Pemberley: "It was just what it ought to be, and it looked like what it was" (*Em* 358). Like Squire Allworthy's estate, Pemberley stands as an ideal, combining beauty of form with worthiness of function. Like any true ideal, it is seemingly inimitable; as Bingley observes, it would be "more possible to get Pemberley by purchase than imitation" (*PP* 38).

The family setup at Pemberley bears a suggestive affinity to the setup at Paradise Hall, so much so that we might regard it as a deliberate allusion. In his first appearance early in the novel, Darcy with his cold reserve might almost be mistaken for Blifil. He is responsible for banishing Wickham from the family estate, just as Blifil is responsible for getting Tom banished. Although legitimate, Wickham is a foster son, like Tom Jones; Darcy's father treated him like one of his own children, supported him through school, and made ample provision for him in his will. Wickham also resembles Fielding's hero in appearance: "he had all the best part of beauty, a fine countenance, a good figure, and very pleasing address" (*PP* 72). Like Tom, too, Wickham inspires tender feelings in many women: Georgiana Darcy, Mary King, and at least two of the Bennet daughters. In eloping with Lydia, he displays a disregard for sexual restraint that is worthy of the unreformed Tom Jones.[28]

Unlike Tom Jones, however, Wickham does not reform. His sexuality is not a mark of misdirected generosity but of vanity; he elopes with Lydia almost as an afterthought, unconcerned with the awkward social position in which he places her. As Elizabeth discovers, he is prodigal, mercenary, revengeful, and mendacious. Murray Krieger points out that Austen turns the Tom Jones model on its head, thus championing upper-class values:

> Wickham is not permitted to make it: it is as if, in *Tom Jones*, Blifil turned out to be the good guy. For it is Darcy, the wealthiest and most highly placed character in the novel, who is its hero and who gets the girl. . . . Wickham does not, like Tom Jones, make the discovery which makes him

> the worthy hero; rather, the discovery is made *about* him to make him the worthless villain.[29]

With regard to the respective fates of her two leading men, Austen certainly reverses the plot of *Tom Jones*, even to the extent that Wickham ends up permanently banished from "paradise."

But Austen's real focus is not on the leading men but on the leading lady. By demonstrating moral development and consequently attaining position, Elizabeth replaces Wickham as the Tom Jones figure. Like Tom Jones, she serves a suggestive supplemental function, for she both renovates the status quo and testifies to its essential goodness. In an effort both to champion "the novel" and to support the status quo, Fielding vacillated between presenting Paradise Hall and Allworthy as exemplary and presenting them as flawed and in need of renewal. Austen similarly vacillates. Krieger comments upon her "uncertainty about Darcy," which causes her to shift between "an unchanging one whose early shyness was mistaken for pride and a prideful one whom love causes to undergo a profound change to humanity."[30] Darcy's dual nature signifies Austen's internal division on feminist issues, enabling her both to criticize patriarchal structures and to validate them. By conferring a transformative power upon Elizabeth, Austen supports her argument about woman's importance as a moral force and raises interesting questions about gender construction in her society. Austen does so, however, only by subordinating Elizabeth's moral authority to Darcy's, which seemingly has been in place all along.

A case can certainly be made that Darcy needs to be reformed. The very first scene in which he appears casts him in a negative light. We can appreciate how the scene functions as a negative indicator of character when we compare it with its probable source in Fanny Burney's *Evelina*. Like Elizabeth, Evelina overhears the aristocratic hero make disparaging remarks about her. Yet her own inexperience and awkwardness have led him to dismiss her as "A poor weak girl!"—as Evelina herself admits—and Lord Orville soon assumes the role of her protector and mentor.[31] Darcy's initial comment that Elizabeth is "not handsome enough to tempt" him, spoken within her hearing, is flagrantly rude, threatening not only Elizabeth's self-esteem but the easy class-mixing of the Longbourn assemblies.[32] When Darcy makes his first proposal, he makes clear that he deplores the inferiority of Elizabeth's connections—not just (understandably) the inferiority of mind apparent in Elizabeth's mother and younger sisters but also the inferiority of the Bennet family's position. In his later confession to Elizabeth, he explains that he was brought up "to think meanly of all the rest of the world, to wish at least to think meanly of their sense and worth compared with my own" (*PP* 369). He has pridefully dismissed others, assuming they lack the worthiness that he has. He must learn to think less of himself and more of others.

Lady Catherine also points to the underlying fissures in the Pemberley structure. Samuel Kliger regards her as "the husk of the doctrine of class, not its inner living spirit" and a representation of "what Darcy might have become . . . had not Darcy met Elizabeth."[33] Donald Greene points out that Austen draws on genuine aristocratic names; Fitzwilliam (Darcy's given name and his aunt's maiden name) was borrowed from the family name of "the Whig magnifico" Lord Fitzwilliam. As Greene suggests, Austen's characterization of Lady Catherine—and of a prideful Darcy—may indeed be a jab at the Whig aristocracy, in keeping with her overall political agenda: "A case might be made out for saying that the unifying thesis of Jane Austen's novels is the rise of the middle class, a process of which the middle class itself became acutely conscious when Pitt, in effect, overthrew the entrenched political power of the Whig aristocracy in 1784."[34] Darcy may not be an aristocrat, but his autocratic behavior and pride, similar to Lady Catherine's, link him with aristocratic behavior—and thus Whiggism—at its worst.

It is not just by her proud, autocratic character that Lady Catherine represents an alternative future for Darcy. She also represents it through the plans she weaves around him. She tells Elizabeth that Darcy and her daughter "are destined for each other by the voice of every member of their respective houses" (*PP* 356). Such plans may be but pipe dreams; as Elizabeth most sensibly responds, why would her refusal of Darcy's hand "make him wish to bestow it on his cousin?" (357). But Lady Catherine nevertheless makes clear that she regards a union of the two cousins as necessary for the perpetuation of family honor. Although a union between Darcy and Anne De Bourgh would be legally sanctioned, the ghostly presence of the old incest taboo gives it a certain symbolic perversity.[35] As if the product of a long process of inbreeding, Anne De Bourgh is "pale and sickly" (162)—a lesser descendant of an unworthy aristocrat—and we might assume that her offspring would have even less to recommend them. The only cousin marriage we find in Austen—that between Fanny Price and Edmund Bertram—has a somewhat unhealthy aspect to it. Austen's more assertive heroines reject such inbreeding: Elizabeth refuses marriage with her cousin, as does Anne Eliot in *Persuasion*. Darcy's rejection of Anne De Bourgh in favor of Elizabeth represents a rejection of an endogamous alliance that threatens Pemberley's moral vigor in favor of an exogamous one that marks a renewal of it. This alliance presents a triumph of solid Tory values against the undeserved pride of the Whig aristocracy.

If we read Darcy as intrinsically flawed, we can thus regard Elizabeth as the necessary agent of his reformation. Elizabeth's force as an instrument of social renewal comes from her class status—or, perhaps more accurately in this case, from her rank.[36] Greene, for instance, notes: "It is the middle-class Bennets and Gardiners who compel the noble Fitzwilliams and Darcys to take them seriously."[37] Yet Austen's slipperiness on the issue raises difficulties. Austen ostensibly makes an egalitarian argument in that Darcy rejects a woman of his own rank in favor of a woman of a lower one—or, to be more precise, a member of the upper reaches of the gentry chooses a member of "the pseudo-gentry."[38] Lady Catherine certainly sees his marriage with Elizabeth as an issue of disparity in rank. Yet throughout the text, rank ends up as an ambiguous indicator of worth. Mrs. Bennet's vulgarity seems to stem from her birth, but her brother has no such defects. Darcy blushes for the highborn Lady Catherine just as Elizabeth blushes for the lowborn Mrs. Phillips. The steward's son turns out bad; the squire's son turns out good. The Bingley family, whose fortune was derived from trade, is made up of ill-bred, social-climbing daughters and a charming, gentlemanlike son who is worthy of Darcy's regard.

Reinforcing the ambiguity of the argument is Elizabeth's "mixed" parentage. Whereas Mrs. Bennet's parents were in trade, Mr. Bennet is a member of the lesser gentry. In order for Austen to make a clear egalitarian argument she would need to make both of Elizabeth's parents from the merchant class—just as Fielding, in order to be truly progressive, would need to make Tom the son of Partridge and Jenny Jones. Of course, Austen's quasi-liberal attitude toward class has come a long way from Fielding's assertions that only those of the upper classes are capable of exquisite feelings and so forth. As Lillian Robinson points out, Austen idealizes the landed elite, yet she also discovers value in the less privileged classes: "Jane Austen never abandons the ideal of the gentry in *Pride and Prejudice*, or calls it by some other name, but she makes its boundaries flexible enough to embrace real worth, in whatever class she may locate it."[39] In effect, the novel acknowledges an ideological shift in the ways of defining "real worth" while it sustains the traditional notion that worth resides in the upper gentry, as embodied in Darcy.

By virtue of its ambiguity, however, the class argument fails to hold up completely. Austen shifts emphasis to a gender argument—a shift marked by the replacement of Wickham, son of a steward, with Elizabeth, daughter of a gentleman—although even this argument is rife with contradictions.[40] Such a shift, however, may itself indicate Austen's attempt to address, or more accurately to defuse, the class issue.

As Nancy Armstrong argues, feminocentric texts of the late eighteenth and early nineteenth centuries tended to transform class conflicts into gender conflicts that could be easily resolved by the happy union of hero and heroine. The resolution of *Pride and Prejudice*, for example, functions in this way: "It is important to notice exactly how such a representation creates personal fulfillment where there had been internal conflict and social unity where there had been competing class interests."[41] Austen's subsuming of class issues to gender issues may indeed finesse the sticky problem of destabilized social categories. The replacement of Wickham by Elizabeth is suggestive. Were Wickham to be the source for moral renewal, he, as the son of a Pemberley dependent, would call the existent social hierarchies into question. Elizabeth, as a woman, however, tends to blur the boundaries of class.[42]

Austen implies that Elizabeth effects a change in Darcy because she is a woman and (more to the point) a "new" woman, capable of intelligence and self-assertion that go beyond what women have traditionally been allotted. Elizabeth refuses to conform to what is expected of her as a woman—an expectation that would include her acquiescence to Darcy as the representative of patriarchal tradition. As she later tells Darcy, defining him to himself, she originally attracted him because she defied his expectations of how a woman would behave toward him: "You were disgusted with the women who were always speaking and looking and thinking for *your* approbation alone. I roused, and interested you, because I was so unlike *them*" (*PP* 381). Instead of "speaking and looking and thinking" according to a male perspective, she does so according to her own. Throughout the text we find that the narrator links Darcy's increasing attraction to Elizabeth with her propensity to speak her mind, defend her position in a rational manner, and dismiss empty conventions and idealized versions of womankind.

Darcy's reformation stems directly from Elizabeth's refusal to play a part in the story in which he has cast her. Before his first proposal he complacently assumes that, bereft of any true position in the world, Elizabeth will gladly consent to his advances. As he later tells her, "I believed you to be wishing, expecting my addresses" (*PP* 369). Darcy attributes his humbling to Elizabeth's thwarting of his expectations: "I came to you without a doubt of my reception. You shewed me how insufficient were all my pretensions to please a woman worthy of being pleased" (369). The worthy woman is thus the woman who resists being just another character in Darcy's flattering story of himself. It is significant that, when he proposes for the second time, Darcy grants Elizabeth the power to silence him, to put a stop to his story: "My affections and wishes are unchanged, but one word from you will silence me on this subject forever" (366). Through the intervention of an intelligent outspoken woman, Darcy apparently becomes a better man.

Austen leaves open the question of whether Elizabeth is an anomaly among women or a representative of their potential. In setting herself apart from other women as she does in the above explanation to Darcy, is she (and, by extension, Austen) regarding self-assertion as a non-womanly characteristic? Do we see here an argument about separate realms of male and female behavior? or a demonstration of human potentiality for reasoned behavior, regardless of gender? Again, Elizabeth's attributes can be traced only to her father, a situation supporting a conservative argument that the sources of traditional authority reside in the male. She seems to have inherited nothing from her mother. Austen indeed emphasizes the lack of maternal ties; to Mrs. Bennet, Elizabeth is "the least dear . . . of all her children" (*PP* 103). We might wonder whether we are supposed to regard Elizabeth as noteworthy only because she is unlike "other girls" and acts like her father rather than her mother. Nancy Armstrong regards Elizabeth as surpassing the other women in the novel because she possesses "traditionally masculine qualities"; although Elizabeth's initial behavior "amounts to direct violation of the female ideal," she later renounces or blunts her more "masculine" characteristics to assume the role of a "softening influence in the world projected at the end of the novel."[43]

Yet Elizabeth does not end up subduing those "masculine" qualities that attracted Darcy to her in the first place. When she checks herself from making fun of Darcy's influence over Bingley, she reflects that "he had yet to learn to be laughed at," and that "yet" tells us that she will teach him to be so eventually (*PP* 371). After Darcy's proposal has been given official parental sanction, "Elizabeth's spirits soon ris[e] to playfulness again" (380), and after her marriage, she alarms Georgiana by "her lively, sportive manner of talking to" Darcy (387). In so doing, she gives Georgiana "knowledge which had never before fallen in her way. . . . that a woman may take liberties with her husband, which a brother will not always allow in a sister more than ten years younger than himself" (387). The term "knowledge" suggests that Elizabeth is in the position of a teacher, supplying Georgiana with a new and viable understanding of woman's role.

Too, it is arguable whether we are to regard Elizabeth's assertiveness as masculine at all. Austen often strips such supposedly masculine qualities of their connection with gender. Margaret Kirkham regards Austen's texts as propounding the tenets of Enlightenment feminism, which argued that women had a capacity equal to that of men for informed, rational behavior: "Jane Austen's heroines are not self-conscious feminists, yet they are all exemplary of the first claim of Enlightenment feminism: that women share the same moral nature as men, ought to share the same moral status, and exercise the same responsibility for their own conduct."[44] Elizabeth's reply after Darcy explains his silence at Longbourn makes a clear case for the equality of their minds: "How unlucky that you should have a reasonable answer to give, and that I should be so reasonable as to admit it!" (*PP* 381).

Indeed, Austen highlights Elizabeth's capacity for reason by placing the scene of her enlightenment midway through the text. Tom Jones's moment of éclaircissement occurs at the end of Fielding's text, and we are given no actual demonstration of his newfound understanding; we simply take it on faith and have done with it. After Elizabeth receives Darcy's letter, however, we are made privy to her rational evaluation of it and her consequent reassessment and reform of her own behavior. Throughout the latter half of the novel, Austen brings to the fore Elizabeth's internal voice, enabling us to see her increased and increasing capacity for reasoned judgments, such as her heightened awareness of her father's failure as a husband and father: "But she had never felt so strongly as now, the disadvantages which might attend the children of so unsuitable a marriage, nor ever been so fully aware of the evils arising from so ill-judged a direction of talents; talents which rightly used, might at least have preserved the respectability of his daughters, even if incapable of enlarging the mind of his wife" (*PP* 237). Significantly, Elizabeth's assessment is inseparable from that of the Austen narrator, her internal voice beginning to take on the authority of the voice that tells her story.

Yet although, through the characterization of Elizabeth, *Pride and Prejudice* makes a case for women's equality, capacity for reason, and ability to reconstitute the estate, it never quite gives over its allegiance to a feminine notion that woman's influence is subordinate. The second version we get of Darcy reinforces this notion. Despite the confession she has her hero make, Austen presents a Darcy who does not need to change internally, who is from the beginning, "the best landlord, and the best master . . . that ever lived" (*PP* 249). His fault lies not in his holding himself superior, but in his neglecting to assume an appearance congruent with his essential goodness. As Elizabeth remarks to Jane, "There certainly was some great mismanagement in the education of those two young men. One has got all the goodness, and the other all the appearance of it" (225). After Elizabeth has been disabused of her prejudices about Darcy, she tells Wickham, "In essentials, I believe, he is very much what he ever was" (234). The only change he need make is matching those essentials to an outward appearance that would do them credit. If Darcy has been intrinsically good all along, Elizabeth's influence becomes less crucial, and her reformation is more significant than his.

By the end of the text we get a sense that Elizabeth has been put in her place—and that place is a subordinate one under the guardianship of the representative of patriarchal tradition, Darcy. Nina Auerbach regards Darcy, along with other Austen heroes, as a "redeemer/jailer" figure.[45] Whereas "jailer" may be too strong a term (Elizabeth retains her high spirits, after all, and Darcy becomes a better man in our eyes), Darcy does assume the stature of a supreme authority. Elizabeth herself regards Darcy as able to provide her with more in the way of instruction than she can him, a situation underscored by his economic superiority: "by her ease and liveliness, his mind might have been softened, his manners improved, and from his judgment, information, and knowledge of the world, she must have received benefit of greater importance" (*PP* 312). Mr. Bennet notes that she will only be happy if married to a superior, an opinion that she does not gainsay: "I know that you could be neither happy nor respectable, unless you truly esteemed your husband; unless you looked up to him as a superior" (376). Elizabeth's proposal to Mrs. Gardiner that they make a daily circuit of the Pemberley grounds suggests that she will be bounded by the estate, staying within the realm prescribed for her.[46]

Austen's portrait of Lady Catherine supports an argument for keeping lively, opinionated women constrained. Lady Catherine does not have to answer to anyone's authority; a widow, she can use her money as she pleases, for, as she tells Elizabeth, entailment "was not thought necessary in Sir Lewis De Bourgh's family" (*PP* 164). Yet she is abusive of her power, wielding her authority in an imperious, intrusive fashion, even to the point of attempting to dictate what the weather will be.

The instrument of Elizabeth's development also provides subtle reinforcement to the patriarchal agenda. Darcy's letter to Elizabeth gives an alternative version of a story already told her by Wickham; it is similar in many details, but different in essentials. After a careful retrospective examination of each man's actions, Elizabeth finally determines for Darcy. Reuben Brower points out that Elizabeth rereads Darcy in the light of her new information.[47] What Elizabeth learns to read is the intrinsic value of the upholder of patriarchal tradition. Her decision is not made on the basis of his wealth, but that such a decision must be made in Darcy's favor implicitly reflects the essential soundness of the status quo.[48]

In his relations to all the major characters in the novel, Darcy functions as a patriarch in the most saturated sense of the word—as wise man, moral authority, and (most important) father. As Gilbert and Gubar note, Austen heroines "reject inadequate fathers . . . for better, more sensitive men who are, nevertheless, still the representatives of authority."[49] Darcy brings about the marriage of Bingley and Jane by, as Elizabeth observes, granting Bingley "permission" (*PP* 370), rather as a father might consent to his son's choice of bride. He acts as a father to Georgiana, and he takes over Mr. Bennet's paternal duties by getting Lydia married off to her seducer. In each case he serves as a sort of moral policeman, saving his sister from possible sexual transgression and saving Lydia from the consequences of hers. He thus controls the disruptive effects of ungoverned and unsettling sexuality by keeping Georgiana in her proper social sphere and by bringing Lydia and Wickham back inside social boundaries. Finally, he saves Elizabeth from future penury and gives her what her father cannot—her rightful (because earned) position in society. It is a higher position than she could ever have achieved through the Bennet line; the more powerful the patriarch, seemingly, the greater the chances of justice being meted out. Darcy literally saves the day.

Elizabeth herself takes only a subordinate position with regard to putting things to rights. She has little or no influence on any character in the novel besides Darcy; she only indirectly helps bring about Jane's happy union with Bingley and does nothing toward effecting Lydia's ill-conceived but necessary one with Wickham. Or is it that she can do nothing? Her father ignores the good advice she gives him about Lydia, and as a woman she cannot presume to give Bingley guidance. So in some sense Elizabeth's inability to bring about change is a reflection of society's unwillingness to let her do so.

The very power she has as a moral force is granted her by Darcy. Her admonishment only takes effect because Darcy has the capacity to recognize his faults (if faults they indeed be) and reform. Elizabeth's rebuff of Collins, we remember, has no such effect. Her empowerment comes through Darcy, as we see when she finally takes her place as mistress of Pemberley, the bastion of traditional values and structures. Patriarchal institutions may benefit from the influence of an intelligent female, but they are essentially sound. Darcy's power as both a corrective force and a *self*-corrective one demonstrates the inherent worthiness of the institutions for which he stands. The traditionally dispossessed may also be worthy, but it is up to the representatives of tradition to validate them. The patriarch finally maintains the necessary order in society, even to the extent of allowing for the absorption of elements necessary for renewal. Austen's critique of entailment gets swallowed up by the Pemberley plot. The comedic ending—the multiple marriages, the inclusion of Lady Catherine into the final tableau—reinforces our sense of the soundness of things as they are.

Again, the inheritance story that Austen tells reflects her relation to her own authorial vocation. Although Austen does not, as in *Northanger Abbey*, make an explicit defense of the feminocentric novel, she makes here an implicit argument about the significance of woman's voice. It is, after all, the speech of Austen's protagonist that seemingly effects change in the representative of patriarchy, and Elizabeth disdains to be "always speaking and looking and thinking for [masculine] approbation alone" (*PP* 381). Just as Elizabeth refuses to flatter Darcy, Austen refuses to tell an altogether flattering story of the man-made situations women find themselves in—an entail can deprive a woman and her five daughters of their livelihood; a blockhead suitor does not pay a forthright woman "the compliment of being believed sincere" (109); an intelligent woman accepts said blockhead "solely from the pure and disinterested desire of an establishment" (122). Austen skewers societal conventions that promote female duplicity or docility as a means of catching a husband, showing us that Caroline Bingley's shallow tricks and Jane Bennet's amiable passivity are just different sides of the same coin. With sly irony the Austen narrator exposes the gap between the characters' professed good intentions and their actual ill-natured actions. Like her protagonist, Austen brings her often acerbic wit to bear upon her surrounding society, creating a satire that takes into account woman's experience and perspective. Austen's text demonstrates the reformative power of woman's voice in the novel genre.

But Austen's position is equivocal, as the fate of her protagonist shows. By drawing on the elements of earlier novels of making good, by inscribing her heroine in a traditional plot, Austen ends up supporting rather than subverting a traditional system of values. In a provocative analysis of *Sense and Sensibility*, Deborah Kaplan argues that Austen revised her own structures as a means of eliding the problem of female assertiveness: "These patterns in *Sense and Sensibility* reveal Austen's resolution of the problem of authority. She circumvented narcissistic or unfeminine assertion by writing revisions."[50] Although Kaplan here alludes to Austen's making her characters do something again in a different manner, Austen's revisions of other texts similarly help her muzzle her assertiveness. By revising the *Tom Jones* plot she makes a case for woman's authority, but she inscribes it within a patriarchal text. The assertion of the entailment plot is kept within bounds by the Pemberley plot, and the woman's voice remains muzzled by traditional structures. Austen ends up validating the law of the father, inscribing a woman into the patriarchal text of the reconstitution of the estate rather than allowing her to take part in the formation of a new kind of text.[51] Unlike Tom Jones, Elizabeth cannot be a founder. Nor can Austen, like Fielding, lay claim to being a founder herself. She can only perpetuate what is, albeit with a female difference.

As a coda to my analysis of *Pride and Prejudice*, I would like to end where Austen began. Along with Melville's "Call me Ishmael," the most famous opening line in the history of the novel is perhaps "It is a truth universally acknowledged, that a single man in possession of a good fortune, must be in want of a wife" (*PP* 3). This sentence has engaged practically every critic of the novel.[52] It epitomizes the sorts of conflict that are apparent not just on the level of story but on the level of ideology. Although the sentence is presented as a maxim, the tendency has been to read it ironically. If Henry Fielding had written the line, we would read it as a straightforward ironic reversal: "It is a truth universally acknowledged, that a single woman lacking a good fortune must be in want of a husband" or "that a single man in possession of a good fortune must be wanted by a would-be wife." And many do read the line exactly in this manner. But such a reading is too simple. As Wayne Booth tells us in *A Rhetoric of Irony*, in assessing irony we should accept the reading that adds the most to our appreciation of the text.[53] Should we take Austen's opening line as mocking the predatory nature of single women? or should we see it also as mocking the society that has brought about this situation?

The word "truth," a term traditionally associated with the male domain of reason, culture, mind, and so forth, has an interesting resonance in the sentence. For the "truth" that we find in the sentence is perhaps the only one that a woman can speak. A woman of Austen's day could not acknowledge her desire for a husband, even though such a desire was not an idle one but one prompted by necessity, as the plight of the Bennet daughters makes clear. Thus the need to prettify the reality that single women were after marriageable men and to confer upon the man the role of aggressor that economic necessity had compelled woman to take. The sentence ironizes woman's plight but in a more complex way than simple mockery. Woman's "truth" must necessarily be one of indirection, for only through rhetorical manipulation can she hope to evade her traditional state of dispossession. Yet with a final turn of the screw, I might point out that the novel itself confirms the un-ironic validity of the maxim: both single men in possession of good fortunes do indeed end up in want of wives, a testimony less to social realities than to wish-fulfillment endings perhaps, but also a final joke at the expense of the reader who reads the line as an indictment of predatory females.[54]

Austen's opening line bears within itself the contradictions and complexities that beset the novel as a whole, and it is emblematic of the doubleness we find throughout. Austen displays and celebrates the authoritative power of the female voice, but she ultimately puts it in the service of the patriarchal myth. She rewrites *Tom Jones* but lets its conclusions stand. Austen's doubleness (of plot, of language) both criticizes and enables the traditional values of her time, and we discover in *Pride and Prejudice* a desire to give credence to the traditionally dispossessed struggling with an unwillingness to reject traditional forms of authority.

Part Three

Questioning the Novel

CHAPTER FIVE

Amelia

Fielding's Dark Sequel

The anxieties of common life began soon to succeed to the alarms of romance. —Jane Austen, *Northanger Abbey* (161)

It would seem as if there never was a book written or a story told, expressly with the object of keeping boys on shore, which did not lure and charm them to the ocean, as a matter of course. —Charles Dickens, *Dombey and Son*

IN *TOM JONES* AND *PRIDE AND PREJUDICE*, Henry Fielding and Jane Austen managed to resolve societal conflicts through plots that neatly knitted all seemingly disparate elements together, and it is the satisfying resolutions of these texts that give them their particular appeal. Both writers, however, took a very different tack in the novels that followed. In some sense, both reworked their earlier material and, in so doing, highlighted rather than allayed conflicts.

Although at least one other writer tried his hand at continuing Tom's adventures (the anonymous *A History of Tom Jones in His Married State*), Fielding never wrote a sequel to his most popular novel. He thus avoided the trap of trying to rewrite what had already been told—a trap into which the control-obsessed Richardson fell when he continued Pamela's story.[1] After all, nothing more needed to be said about Tom. His adventures had come to a satisfying close: he had taken his place as the true "heir" to Paradise Hall, he had defeated the devilish Blifil, and he had won Sophia (both the person and the quality).

In some sense, however, *Amelia* serves as a skeptical sequel or counterpoint to *Tom Jones*, giving us a picture of what might happen to a lively and loving young couple (such as Tom and Sophia) once the nuptial ceremonies ended and they had to settle down to domestic concerns. Moving beyond the happily-ever-after romance ending of the earlier text, focusing on "the anxieties of common life" rather than "the alarms of romance," *Amelia* calls into question the institutions and values that Fielding had ultimately validated in *Tom Jones*. Ostensibly Fielding's most conservative text, *Amelia* offers little hope for social renewal or literary authority under existing circumstances. Although interestingly located in the domestic realm, moral authority is shown to have little impact on society at large. As in his previous novels Fielding authorizes his text by claiming a classical lineage for it, but he is uncertain about the nature of the text's affiliation to its classical forebears and is uncharacteristically reticent about its generic novelty.

In *Amelia*, Fielding draws on familiar elements, but he employs them in new ways. Similar character types and plot structures link the fictional worlds of *Tom Jones* and *Amelia*. At the margins of each hovers the shadow text of Fielding's own courtship and marriage, and it serves as an extratextual link between them. The heroine of each text is a fictionalized version of Fielding's beloved first wife, Charlotte Cradock. In *Tom Jones*, the narrator explicitly connects Sophia with Charlotte: "but most of all, she resembled one whose Image never can depart from my Breast" (*Tom* 1:156). Although the narrator makes no such direct assertion in *Amelia*, Charlotte once again serves as Fielding's model. As Wilbur Cross points out, Charlotte, like Amelia, came from Salisbury, was favored by her mother in her will, and had suffered an injury to her nose.[2] One of Samuel Richardson's typically acrimonious comments confirms the connection: "Amelia, even to her noselessness, is again his first wife."[3] Of course, the fictionalizing process (coupled, perhaps, with Fielding's understandable idealizing of his dead wife) has transformed the human Charlotte into almost inhuman versions of exemplary womanhood, especially in the case of the angelic Amelia. But the traces of Fielding's real-life model nevertheless appear in each heroine, enabling them to join with Charlotte in a triumvirate of actual and fictional heroines. Amelia, ridden with sensibilities, may lack some of Sophia's pluckiness, but we would not be too off the mark to see her story as a "History of Sophia in her Married State."

Certain general traits connect Tom Jones and Booth. The key trait is good nature, a trait so noteworthy it can cancel various character flaws. Each fellow falls into error because of his inadequately grounded moral system and (according to the explicit textual arguments) ultimately rejects that error.[4] More important, Booth's story of his obstacle-ridden pursuit of Amelia—retrospectively recounted to Miss Mathews—bears striking similarities to that of Tom's pursuit of Sophia. Each couple is brought together by an accident—Tom and Sophia by Sophia's being thrown from her horse, Booth and Amelia by Amelia's being thrown from her carriage. Tom's wild reputation initially hurts his chances with Sophia, and Booth's reputation is apparently bad enough to earn him the initial disfavor of Dr. Harrison, the novel's zealous but unprepossessing moral authority. At the outset of the courtship neither hero has the gold that might gild his tarnished name, and the guardians of each heroine—Squire Western and Mrs. Harris—each try to block the match on the basis of the hero's penury. Yet, despite the obstacles put in their way Tom and ostensibly Booth achieve happy endings for themselves, winning through their noble actions both the hand of a model wife and the good opinion and patronage of the older man who functions as the novel's moral authority. Although (unlike Allworthy) Dr. Harris cannot confer an estate upon the couple, he nevertheless helps them financially and rents them his own parsonage once Booth has returned from Gibraltar.

But that Booth tells his courtship story while he is locked up in prison makes clear that Booth's history does not, like Tom's, come to a close with the happily-ever-after marriage. The marriage that concludes *Tom Jones* ties together not only all the loose ends in the story but also, on a symbolic level, the conflicting impulses that beset the text. Marriage, after all, serves as one of the archetypal ends to narrative, signifying a quintessential reconciliation of opposites. It is the metaphor for metaphor, that joining of opposing forces in a new unity, a unity presupposed as merging sign and content, as Tom himself has done. Naturally, any sequel to a courtship story must depend on the rupturing of that metaphoric marriage, for narrative cannot exist without its discontents; as Tony Tanner reminds us, the stasis of metaphoric coincidence is not the stuff of novels: "the novel—indeed, all narrative—emerges from, is dependent upon, 'mixture' and 'unsatisfiedness,' the maculate conditions of life in which nothing is 'for evermore,' except death."[5] Narratives of mysterious births and thwarted courtships—narratives drawing on traditional romance themes—have built into them the "unsatisfiedness" or lack that will drive them forward (the search for origins, the search for love), as well as the sufficiency that will bring them to closure (discovered parentage, successful suits). The domestic narrative—specifically, one centering on married life—runs the risk of having nothing to drive it forward once the nuptials are concluded, as Fielding himself points out in a passage from *Jonathan Wild:*

> Most private histories, as well as comedies, end at this period; the historian and the poet both concluding they have done enough for their hero when

> they have married him; or intimating rather that the rest of his life must be a dull calm of happiness, very delightful indeed to pass through, but somewhat insipid to relate; and matrimony in general must, I believe, without any dispute, be allowed to be this state of tranquil felicity, including so little variety, that, like Salisbury Plain, it affords only one prospect, a very pleasant one it must be confessed, but the same. (142–43)[6]

The narrative can move forward only when something threatens domesticity, when some lack belies the integrity of the marriage bond.

To some extent, all postnuptial narratives are sequels, for all take as their starting point the apparent closure of a prior story. As such, they are inherently skeptical, for all implicitly demonstrate the speciousness of such closure. The initial demonstration may indeed undercut a subsequent well-knit resolution, a reason perhaps why many such novels leave us with a sense of open-endedness. Rather than a movement through metonym to metaphor we have movement from metonym to yet another metonym, with no perfect marriage to wed all tropes at the end. *Amelia* calls into question the possibility of textual closure. Moreover, in so doing it throws doubt upon the reconciliation of opposing forces that we saw in *Tom Jones*, and the resulting exposed seams account for some of the difficulty we have with the text.

The Gibraltar episode in *Amelia* initiates the structure of deferral that will occur throughout the text. As Booth tells Miss Mathews, his prison confidante, he and Amelia have scarcely settled into married life before he is called away to war, which leads to a temporary severance from Amelia followed by several trials that the couple face together. Even when Dr. Harrison rents the parsonage to Booth once the war has ended, our expectations that we shall now see the deferred happy ending are thwarted. Booth seems to have achieved an earthly paradise. He is settled in a fixed place with his ideal wife and exemplary mentor, on his way to fulfilling Dr. Harrison's sanguine prediction: "a Country Life, where you could be always together, would make you both much happier People" (*Am* 146). Initially, the country does indeed function as a place of ideal stasis upon which time and trouble make no inroads: "'Why then, I do assure you, Miss Mathews,' cries Booth, 'I scarce know a Circumstance that distinguished one Day from another. The whole was one continued Series of Love, Health, and Tranquillity'" (147). The narrative line would seem to describe a circle at this point. But snakes live in Booth's Eden. The extended absence of his mentor, Booth's own pride, the neighbors' malice, the jealousy of the clergyman's wife—all contribute to drive him out, compelling him to wander through the labyrinthine byways of London.

Once Booth is in London, the meaning of the courtship story he tells

Miss Mathews is cast into doubt by the context of its telling. Whereas it should serve as an inspiration to him about what he was able to gain through noble actions (the exemplary Amelia), it instead serves as an elaborate means for one of Fielding's typical deflations, whereby Fielding undercuts a person's generally virtuous professed intentions by a generally faulty opposing action. Immediately after talking of his great love for Amelia, of reminding himself of her manifold charms, Booth succumbs to the wiles of the lecherous Miss Mathews. His story, rather than filling Miss Mathews with suitable awe at the Booths' sacrosanct relationship, instead prompts her to vie to supplant Amelia in Booth's affections. The storytelling ends up functioning as an extended means of foreplay, and the knitting up of the story coincides with a rending apart of the marriage ties.[7] Booth's present thus commences with the breaking apart of the union that gave meaning to his past. The embedded narrative—Booth's history—is recontextualized by the events that come after it. When we read it back in light of these subsequent events, we tend to regard the picture of marital perfection it paints as a counterfeit; what Booth describes in such glowing terms must already have contained the seeds of its own destruction. That he tells the story while locked up in prison further undercuts its meaning.

Moreover, Booth's story consistently draws our attention to the gap between a narrator's assertions and a narrative's implications—a situation that will trouble Amelia as a whole. It points to the difficulties involved in assessing the "truth" in any subjective account of the self, a difficulty Fielding had already addressed in his parody of *Pamela*. Booth tends to paint a fairly blameless picture of himself, telling his story as Tom Jones might have told his own in retrospect. As Fielding points out in *Tom Jones*, all autobiographical accounts tend to color the truth:

> For let a Man be never so honest, the Account of his own Conduct will, in Spite of himself, be so very favourable, that his Vices will come purified through his Lips, and, like foul Liquors well strained, will leave all their Foulness behind. For tho' the Facts themselves may appear, yet so different will be the Motives, Circumstances, and Consequences, when a Man tells his own Story, and when his Enemy tells it, that we scarce can recognize the Facts to be one and the same. (*Tom* 1:420)

From unwitting hints Booth gives us in his account and from his behavior in the rest of the novel, we can imagine that he is presenting himself in a better light than he deserves.

In effect, the authority of Booth as narrator is consistently undermined by the evidence he puts forward in his narrative—and undermined as well by the evidence put forward in the main narrative. Fielding's authoritative pronouncements are similarly belied by what actually occurs in the story of Booth and Amelia. In *Tom Jones* the gaps between assertion and evidence are often deliberate. Fielding thus pokes fun at authorial omniscience even as he insists upon authorial authority. Here, however, they apparently result from authorial blindness, indicating Fielding's unwillingness to confront irresolvable cultural conflicts.[8]

By starting with Booth's imprisonment, narrative, and adultery, *Amelia* demonstrates that a golden age, wherein occurred unity and closure, cannot be sustained—and thus was never really there to begin with. And despite his attempt to knit together the threads he had pulled apart at the outset, Fielding never achieves the seamless presentation that he manages at the end of *Tom Jones*. The exemplary heroine is unrecognized and ineffectual. The "hero's journey" comes across as more casual than causal, demonstrating society's power over the individual rather than the individual's power to transform society. Here appears no foundling/founder to gather all disruptive elements into a comic vision of societal renovation. Undercutting the marriage ideology of *Tom Jones*, adultery serves as the driving force for the plot and an indicator of societal corruption. Rather than the wryly benevolent author/narrator of the earlier work, we find an inconsistent narrative voice, veering wildly from a fairly unobtrusive objectivity to an almost wild-eyed didacticism. The narrator wrestles anxiously for control over the text's meaning, while the text itself repeatedly deals with the inability of authors to control their issue. Fielding's "sequel" highlights the discontinuities that were downplayed and defused in the earlier work, casting doubt on whether moral or literary authority can stand up against the forces that would undo them.

THE DEFERRED HEROINE AND THE OBSCURE "EPIC" HERO

Amelia features dual protagonists, and although they undergo similar experiences by virtue of their union they each assume a different kind of heroic role in the novel. Fielding intends Amelia as the embodiment of immutable perfection, holding her up as a moral exemplar, but a countervailing subtext works against such transcendence, testifying to Fielding's bleak view of the reception of the good in a world gone bad. Amelia is pulled down to earth by her surroundings, and what emblematic function she has seems unconvincing and anachronistic.[9] Because subterranean forces work against the narrator's explicit claims for Amelia's perfection, the reality of the good is itself called into question.

In one regard Amelia's role in the novel comes closer than Booth's to the role Tom Jones plays in Fielding's earlier work although, unlike Tom, she has already conjoined essence and appearance—a crucial difference.[10] The plots of both *Tom Jones* and *Amelia* turn upon the discovery of the proper heir to a particular estate. The legacy is a moral as well as a material one, and the estate serves as a synecdoche for the whole of society. Amelia, not Booth, is the true heir in this text, a fact that Booth's head-of-the-family status does not mitigate. Tom Jones, we recall, proves himself the spiritual heir of Allworthy, and Bridget's deathbed letter reveals him as an actual member of the family, the two factors that prompt Allworthy to bequeath Tom his goods. At Allworthy's death Tom will not only assume Allworthy's estate but also presumably his role as moral authority. In *Amelia* we have no mysterious birth and subsequent quest for identity; Amelia's lineage is obvious. Mrs. Harris, Amelia's mother, has the power to give her material worth. Dr. Harrison serves as Amelia's spiritual father, a relationship reinforced by the similarity between their names. Amelia's real father being dead at the beginning of the text, Dr. Harrison assumes the paternal role—giving his permission to Booth to marry Amelia and bestowing a farm upon the couple, helping them out of debt, and providing them with useful instruction. Dr. Harrison often refers to Amelia as "daughter," and she refers to him as "father," additional reinforcement of the spiritual kinship between them. Mrs. Harris intends to provide Amelia with a material estate; Dr. Harrison has already conferred upon her a spiritual one.

Amelia has neither to discover her heritage nor to establish her identity—she already is at the outset what she will be at the close. Throughout the text the narrator extols her unchanging perfection. At times he praises her to such excess that we begin to suspect the epithet "excellent woman" has the same ironic force as does "great man" in *Jonathan Wild*. The following passage provides an especially apt example: "This it was that enervated his Heart, and threw him into Agonies, which all that Profusion of heroic Tenderness that the most excellent of Women intended for his Comfort, served only to heighten and aggravate; as the more she rose in his Admiration, the more she quickened his Sense of his own Unworthiness" (*Am* 163). We might question an excellence that has the effect of heightening agony. But our cynical suspicion is undermined by the evidence supplied by Fielding to demonstrate that the epithet fits: Amelia provides her beloved children with moral instruction; she pawns her clothing to pay Booth's debts; she cooks her husband dainty suppers and forgives his adultery; and so on and so forth. Amelia keeps the family together and maintains the values necessary for the proper operation of the social order. With our modern sensibilities we may find this heroine of sensibility somewhat irritating (and more than somewhat incredible), but we cannot find her contemptible.[11] Influenced no doubt by his admiration for Richardson's *Clarissa*, Fielding presents a heroine who out-clarissas Clarissa, never allowing her to lapse into the kind of blindness to self that leads to the latter's downfall. Clarissa's chilly chastity renders her somewhat ethereal whereas Amelia's healthy sexual relationship with Booth serves as evidence of her loving and generous, eminently human, nature, Fielding's text indeed serving as an implicit refutation of the antimarriage ideology of *Clarissa*.[12] Unlike most of the novel's characters, Amelia has no hidden character flaws that will come to light hereafter; she is as she appears to us. If certain motifs undermine her exemplary function, they do not appear in the actual descriptions of her actions or the narrator's enthusiastic assessment of them.

In the world of *Tom Jones*, such a conjunction of appearance and essence would call for immediate reward, as demonstrated by Tom's story. But in the world of *Amelia*, such reward is deferred. Whereas the withholding of Tom's inheritance enabled Tom to discover himself, the withholding of Amelia's serves no such purpose. It does enable her exemplarity to shine forth so that she ends up reminding us of a latter-day Griselda, patiently enduring her increasingly difficult trials. J. Paul Hunter even regards her as a Christlike figure, arguing that her trials resemble the three temptations of Christ in *Paradise Regained*.[13] In Amelia we seem to have an immovable object steadily resisting forces of change and corruption. Whereas *Tom Jones* demonstrates the development of the individual as a worthy member of society and his subsequent reward, *Amelia* demonstrates society's deferral of reward to the worthy individual.

The text reinforces this notion of deferral of the good by deferring the very appearance of the heroine. Despite the novel's title, we might think that Miss Mathews will assume the role, for Fielding introduces her trailing clouds of glamour and mystery and indeed mentions her before he gives us the least hint of Amelia's existence. This hint, so oblique as to be almost negligible, occurs when Booth remarks that he values his stolen snuffbox "for the Sake of the Person who gave it him" (*Am* 40). Miss Mathews's detailed narrative further confuses us; we expect that its prominent position is indicative of her significance to the rest of the novel—an expectation we gradually realize is false when Miss Mathews dwindles away into an intermittent and clumsy plot device. We do not know that Booth even has a wife until Miss Mathews, already vying for Booth's affections, reminds him: "your affections were more happily disposed of to a much better Woman than myself, whom you married soon afterwards" (48). Amelia's name does not come up until the first chapter of book 2, and we get no idea of her present situation until the conclusion of Booth's story. She does not appear in person until book 4. In the meantime she does appear at one remove in Booth's story, although (significantly) she wears a mask, as if to indicate the hidden nature of the good.

The motif of doubling also ends up being crucial to the implicit argument of *Amelia*, and nowhere is this more apparent than in the masquerade episode, wherein Amelia deceives her husband and allows Mrs. Atkinson to take her place. Amelia's exemplarity throughout the text is problematized by her tendency to resort to deception—a point Samuel Johnson might have considered before he elevated Amelia over the less-than-truthful Clarissa.[14] She deceives Booth about her reasons for leaving Bagillard's lodgings, the extent of Col. James's advances, and James's letter challenging him to a duel. Although we may feel a certain uneasiness when the paragon stoops to subterfuge, both Amelia and the narrator attempt to justify these lapses on the grounds that they are concealments, not outright lies, and necessary to avert some greater evil. The imperfections of the world require these omissions, or so Fielding's argument goes. Amelia's greatest deception—allowing Mrs. Atkinson to double for her at the masquerade—enables her (though not her thus compromised substitute) to avoid encountering, in Dr. Harrison's words, "Scenes of Riot, Disorder, and Intemperance, very improper to be frequented by a chaste and sober Christian Matron" (*Am* 423).[15]

The deception is not just Amelia's but also Fielding's, a textual feint that makes us aware of our inability to differentiate between the ostensible good and its opposite. Although Fielding scrupulously avoids calling the false Amelia by the heroine's name, he deceives us as to the identity of this strangely forward domino by concealing a crucial clue—that Amelia ran back into the house before the four Masques set out for the ball. This elision (a real cheat were Fielding a mystery writer) causes us, albeit puzzledly, to read the scene as if it were indeed Amelia whose "bewitching softness" makes the rapacious Noble Lord fly into raptures (*Am* 411). Only at the end of the episode does Fielding give us a hint by calling the domino "the supposed Amelia" (419). But until this hint, we may confuse the true Amelia with an imitation of her.

As the episode makes clear, it is difficult to tell the true from a specious double of it. And Amelia has many such doubles, Mrs. Atkinson being the most obvious.[16] Mrs. Ellison discovers this resemblance, citing it as her reason for liking Mrs. Atkinson: "what I like her the best for is a strong Resemblance that she bears to yourself in the Form of her Person, and still more in her Voice" (*Am* 237). Since Mrs. Ellison befriended Mrs. Atkinson before ever meeting Amelia, the statement seems rather odd, but it both reinforces the notion of Amelia as the original, against which all imitations are judged, and problematizes that notion by confusing the issue of priority. Fielding later remarks on this resemblance when he explains the ease with which Amelia effected the substitution of Mrs. Atkinson for herself. Mrs. Atkinson's narrative of her life story (similar to the narratives of the Old Man of the Hill and of Mrs. Fitzpatrick in *Tom Jones*) serves to show the heroine (and the readers) an alternative route that her life might have taken, Mrs. Atkinson thus acting as an off-center Amelia in a parallel universe. Like the False Maria in Fritz Lang's *Metropolis*, Mrs. Atkinson performs actions in the heroine's name, possibly even granting sexual favors to the Noble Lord and certainly undermining Amelia's reputation.

Mrs. Atkinson is not Amelia's only double. Blear-Eyed Moll, the most grotesque of the prison inmates, is, like the heroine, noseless. Terry Castle notes that we feel anxiety when Amelia unmasks because we fear that the face of Moll herself will be revealed.[17] In some sense Moll is an anti-Amelia, her prison "propriety" the reverse of Amelia's proper dress and behavior. Within the prison resides yet another of Amelia's doubles, Miss Mathews, who attempts to play the role of Booth's wife; she shares his bed and provides him with suppers, solace, and money, just as Amelia is wont to do. Once perhaps, as her tale indicates, she inspired Booth to the same kind of gallantry with which Amelia now inspires him. Again, at the outset of the novel, she doubles as the heroine—a structural reinforcement of the doubling motif. Toward the end of the novel it is not Amelia herself but a representation of her—the picture she pawns—that inspires Robinson's confession about the forged will. Of course, here the double of the good serves to bring about good, but it is nonetheless only a copy. This same copy prompted Atkinson to commit a theft and served him as a substitute for the unattainable original.

Such imitations can usurp the position of the original, as when Miss Mathews briefly assumes Amelia's conjugal role and Mrs. Atkinson assumes her name as a way of tricking the Noble Lord into helping Atkinson. Amelia exists in a world that cannot recognize the good because it is full of imitations of it. The imitations themselves reflect back upon the true itself, causing it to be regarded as what it is not. Amelia herself is at one time mistaken for an anti-Amelia, for "the Greatness of her Beauty, and the Disorder of her Dress" cause the bailiff's wife to suspect "that she was a young Lady of Pleasure" (*Am* 496). But it may be that the landlady's portrait of a whorish Amelia will be credited as much as the narrator's portrait of an ideal Amelia in a world where the good is deferred, disguised, and doubled.

Although we may buy the narrator's explicit argument that Amelia is exemplary, we cannot neatly separate her from her doubles. Miss Mathews gives vent to the jealousy that our knowledge of human psychology makes us suspect Amelia of suppressing, and Mrs. Atkinson engages in the sexual encounters that Amelia initiates. Moll's hideous noselessness, a consequence of syphilis, casts a shadow across Amelia's beauty—and perhaps across her character. Granted, Amelia's nose is repaired, but we never quite see her whole. The little scar, which some characters claim enhances her beauty, shares symbolic affinities with the crack in the golden bowl—that barely perceptible flaw undermining the integrity of the whole.[18] In a sense, Amelia's very power seems to reside not in her ideality but in her ability to manipulate representations of herself: by sending out a surrogate to the masquerade, she can disobey her husband's wishes, and by sending out her picture, she can recover her wealth. Although we cannot finally deny the narrator's claims for Amelia's exemplarity, the motifs of doubling and scarring serve as a troubling symbolic counterforce. In the world of imitations that Fielding describes, ontological integrity is itself suspect. The ideal is a problematic entity in a world bereft of ideality.

As a developing rather than an ideal character, the text's other protagonist—Amelia's erring husband, Booth—is more in keeping with the novel genre, a genre predicated upon the inexorable movement of time. Whereas Amelia's role as hero conforms to the traditional sense of noble being (a type of epic figure), Booth's role as hero conforms only to the sense that came into currency at the outset of the eighteenth century: the primary personage of a work.[19] Fielding undermines any sort of noble stature on Booth's part. A paradigm of ordinariness, Booth begins with a flawed philosophical outlook, which causes him to behave badly, and moves throughout the text toward a moment of self-discovery and subsequent transformation. His conversion from his cynical philosophy of the passions to his Christian self-determination may strike us as an instance less of credible psychological development than of authorial fiat, but he nevertheless undergoes a change that if it will not render him heroic will at least render him an upstanding member of society.

That Booth's character develops while Amelia's remains static is in keeping with contemporary notions of gender. Ronald Paulson points out that "the central moral action . . . is Booth's—a man's, in what is clearly still, in Shaftesbury's sense, a man's world in which Amelia remains a symbol or, as we have seen, both a moral and an aesthetic object."[20] But it is not simply that Amelia is a symbol or an object, although at times she is both. As a heroine, she cannot be allowed to fall into the same sort of error as Booth. Certainly, heroines of the mid–eighteenth century could err; the exemplary Pamela and Clarissa often do the wrong thing, and Charlotte Lennox's female Quixote, appearing in the year following *Amelia*, is intended to keep readers amused with her delusions and antics. But, although these heroines make mistakes of judgment, they are not guilty of moral lapses. Such lapses would call into question the decarnalized version of female nature that was coming into ascendance, thus placing them outside the bounds of heroine-ism. The "man's world" is one wherein males can recover from moral lapses, but females cannot—a situation that the burgeoning novel genre does not so much describe as prescribe.[21] Although basing his heroine on the Richardsonian model (as would so many writers in the latter half of the century), Fielding patterned his hero upon his own Wilson and Tom Jones. Booth's development both anticipates a particular sort of novelistic structure that would become a standard in the nineteenth century (the bildungsroman) and reinforces a particular conception of gender differences that disallows female development because it would presume female error.

From the outset of the novel Booth is rendered in a decidedly unheroic fashion. Rather than a doer of extraordinary deeds, he is a fairly undistinguished Everyman. He does not even have the lingering romantic accoutrements of portentous birth and discovered noble heritage of Fielding's earlier Tom Jones. Rather than initially appearing as a babe swaddled in mystery, Booth initially appears as one in a crowd. The text opens in a Balzacian, even cinematic fashion, giving us a sense of Booth's anonymity, his facelessness among the masses. The narrator first gives us the wide pan of the courtroom, sweeping over an indifferent judge and the falsely accused victims. He then zeroes in on the figure of a man, one of the many defendants up before Judge Thrasher: "A young Fellow, whose name was *Booth*, was now charged with beating the Watchman, in the Execution of his Office, and breaking his Lanthorn" (*Am* 24). The syntax of the sentence introducing Booth reinforces this zeroing-in process, for Booth's name is subordinated to the subject "young Fellow," just as Booth himself will be subordinated to a generic conception of himself on the part of society. Not until the third chapter does the narrator make clear that Booth will be the subject of the story. We can never quite escape that first impression of Booth as only one of many—many whose stories might have equal importance.

Booth's origins are unimportant, in fact nonexistent, as far as the text is concerned. Booth lacks ostensible forebears and any connection to an established line. The brief reference to his father is intended only to account for his classical education (*Am* 324). Although we do hear of a sister, her position in the story is insignificant and, as Martin Battestin argues, may have resulted from Fielding's psychological quirks rather than the exigencies of the plot.[22] Although Dr. Harrison mentions that Booth has been "a dutiful Son, and an affectionate Brother" (90), this information serves to establish Booth's character, not his genealogy. For all intents and purposes Booth may as well be an orphan. And he is one literary orphan who eludes being found.

Indeed, he eludes founding. Booth does end up in a small exemplary social circle, but he is neither responsible for its founding nor presumably vital to its continuation. We never see him assume any actual duties. Although he is married to the "best of Wives," his most significant quality is that he has apparently made Amelia "the happiest of Women" (*Am* 533). The line to which he belongs is essentially matrilineal, moral authority and material worth being transmitted through and inherited by the females of the family.

By making Booth propertyless in his own right Fielding acknowledges the decreasing significance of the notion that ownership guarantees virtue. As J. G. A. Pocock argues, by the late seventeenth century, this notion was regarded as anachronistic:

> the ideal form of property thus came to appear the inheritable freehold of fee simple in land, on which the Roman or Gothic citizen warrior had based his capacity for self-defense and self-government. But this ideal existed in the past. By the closing decade of the seventeenth century, English and Scottish social critics were increasingly disturbed by the rise of professional armies, in which the citizen alienated the vital function of self-defense to a hired and banausic specialist, and thus became in some measure corrupt.[23]

Booth is not only propertyless; he has also been a member of the professional army, that sign of civic corruption. Throughout the text Booth's lack of property both real and mobile makes him prey to the corrupt system of patronage that runs rife in London. Fielding is aware that the propertied, incorruptible squire such as Allworthy is a thing of the past, and he wants to demonstrate how difficult it is for virtue to triumph when a person has no property with which to counter the blandishments of corruption, as we see in the case of the erring Booth.

Drawing on several explicit comments by Fielding, critics have often discussed Booth in terms of an epic hero, but the text implicitly works against such an identification. From the outset of *Amelia*, Fielding makes allusions to the *Aeneid*, a connection reinforced in his defense of the text that appeared in *The Covent-Garden Journal* on January 25 and 28, 1752. Referring to *Amelia* as his "favourite Child," he therein argued that he had used Virgil as his model: "she will be found to deviate very little from the strictest Observation of all those Rules; neither Homer nor Virgil pursued them with greater Care than myself, and the candid and learned Reader will see that the latter was the noble model, which I made use of on this Occasion" (*CGJ* 65). Lyall Powers sees the text as demonstrating the Christianization of the epic hero, apparent in Booth's being freed "of the need to justify himself by recourse to the foil" when Col. James challenges him. Robert Alter sees the novel as demonstrating an individualization of epic themes; Booth is a Christian hero who must assume his proper duties in the domestic realm.[24] But Booth's incapacity to found a new society—one based on the values of a venerable, but vanished one—and the general ignobility of his actions marks off his difference from his supposed epic model.

Obscure and ineffectual, Booth is not a hero of epic proportions but merely an ordinary fellow incapable of contending with society's forces. He may be good-hearted, tender to his wife, and fairly upright, recoiling from the thought of selling Amelia's honor for his own advancement. But as qualities of the heroic temperament these wear pretty thin. Although he apparently displays valor on the field of battle and bravery in his fruitless attempt to rescue an unknown fellow from two assailants, these are the only instances that come close to being heroic, and they are described only in summary. The first of his actions that we actually witness (at least until Fielding discreetly draws the curtain on the scene) is his adulterous coupling. Miss Mathews, the putative Dido figure in *Amelia,* is no tragic queen but a vengeful demimondaine holding court in a sordid prison. Booth's liaison smacks of no noble passion. Fielding instead highlights Miss Mathews's bold stratagems and Booth's willing and certainly not uncomprehending participation in her games. Booth knowingly wrongs "the best Woman in the World" (*Am* 154) and leaves himself open to further complications.[25] He also ends up doing what Tom Jones did at his moral nadir—accepting money from his mistress—and even his figurative impotence in the prison system caused by his lack of funds does not make his actions seem any less excusable than Jones's. Miss Mathews gives Booth money that Col. James gave her, and Booth later borrows the sum from the Colonel in order to pay his debt to her. Passed back and forth among the three the money points to the transactional nature of their sexual relationships, reinforcing Fielding's theme of debased sexuality.

Booth appears throughout not as active agent for social change but as hapless victim of society, incapable of making the slightest dent in its bulwark of corruption. He actually adds to this corruption by tendering a bribe to the corrupt "great Man" in the War Office and by gambling away his remaining funds along with those he borrows from Trent in an attempt to get a lot for a little. Although we must take all of Samuel Richardson's assessments of Fielding with a generous helping of salt (he typically put *Amelia* aside in disgust after only the first volume), his undermining of Fielding's epic claims is not far off the mark: "he must mean Cotton's Virgil Travestied; where the women are drabs, and the men scoundrels."[26] Booth himself is to the epic what Willy Loman is to tragedy.

The dueling motif in Amelia, which critics have linked to the battle scenes in the *Aeneid,* further demonstrates the text's distance from its epic forebear and the difference between Booth and Aeneas. Powers regards Booth's duel with Col. Bath as analogous to Aeneas's battle with Turnus and as symbolic of his "triumph over that passé code of honor which Bath represents here."[27] Yet the duel they fight shows how Bath's code of honor is not just passé; it is ungrounded. Rather than resulting from a genuine affront the challenge issued by Bath arises from a series of misrepresentations. Angry about Booth's rebuff of her advances Miss Mathews lies to Col. James, recounting that Booth's vilifications of James led to her capricious behavior. Evidencing an all-too-willing suspension of belief in his proven friend, Col. James treats Booth badly and then lies to Bath, putting Booth in the wrong. The duel is thus based on "the thing which was not," to borrow Swift's apt phrase, conforming to Richard Steele's definition of contemporary dueling as "this chimerical groundless humor."[28] Bath epitomizes the fighter of chimeras; early in the text he even takes offense over a compliment Booth pays him. Of course, Bath is no *miles gloriosus;* he does fight, not just boast of doing it, and eventually dies "in battle." But he defends what does not matter, involving Booth too in a contention over the meaningless. Whereas the stakes are high in the world of epic, here they are paltry. A man can die dueling, granted, but he dies for no noble cause, as is demonstrated by Col. Bath's death over a mere difference of opinion.

Fielding's earlier novels can parody epic motifs in various set pieces yet nevertheless draw on the epic genre itself to authorize themselves. We may at times question Fielding's claims that *Joseph Andrews* and *Tom Jones* derive from Homer's line, but we can regard those claims as serious attempts by Fielding to place his texts generically and thereby to legitimate them. Despite a similar claim for the epic status of *Amelia,* however, the text emphasizes the gap—not the congruence—between itself and its supposed noble forebear, and it provides no consistent critical commentary to remind us periodically about its noble lineage. In order to counter the authority of the society it describes, the text must diverge from the authoritarian impulse of epic, even against Fielding's professed aims. As Mikhail Bakhtin points out in his essay "Epic and Novel," the epic depicts a society of the past that is the source for all good in the present: "The world of the epic is the national heroic past: it is a world of 'beginnings' and 'peak times' in the national history, a world of fathers and of founders of families, a world of 'firsts' and 'bests.'" Even when the epic deals with contemporary events, it gives "to these events the time-and-value contour of the past, thus attaching them to the world of fathers, of beginnings and peak times—canonizing these events, as it were, while they are still current."[29] For example, although it certainly goes back to the beginning, *Paradise*

Lost, the last true English epic, essentially canonizes the Puritan ideology of its time. Of all Fielding's novels *Amelia* most clearly sets itself against a world of beginnings, peak times, firsts, and bests.

Amelia, by highlighting the incongruity between itself and its epic forebear, makes clear that the world it depicts is not complete but is in need of completion. The epic world, however, is sufficient unto itself; according to Bakhtin, "the epic past is absolute and complete. It is as closed as a circle; inside it, everything is finished, already over. There is no place in the epic world for any openendedness, indecision, indeterminacy."[30] As a faulty but developing hero with potential as yet unrealized Booth can, on an individual level, point toward the possibilities for change in the society for which he stands. His misguided philosophy of the predominant passions links together the notions of individual error and social problems. Fielding attempts to show that Booth's passivity and faults stem from his philosophical system and that his conversion from this philosophy will make him a better man. Unlike Tom Jones, Booth actually has a coherent philosophy, however faulty; whereas Tom runs into problems because he has not learned to control himself (and has not yet learned who "himself" might be), Booth runs into problems because he incorrectly believes that he is inevitably subject to his passions and thus cannot consciously control his own destiny. As George Sherburn suggests, because of his belief that people act from their passions, Booth "lacks moral courage to struggle against misfortune."[31] Booth seems to lack any real direction in life, and he seems to let whim take him where it will—whether into Miss Mathews's willing arms or into a gambling den.

By relieving him of responsibility Booth's philosophy encourages not only passivity but wrongdoing, as the following passage illustrates:

> *Booth* answered, that the Doctrine of the Passions had been always his favourite study; that he was convinced every Man acted entirely from that Passion which was uppermost; "Can I then think," said he, "without Contempt for myself, that any Pleasure upon Earth could drive the Thoughts of *Amelia* one Instant from my Mind?" (*Am* 109)

By telling himself that he cannot act otherwise Booth evades moral decisions and justifies his embrace of pleasure over duty. This passage, incidentally, serves a proleptic function, for within a short space the pleasures held out by Miss Mathews have effectively driven all thoughts of Amelia from Booth's mind.

Although the doctrine of the passions serves as a leitmotif throughout, Booth expounds upon it at three crucial points in the text, and each discussion marks an advancement over the one before. Booth debates with another "philosopher" during each of his three incarcerations—an appropriate situation considering that the prison, as Battestin points out, serves as the metaphor for "the hero's crippling spiritual bondage to a false philosophy."[32] In the first debate, although Booth opposes the gambler Robinson's fatalistic philosophy overall, he nevertheless agrees with Robinson that all human action is determined by necessity: "that every Man acted merely from the Force of the Passion that was uppermost in his Mind, and could do no otherwise" (*Am* 32).[33] In his second debate, Booth opposes his doctrine to the stoicism of the spunging-house gentleman. Although he agrees in theory with the gentleman's contention that people should desist from "all violent Joy and Grief concerning Objects which cannot endure long, and may not exist a Moment" (350), he regards Stoicism as an untenable philosophy in a world where people act according to their passions: "however true all this may be in Theory, I still doubt its Efficacy in Practice. And the Cause of the Difference between these two is this; that we reason from our Heads, but act from our Hearts" (350). The gentleman himself proves a faulty stoic, crying that he will be "the most miserable man alive" if he cannot sup with his wife. He nonetheless points toward a course of action that Booth will embrace by the third debate: "By Philosophy, I do not mean the bare Knowledge of Right and Wrong; but an Energy, a Habit, as *Aristotle* calls it; and this I do firmly believe, with him and with the Stoics, is superior to all the Attacks of Fortune" (351). Against Booth's notion of the inevitability of human action, the gentleman opposes the notion of a learned behavior, which, even if it cannot change the status quo, can at least lead to individual improvement.

This notion that individuals can improve through habituating themselves to right behavior is raised in the third debate. After reading a number of Barrow's sermons, Booth renounces the doctrine of the passions and its corollary that people are not accountable for their actions: "my chief Doubt was founded on this, that as Men appeared to me to act entirely from their Passions, their Actions could have neither Merit nor Demerit" (*Am* 511).[34] The text makes an explicit argument that Booth's renunciation signifies a change for the better: Booth is now able to take responsibility for his actions and, presumably, to act according to some kind of moral imperative rather than according to the whim of the moment.

Yet Booth's renunciation of his necessitarian doctrine is a problem area of the novel. Many critics point out that there is a discrepancy between the text's explicit commentary and the evidence put forth by the story.[35] Booth's embrace of self-determination and self-accountability seems to go against what experience has taught him and what the text plainly demonstrates. Amelia, of course, does not act according to her passions but according to moral imperatives, but she is as beset by forces outside her control as her erring husband. Often the people who act according to a rule of right end up in prison, the omnipresence of the prison motif indeed working as a symbolic counterforce against notions of free will. This tension between explicit claims and implicit counter-examples points to an unresolved conflict in the text between hope and doubt in the possibility of self-determination.

Booth's philosophical conversion is integral to the notion of societal reformation, for only by arguing that people's choices are responsible for how things are can Fielding demonstrate how things can be changed; if people regard their actions as rationally determined and intrinsically good or bad, as Booth learns to do, they can make the choices that can begin to heal the diseased nation. Through Booth's fate Fielding demonstrates that, although the propertyless individual is subject to corruption, he can rise above it—although, as with Tom Jones, we have little opportunity to see the reformed Booth in action. In effect, Booth's initial state of undeveloped potential symbolizes his nation's dilemma, and his renunciation of his fatalistic philosophy points the way toward a renunciation of national fatalism and corruption. Although Amelia may maintain the moral values necessary to society, it is her erring husband rather than her exemplary self who points to the possibility of societal reform, precisely because of this capacity for change and development.

The instrument of Booth's conversion is also important to the argument about social reform. By attributing that conversion to Booth's reading of Barrow, Fielding makes a case for his own text's being instrumental in societal reform. Like Saint Augustine in the *Confessions*, the prototypical novel of conversion, Booth finally sheds his mistaken beliefs as he is moved by the text he is reading. *Amelia* aims for the same sort of reformative power it ascribes to Barrow's *Works*, for its "lesson" is the same as the one Booth finds in Barrow: that people need not be swayed by predominant passions, that actions do have merit or demerit.[36] The novel itself attempts to mediate between a seemingly hopeless social situation and the individual confronting it, for the novel holds out the possibility that an erring individual may learn by reading texts such as itself to renounce the erroneous thinking that nothing can be changed and may gain the capacity to bring about just such a change.

The critically panned "providential ending" that follows on Booth's conversion is an attempt to validate the appropriateness of Booth's action, but it also serves as acknowledgment that the only way to prove such appropriateness in the teeth of the evidence is by miraculous intervention. Once Booth has dropped his unsound beliefs, he is put in the way of fortune and happiness. But most critics have been rightly dissatisfied with the seemingly arbitrary bestowal of riches upon the Booths at the end of the novel.[37] A providential ending implies that all the bad, seemingly random things that take place occur for a reason—in Pope's succinct phrase, "All partial evil, universal good." Thus the original impetus for the action takes on the nature of a "Fortunate Fall," and the plot follows this structure: commission of sin and consequent expulsion, journey to enlightenment or improvement, and ultimate return.

However, this Fortunate-Fall structure is problematized in *Amelia.* We never feel the aesthetic appropriateness of the notion of providential design as we do in *Tom Jones*, for example; the connection between Booth's conversion and his accession to fortune appears more casual than causal. Too much of the chaotic in *Amelia* remains as such. Amelia herself has no need of a Fortunate Fall because she is already seemingly perfect; her fall into narrative actually endangers her exemplary status. Booth, on the other hand, does need to develop—in this case, the self-determination and self-accountability that will make him a better man. But we simply do not get a sense of inevitable progression here or of a developing moral entity. Booth's experiences make him aware of the wickedness of others, not of himself. He is jailed three times, but the number, though recalling a fairy-tale charm, ultimately seems arbitrary. His final incarceration seems no worse than his earlier ones—perhaps even less so, for he has justifiable hopes that the Doctor will come to his aid, and he is quickly forgiven by Amelia. He is never confronted with the enormity of his actions, as Tom is during his imprisonment. Booth could have picked up Barrow's sermons at any time during his career.

Many of the scenes in the novel, as has been remarked, have the quality of satiric set pieces and add little to the actual plot.[38] Certain encounters have significance, but just as many do not. Granted, we do get a sense of design when we discover that the lawyer and the gambler Booth meets during his first incarceration are, respectively, the man who is responsible for Amelia's being deprived of her inheritance and the man who will be responsible for the restoration of it. Yet Fielding does not give us enough of a sense of mystery at the outset to let us revel in the inevitability of its solution. Booth's actions do not lead to the restoration of Amelia's inheritance, except in the most incidental way. Although Booth benefits from it, the inheritance is actually Amelia's; the causal connection between conversion and restoration of fortune is thus further undermined. Considering how the plot progresses, Mrs. Atkinson's misapprehension at the end of the novel that Booth has been committed to prison for forgery seems just as logical a conclusion (or perhaps even more logical) than what actually occurs.

Fielding the characterized author figure is but an occasional god, and the sporadic nature of his controlling presence undermines the tightness of the providential scheme. The narrator of *Amelia* does not demonstrate his control over the events in the text to the extent that the author/narrator of *Tom Jones* does. It may be that Fielding's other alter ego in *Amelia* does a better job of saving Booth than does the author himself. As Cross points out, the honest justice who helps the Booths retrieve their stolen fortune is modeled upon Fielding himself.[39] It is almost as if Fielding felt that in order to rectify the injustice meted out to the Booths he needed to intervene personally. After all, the world he described seemed to have no place for an incorruptible magistrate. Only by making this sort of metaleptic gesture could Fielding introduce true justice into this world. Fielding essentially saves Booth on two levels.

Overall, with its spuriously causal connection between Booth's reformation and the restoration of Amelia's inheritance, the providential scheme functions as a necessary device that Fielding jams onto unwieldy and unsuitable material in an effort to validate the crucial argument for conversion and reformation. Its unearned status makes it seem like an attempt to assert an orthodox belief in the rightness of things against the overwhelming evidence of their essential wrongness, an attempt to close off Booth's story from troubling counterforces and to make the text's didactic point appear attractive. Although the text may contemplate the possibilities of societal reform and its own capacity to effect it, the picture of society it paints inspires little hope in the reader.

Dr. Harrison and the Adulterate Society

When Amelia mistakenly believes that Dr. Harrison has turned against her family, she loses faith in all humanity: "'Dr. *Harrison*!' cries *Amelia*.—'Well then, there is an End of all Goodness in the World. I will never have a good Opinion of any human Being more'" (*Am* 307). She voices a sentiment that we might all feel after encountering the corrupt world she inhabits. In light of our previous experience with the text, we have little trouble accepting that he who has been represented to us previously as "one of the best Men in the World" (77) has maliciously turned against the hapless Booths, as so many of their supposed friends do. Subsequent events exonerate the good Doctor, but they do not exonerate society: there does seem to be an end to all goodness in the world Fielding depicts. Although *Amelia* provides a thorough list of social evils, it focuses especially on adultery. Adultery appears as both cause and symptom of society's lack of moral grounding, serving as the text's most eloquent symbol for the diseased world described therein and problematizing the very possibility that moral authority might be enforced.

Amelia may be presented as the novel's moral exemplar, but it is her "father" Dr. Harrison who—despite the temporary questioning of his character—is presented throughout the text as the actual moral authority. In his relationship with Amelia the Doctor has the final say, as we see by his explanation of what constitutes wisdom in her: "'Why, whenever you act like a wise Woman,' cries the Doctor, 'you will force me to think you so; and whenever you are pleased to act as you do now, I shall be obliged, whether I will or no, to think as I do now'" (*Am* 372).[40] Dr. Harrison is one in a series of Fielding's spokesmen, with a function similar to that of Abraham Adams or Squire Allworthy in the earlier novels. Although we should not assume that these spokesmen unequivocally voice the sentiments of Fielding the man, we can see that their sentiments are closely aligned with those put forth in Fielding's nonfiction works such as the essays.[41] Fielding treats Dr. Harrison with greater respect than he treats his other moral spokesmen, a sign perhaps of his unwillingness to let the Doctor's precepts be associated with any levity. Lacking the naive sweetness of Abraham Adams and the good-natured benevolence of Allworthy, Dr. Harrison functions as a chastening rather than a merciful god, unprepossessing rather than endearing.[42] He plays the role of stern punisher when, under a misapprehension, he has Booth jailed for debt. His derision of Mrs. Atkinson's admittedly dubious intellectual accomplishments verges on the mean-spirited. He high-handedly devises tests of character for those around him. Yet Dr. Harrison's very austerity gives him the moral forcefulness that is lacking in Fielding's more pleasant spokesmen.

This austerity also renders him more mouthpiece than fully realized character. At the masquerade ball (this novel's version of the inn at Upton), all the principal characters appear, including a surrogate of Amelia. Dr. Harrison, however, appears only as text, a sort of bodiless mouth preaching an apt sermon on adultery. His words often seem like inserted chunks of didactic commentary; as Hugh Amory observes, he is "a pure role, not a character, an exhibit of the potentiality of an ideal clergyman for good and evil, not a revelation of the 'real' human being beneath the mask of a profession."[43] Whereas we can easily form a mental picture of, for example, Abraham Adams and perhaps even Squire Allworthy, Dr. Harrison eludes us. We have not so much a sense of a man as of a moral force.

Dr. Harrison opposes the vicious drives of society, launching his moral "should-be" against its immoral "is." But he preaches values to a society that has rendered them meaningless. From the outset of the novel appear examples of a system of influence peddling and bribery so pervasive as to seem ineradicable—like the self-perpetuating "wiglomeration" in the chancery courts of *Bleak House*, a novel that *Amelia* in many ways anticipates. Corruption perpetuates itself, as the influential nobleman—a representative of the nation's leaders—indicates: "Do you not know, Doctor, that this is as corrupt a Nation as ever existed under the Sun? And would you think of governing such a People by the strict Principles of Honesty and Morality?" (*Am* 460). The nobleman likens the nation to a body in decline, whose inevitable destruction renders palliatives unnecessary: "It is enervated at home, becomes contemptible abroad; and such indeed is its Misery and Wretchedness, that it resembles a Man in the last decrepid Stage of Life, who looks with Unconcern at his approaching Dissolution" (461).[44] By naturalizing the social process of corruption the nobleman promotes its unquestioned acceptance; by being in a position of power he will guarantee its perpetuation. The text's other representation of nobility—the lecherous Noble Lord—reinforces the argument that the nation is in the hands of the corrupt. As critics have often pointed out, his lack of a name confers a generic quality upon him, so that he becomes not just an individual but a representative of the nobility—those who should be guiding the lower classes, not leading them astray.

Religion, argues Dr. Harrison, "would have prevented this decrepid State of the Constitution" (*Am* 461), but religion is permeated with the very corruption to be mitigated. Although Dr. Harrison adheres to the tenets of his religion, zealously promoting them among his parishioners, he is an exception, not a rule. Contemporary churchmen, represented by the newly ordained Tom, twist Scripture to their own selfish purposes, presumably passing on to their flock a debased version of religious truth. Yet the self-interested clergyman will seemingly thrive while he who speaks truth will have decreasing influence. Tom has the potential to achieve an influential position if he (as is probable) follows the sycophantic strategy that his worldly father advises: "If thou art wise, thou wilt think every Man thy Superior, of whom thou canst get any thing; at least thou wilt persuade him that thou thinkest so, and that is sufficient" (404). We can envision a dynasty of yes-men, happily agreeing to any corrupt doctrine as long as it leads to advancement.[45] Dr. Harrison blames the clergy's laxity toward its doctrines for the general disrespect for religion. Although England styles itself a Christian nation, the designation is empty, according to Dr. Harrison: "in a Christian Society, which I no more esteem this Nation to be, than I do any Part of *Turky*, I doubt not but this very Colonel [the treacherous Col. James] would have made a worthy and Valuable Member" (375). Clergymen lead their flocks astray, and the flocks happily acquiesce in being so led. It is no wonder that the lawyer Murphy can designate the Bible—that authority upon which Christianity is based—as "but a Bit of Calves-skin" (63).

The very clergymen who could bring meaning back to religion, such as Dr. Harrison, lack position in the contemporary church, and the rot has seemingly set in too deep for them to ever regain influence. As Tom's father points out, Dr. Harrison lacks the "wisdom" to advance in the church: "If he had any understanding, he would have been a Bishop long ago, to my certain knowledge" (*Am* 404). Dr. Harrison is precluded from advancement and bereft of influence because he will not go against his moral beliefs. In *Tom Jones*, as the master of Paradise Hall and a county magistrate, Squire Allworthy maintains his position of moral authority for both readers of the text and characters in it. Yet, although Dr. Harrison may signify moral authority for readers of *Amelia*, he is essentially disregarded by most of the other characters.

Fielding reinforces the lack of society's moral grounding through his portrayal of the secondary characters. In *Tom Jones* there is a balance between bad characters and good, so that for each Lady Bellaston plotting Tom's ruin there is a Mrs. Miller attempting to restore his good name. Fielding also makes clear at the outset the nature of each character, summing up the person in a few (generally ironic) sentences. In *Amelia*, however, there is an imbalance of bad and good, with the scales tipping toward the bad. More important, the text frustrates our attempts to determine quickly which category a character fits into by cutting back on the amount of pithy character summations. As Eric Rothstein notes, this lack of commentary puts us in the position of the characters themselves, who have no helpful narrator exposing the contents of another's mind: "*Amelia* lowers us almost to the level of the characters, strips us of comedy and comfort, and creates in us what one might rather lumpishly call 'epistemological empathy.'"[46] Not only do we feel puzzled; we end up suspecting the motives of all subsidiary characters and anticipating the inevitable unmasking of each. When Amelia does not know "whether to conclude Mrs. *Ellison* to be a Friend or Enemy to Mrs. *Bennet*" (*Am* 260), her plight mirrors that of the reader.

From the outset apparent friends easily metamorphose into actual enemies. In the story he tells Miss Mathews, Booth describes the friendly Bagillard, who plotted against his Amelia's honor, and the solicitous Betty, who plotted against her fortune. In retrospect he can assess their duplicity, but he is nonetheless unable to learn from his experience, as his relations with the lecherous Col. James and the pimping Trent show. In Gibraltar when a once friendly Colonel refuses to help Booth financially, he turns to Col. James. But later Col. James, piqued over Booth's affair with Miss Mathews and himself enamored of Amelia, proves false. His friendship with Col. James undermined, Booth renews acquaintance with the amiable Trent, but he, by trying to drive Booth into debt so that he will "sell" Amelia to the Noble Lord, proves the greatest scoundrel of all. The Booths leave their country home because of the malice of the clergyman and his wife. The landlady Mrs. Ellison, with her solicitude for Amelia's health and her concern over Booth's indebtedness, seems genuinely good-hearted, but she turns out to be no better than a procuress.

Amelia's surrogate, Mrs. Atkinson, is the most audacious shape-shifter in the text. She shifts from friendly young lady to tragic victim to worldly schemer to high-tempered drunkard and finally back to concerned friend. In his essay on Fielding's "conservation of character," John Coolidge argues that, due to the complex idea we get of her, she "saves the novel": "The character of Mrs. Atkinson seems the product of a more thoroughgoing, in a sense a less controlled, process of imagination than Fielding had hitherto ventured upon. In that process he developed a conception of the relation between good and evil in human life which challenges that represented by Amelia."[47] In Mrs. Atkinson, we see that mixture of good and bad motives that Fielding regarded as vital to presenting a character such as Black George in *Tom Jones:* "Life most exactly resembles the Stage, since it is often the same Person who represents the Villain and the Hero" (*Tom* 1:327). But the effect here is not just to make us aware of the complexity of character, aesthetically admirable as that might be. The metamorphoses of Mrs. Atkinson are like those of the wolf and sheepdog in a classic *Looney Toons* cartoon; shifting back and forth between their own form and the assumed form of the other, they confuse us—and themselves—as to which is which. As with Amelia and her doubles, we have the vertiginous sense that no one has ontological integrity. By the time we finish with Mrs. Atkinson, we are unsure how to assess her; she herself provides the most apt summation of her character: "I was . . . turned all at once into a Cypher" (*Am* 275). Epitomizing the variable "friends" throughout the text, she destabilizes our sense of moral certainty.[48]

Whereas the narrative technique underscores the lack of moral grounding, the narrative focus on adultery symbolically drives home that all values are lost.[49] The value of marital fidelity, for which Dr. Harrison argues so fervently in his epistolary masquerade "sermon," has become meaningless in the society Fielding describes. Adultery—both actual and threatened—permeates Amelia. This is not the ungoverned, essentially high-spirited sexuality of *Tom Jones*, but a rampant, mirthless lust, a near frantic quest to satisfy an unquenchable thirst. The novel depicts adultery both as the *primum mobile* that sends society careening off course and as a consequence of society's debasement.

Booth's first actual act in the novel (besides the storytelling) is to engage in an adulterous coupling with Miss Mathews. But adultery leaves its mark on all the characters and threatens not only the Booths' unity but that of society in general. Miss Mathews specializes in adultery. Before Booth she consorts with what she thinks is a married man, and after him she takes up with the certainly married Col. James. Mrs. Atkinson engages in both forced and possibly willing adultery. Although she denies that she granted the Noble Lord "the last Favour" during their interview at the masquerade, his raptures over "those two short Minutes" that he had with her and her own hesitations and equivocal answers suggest that the Clarissa-like victim has become a Becky Sharp–like opportunist (*Am* 442, 446). The erstwhile Trent has turned his wife into a whore, and both he and Col. James hint to Booth that he should do the same.[50] Both Col. and Mrs. James scheme to commit adultery with Mrs. and Mr. Booth, respectively. And finally, Dr. Harrison, although he neither feels nor precipitates adulterous impulses, preoccupies himself with putting a stop to them in others.

Amelia herself becomes a focal point of adulterous intentions, like some steady light to a flock of highly overcharged moths. Bagillard, the Noble Lord, and Col. James all set snares for her virtue. Although she maintains her honor in these instances, she is perhaps not entirely free of adulterous impulses herself. Her affection for Sgt. Atkinson is refined to the point of ethereality, but it nevertheless causes her to think of another man in a manner with "which Booth, if he had known it, would perhaps have been displeased" (*Am* 483).

Adultery—both potential and actual—drives the plot, controlling the actions of the two protagonists, to whom we might give the epithets of "imperiled wife" and "adulterous husband." The attempt to make an adulteress of Amelia results in the Noble Lord's gifts and Dr. Harrison's consequent arrest of Booth, Col. James's plot to send Booth away, Trent's entrapment of Booth with gambling debts, and the frequent moves of the Booths. Booth's liaison with Miss Mathews occasions his estrangement from Col. James and his subsequent duel with Col. Bath. The novel climaxes with the two adultery strands being brought together. To put a stop to Miss Mathews's importunities, a consequence of his liaison with her, Booth ventures out of the safety of the Verge of the Court and visits her lodging. Col. James's spy reports the visit, thus enabling James to fulfill two objectives: to confirm his suspicion that Miss Mathews still cares for Booth and to destroy Booth's credibility and thus ingratiate himself with Amelia. But the spy also notifies Trent, and he, under orders from the Noble Lord, has Booth arrested for debt so that Amelia will be vulnerable to the lord's advances. Within this small area of London occurs a veritable gathering of former adulterers, current adulterers, would-be adulterers, and aides-d'adulterers; it is a convergence point for each character's trajectory in adultery-space, so to speak.

Although this episode demonstrates the consequence of adulterous behavior to Booth, he is ultimately let off. The burden of the text falls on the adulterous woman rather than the adulterous man. The explicit commentary of the text makes clear that any person who commits adultery, whether male or female, is a scourge to society. We have the Doctor's denunciation of Col. James, both in a letter and in a discussion with Amelia, and several statements by the narrator to that effect. But when commentary focuses on the male, it generally is warning him against leading a married woman astray. We see, for example, no similar warnings meted out to the women such as Miss Mathews who lead married men astray.[51]

Certainly Booth's experience does not enable the text to make a convincing case for the consequences accruing to the adulterous male. Despite landing in a few sticky situations because of his affair Booth is extricated from them easily enough, and overall he suffers little from his breach of the marriage bond. Although he wallows in guilt after he is released from Newgate, within a few days he regains his high spirits and can pass a day "without the Interruption of almost a single Thought concerning Miss *Mathews*" (*Am* 170).

Granted, we are led initially to think that his adulterous affair may lead to marital discord. In book 4, after Booth receives a letter from the enraged Miss Mathews, he worries for a time that Miss Mathews will expose him to his wife:

> Nothing now lay on his Mind, but to conceal his Frailty from *Amelia*, to whom he was afraid Miss *Mathews* in the Rage of her Resentment would communicate it. This Apprehension made him stay almost constantly at home; and he trembled at every Knock at the Door. His fear moreover betrayed him into a Meanness, which he would have heartily despised on any other Occasion. This was to order the Maid to deliver him any Letter directed to *Amelia*, at the same time strictly charging her not to acquaint her Mistress with her having received any such Orders. (*Am* 178)

His subterfuges here make the possibility of exposure appear fairly onerous; this is the only passage in the text that actually drives home the consequences of male adultery. And lest we forget this possibility Miss Mathews pops up like a bad fairy at a couple of other points in the text, threatening Booth that she will tell all.

But the text is structured so as to downplay and even forget the enormity of Booth's action. In book 12 we discover that Amelia had received a letter "some Time ago," and in it Miss Mathews "acquainted *Amelia* with the infidelity of her husband" (*Am* 498). Although Fielding makes forays into Amelia's mind at crucial instances, he gives us no indication as to when this presumably significant event occurred. No ripple disturbs the complacent surface of Amelia when she hears of Booth's transgression; no change appears in her feelings. It is as if the letter and its shameful revelations were swallowed up in some black hole of forgiveness—as if his adultery never happened. The narrative elision almost serves to cancel the incident. Amelia's easy forgiveness is matched by the forgiveness of the text itself. We might compare Amelia's reaction to that of Pamela in Richardson's sequel. When Pamela fears that Mr. B. is engaging in an adulterous liaison with a young countess (a mistaken surmise), her sufferings are presented in detail, as we see in her heartfelt words to Lady Davers: "I weep in the night, when he is asleep; and in the day, when he is absent: And I am happy when I can unobserved, steal this poor relief. I believe already I have shed as many tears as would drown my baby."[52] Although Richardson's text itself contrives to forgive egregious male behavior, it nonetheless drives home that adultery has painful consequences on all members of a family. *Amelia* elides that point.

Booth's sporadic twinges of guilt and his brief final confinement—an indirect consequence of his original transgression—hardly serve to paint a bleak picture of the male adulterer's fate. Overall, his adultery assumes the proportions of a minor lapse rather than a major transgression. When Col. Bath gives him Dr. Harrison's letter on adultery, he sees no personal application to himself. He even bristles at the implication there might be: "To say the Truth, I am a little surprised that he should single me out of all Mankind to deliver the Letter to; I do not think I deserve the Character of such a Husband. It is well I am not so forward to take an Affront as some Folks" (*Am* 423). In Fielding's earlier works such a self-deluded statement would not have been allowed to pass without some ironic commentary, but here it occurs without accompaniment, almost as if Fielding as well as Booth has suffered a case of amnesia. In front of the man who should seemingly be his moral confessor, Booth forgets entirely about his transgression. If he were indeed filled with guilt (as some critics have argued) we would expect that he might eventually confess his sins to Dr. Harrison, yet Dr. Harrison never learns that the man he took under his wing wronged his spiritual daughter. Booth escapes the moral accounting that poetic justice would seem to require.[53] In all, male adultery receives absolution.

Not so female adultery. In Amelia's case we feel a continual sense of peril that we do not feel in Booth's. The novel generates real suspense as to whether Amelia can escape the snares laid for her virtue, for it makes clear that female adultery is a grave offense indeed. Fielding lets us in on most of Amelia's strenuous shifts and stratagems to escape from one importunate male or another, thus enabling us to feel the weightiness of the threat. Booth's horror at the thought of his wife associated with adultery reinforces our sense of the crime's dire nature: "'Is not *Amelia* then,' cried he, 'equally jealous of my Honour? Would she, from a weak Tenderness for my Person, go privately about to betray, to undermine the most invaluable Treasure of my Soul? Would she have me pointed at as the credulous Dupe, the easy Fool, the tame, the kind Cuckold of a Rascal, with whom I conversed as a Friend?'" (*Am* 437). As Robert Folkenflik points out, Booth's jealous rantings echo those of Othello, and the allusion to Shakespeare's tragedy helps give us that sense that Fielding's novel could easily veer into the tragic mode.[54] Those Shakespearean echoes keep us from regarding Amelia's predicament as comedic. It is interesting that Booth claims he has not "the least Suspicion" of his wife's honor; his impassioned speech stems only from her refusal to confide in him. Merely the threat of adultery—a seemingly empty one in light of Amelia's faithful nature—is enough to drive him near mad.

Mrs. Atkinson's tale makes clear why the Booths recoil at the thought of female adultery—it leads to the destruction of the family. As the double of Amelia, Mrs. Atkinson marks out the alternate route Amelia could have followed had she continued in her friendship with the Noble Lord. Drugged and essentially raped by him, Mrs. Atkinson contracts venereal disease and in turn passes it on to her husband. Enraged by her supposed betrayal of him, the husband falls into a self-destructive fit, which perhaps helps bring on the "polypus" that dispatches him. On the heels of this loss, Mrs. Atkinson loses her health, her remaining funds, and her child. Her misfortunes do not directly stem from her adulterous liaison, perhaps, but the text is structured so as to make a *post hoc, ergo propter hoc* argument—an argument that Mrs. Atkinson's vociferous self-recrimination reinforces. The adulteress ends up as a source of contagion, destroying her own family. Amelia cannot engage in adultery (the act would irrevocably undo her paragon status), but her double can make clear to us the collapse that would ensue if she did.

As Tony Tanner points out in *Adultery and the Novel*, adultery undermines that which John Locke regards as the premier binding force upon the social order—contract: "adultery can be seen as an attempt to establish an extracontractual contract, or indeed an anticontract that precisely threatens those continuations, distinctions, and securities that Locke outlines."[55] Tanner confines himself mainly to nineteenth-century novels, arguing that sexuality in the eighteenth-century novel "in no sense threatens the structure of society or the institution of marriage" (*Am* 13). But *Amelia* anticipates the nineteenth-century novels explored by Tanner; it makes a very clear connection between adultery and social disintegration.

Adultery herein threatens to lead not only to the collapse of the family but to the collapse of society, the disrupted family bonds serving as a synecdoche for disrupted societal bonds. In his epistle on adultery Dr. Harrison describes how the breech in the marriage contract can rend the entire social fabric:

> The Ruin of both Wife and Husband, and sometimes of the whole Family, are the probable Consequence of this fatal Injury. Domestic Happiness is the End of almost all our Pursuits, and the common Reward of all our Pains. When Men find themselves for ever barred from this delightful Fruition, they are lost to all Industry, and grow careless of all their worldly Affairs. Thus they become bad Subjects, bad Relations, bad Friends and bad Men. Hatred and Revenge are the wretched Passions which boil in their Minds. Despair and Madness very commonly ensue, and Murder and Suicide often close the dreadful Scene. (414–15)

Adultery breaks the bonds of friendship, results in bad citizens, and leads to a state of mind incompatible with religion—conditions indicative of societal breakdown. In *Amelia* we see adulterous impulses undermine the friendship between Booth and Col. James, prompt the Noble Lord to behave ignobly, lead to misuse of the courts, and precipitate potentially fatal misunderstandings, as in the case of Booth's duel with Col. Bath.

Yet adultery is not only a cause of disease but also a symptom of it. Dr. Harrison, echoing Fielding's *Covent-Garden* essays on adultery, points out that society enables this vice to persist: "In the great Sin of Adultery for instance; hath the Government provided any Law to punish it; or doth the Priest take any Care to correct it?" (*Am* 375). The exemplary Amelia is herself implicated in this process, for her easy forgiveness of Booth deprives him of both correction and punishment. In effect, both because it is caused by a system in decline and because it hastens that decline, adultery serves as a sort of positive feedback loop, bringing society ever closer to the verge of collapse.

Mrs. Atkinson affixes the blame for such collapse not on the deceptive male but on the too-credulous female. Even though the Noble Lord, with Lovelacian guile, masterminded a well-nigh foolproof plan to snare her, she nevertheless blames herself in part for the affair: "it is now my stedfast Opinion, that the Woman who gives up the least Out-work of her Virtue, doth, in that very Moment betray the Citadel" (*Am* 295). Her statement smacks of the asking-for-it argument: although she "never consented" to the act, she implicitly said yes because she flirted with the Noble Lord. Thus she can so dramatically avow herself "an Adulteress and a Murderer" (267). Even such patently histrionic pronouncements have rhetorical force, reinforcing our sense of the destructive potential of female adultery.

The attitudes toward adultery we see in *Amelia* reflect those of the period. Lawrence Stone notes the prevalence of the double standard whereby "both fornication and adultery were exclusively male prerogatives" and "wifely infidelity was unpardonable."[56] In his letter Dr. Harrison provides us with the rationale behind the double standard; adultery "includes in it almost every Injury and Mischief which one Man can do, or bring on another. It is robbing him of his Property" (*Am* 414). When a husband strays he disposes only of what belongs to him; when a wife strays she disposes of what belongs to another.

Fielding's text not only reflects but also composes the values of society. By almost canceling Booth's transgression, *Amelia* (as well as its eponymous heroine) makes a case for a shrugging toleration of adultery in the male; by emphasizing the consequences of Mrs. Atkinson's, it makes a case for the abhorrence of such behavior in the female. Although an actual chastisement of the seducer rather than the seduced, Dr. Harrison's letter reinforces the notion that a female's transgression leads to ruin. To a certain extent this emphasis on female fidelity is necessary. In *Amelia* Fielding wishes to locate moral authority in the domestic realm. If Amelia—as well as the women who read her story—is to assume responsibility for promulgating and enforcing morality, the preservation of purity becomes especially important.

Only the exemplary figures—Amelia and Dr. Harrison—do not succumb to adulterous impulses, and the retreat to the country at the novel's conclusion suggests that freedom from contagion can be found only outside the city/society. The novel's apparently happy ending reinforces its overall skepticism, for it suggests that there is little hope for societal redemption. Although Amelia is restored to her proper station at the end of the novel, we do not have a sense that all is now right with the world, as we do in *Tom Jones*, for example.

Like many eighteenth-century writers, Fielding tended to draw up a distinction between country and city, regarding the former as a fairly idyllic locale and the latter as an overall hotbed of corruption. In both *Tom Jones* and *Amelia* the protagonists leave the city and return to a country estate. But whereas Tom's return is in the nature of a restoration, the Booths' is in the nature of an abdication. By ending with Tom as the eventual heir of the county's largest estate, *Tom Jones* symbolically suggests that moral authority has assumed its rightful place in the world. The city, though more corrupt than the country, does not appear beyond redemption. Good people live there—the Millers and Nightingale, for instance. Tom and Sophia marry there, and they are able to move between county and city at no apparent detriment to themselves. The many marriages suggest that there is an overall unity and goodness in the world. The dreadful Blifil himself stands poised on the brink of matrimony, and even if his intended is one of Fielding's despised Methodists he will seemingly find comfort in her large estate. The ending of *Tom Jones* includes rather than excludes, and this inclusive gesture expands outward to society as a whole, giving us a sense that Tom's ascension has helped put things to right.

Not so with Amelia's ascension. The novel shows that Amelia, intended to represent an immutable moral perfection, can barely maintain her own integrity (let alone inspire others) in a corrupt world. Her influence throughout the novel is negligible; in fact, the very person she should inspire—her feckless husband, Booth—is often impervious to this good angel, especially at the most crucial instances. Like Dr. Harrison, she is a voice crying in the wilderness, and like him she ends up fleeing the place where she might do the most good, the text thereby acknowledging the receding power and presence of moral exemplars. The Booths must escape the city, it seems, in order to save themselves, as Dr. Harrison's words indicate: "do you pack up every Thing in order for your Journey To-morrow; for, if you are wise, you will not trust your Husband a Day longer in this Town—" (*Am* 505). Once back in the country, the Booths make no further forays into the wicked city: "In about six Weeks after *Booth's* first coming into the Country, he went to *London*, and paid all his Debts of Honour; after which, and a Stay of two Days only, he returned into the Country, and hath never since been thirty Miles from Home" (532). London is left to its own wicked devices.

And except for the Atkinsons, London might as well be Sodom. Certainly, the punishments that are meted out to the bad characters at the end have a wrath-of-God touch to them—or should we call it an influence-of-Richardson touch? Col. James's reward is concurrently his punishment, for to possess Miss Mathews he must submit to her ill treatment of him. Mrs. Ellison, the Noble Lord, the lawyer Murphy, the thief Robinson, and Betty Harris all die horrible deaths. Even the humorous, duel-prone Col. Bath is killed off, a sorry fate for an essentially good-hearted soul. Rather than concluding with multiple marriages signifying unity and well-being, *Amelia* concludes with multiple deaths.

Granted, a little group of good characters form a society for themselves in the country, and Fielding provocatively suggests that moral authority resides in the domestic realm, the province of women. Amelia, not Booth, is heir of both her mother's estate and Dr. Harrison's wisdom. She presumably has control over her own estate, for after his marriage Booth promised Mrs. Harris he would settle the Harris fortune on his wife. Amelia may defer to Booth, but it is she who enforces morality, a role so many of her literary "daughters" would perform over the next fifty years. Fielding indeed suggests that moral authority descends matrilineally. Although Amelia and Booth have sons, it is her eldest daughter who is presented as the "heir." She, too, is named Amelia, and Dr. Harrison has settled his estate—both spiritual and material—upon her.

Yet the text suggests that the line will stop with her. In the penultimate paragraph of the novel, the narrator gives us information that bodes ill for the line's continuation: "A Marriage was proposed to her the other Day with a young Fellow of a good Estate, but she never would see him more than once; 'for Dr. *Harrison*,' says she, 'told me he was illiterate, and I am sure he is ill natured'" (*Am* 533). Despite the cheerful picture it paints of the happy life the Booths now lead, *Amelia* ends on a discordant note, subscribing to an antimarriage ideology it had earlier rejected and giving us little hope for societal reconstruction.

The shift in narrative stance also indicates Fielding's bleaker purpose. Fielding drops the stance he had assumed in earlier novels of the genial author/narrator, self-professedly shepherding his text and controlling its reception. The only portrait of an author we get here is a character in the text, and a rather unsympathetic one at that. The author that Booth meets in Bondum's spunging-house is an ignorant, money-grubbing wordmonger. The satire falls also on the publishers who pay for quantity, not quality, and the readers who prefer scandalous romances to epic poems. But the author himself compromises the literary profession with his made-up Parliamentary speeches, his faulty criticism, and his solicitation for subscriptions to nonexistent publications. The chapter in which he appears has the ambiguous title "Comments upon Authors" (*Am* 323); although it could refer to the subsequent literary discussion between Booth and the author, it could also imply that the negative portrait of this particular author applies to the profession in general.

Rather than the characterized author figure we have a narrator who alternates didactic commentary with self-effacement, letting the characters do most of the evaluations. John Bender points out, "both as regards the comparatively elusive presence of the narrator and the characterization of omniscient authority in the benevolent Dr. Harrison, we find significant movement toward the transparency of the later realist novel."[57] The narrative voice here points to what would become a standard by the end of the century. Thus Fielding once again provides a partial blueprint for the novel genre, albeit without the self-conscious discussion of what he is doing.

However, the narrative voice suggests too a more skeptical notion of authority than we saw in *Tom Jones*. The transparent narration, especially as it applies to the presentation of various secondary characters, has the effect of destabilizing our expectations; Fielding shows the difficulty of making authoritative assessments in a society lacking moral grounding. The chunks of didactic commentary are Fielding's attempt to provide that grounding, although, as Bender suggests, many of the authoritative moral pronouncements are transferred to Dr. Harrison. This alternation between narrational transparency and didacticism suggests that Fielding has no clear idea what will work to get his message across. Fielding desires that the story tell itself, but he fears that it cannot do so; he thus resorts sporadically to a more strident commentary than he had employed in the more consistently mediated early novels. Throughout *Amelia* Fielding makes a case for the moral authority of his characters and the literary authority of himself, but an insistent subtext calls into question any pretense to authority.

Implicit threats to the authorial voice recur. According to the evidence put forth in the text, whether an author writes well or ill, he has little control over his issue. In all of Fielding's texts, words tend to slip away from any denotative moorings, but the situation is exacerbated here. The misunderstanding over the word "satisfaction," for instance, provides an amusing instance. After Booth's arrest for debt, Col. Bath assumes that he will want "satisfaction"—the chance to defend his honor in a duel—from the person who had him arrested. Dr. Harrison, the very person who instigated the arrest, interprets the word to mean Booth's settlement of his debt and kindly absolves Booth of the immediate obligation: "'I beg, Sir,' says the Doctor, 'no more may be mentioned of that Matter. I am convinced, no Satisfaction will be required of the Captain, till he is able to give it'" (*Am* 364). Throughout the scene the Doctor and the Colonel talk at cross-purposes. The scene not only shows us the confusions inherent in language but also sets up a distinction between a bad use of a word (the Colonel's) and a good use (the Doctor's), the former usage abetting the ideology of dueling and the latter reinforcing the principle of repaying one's debts.

A similar and related confusion results from the use of the word "honor," for whereas it once meant integrity it now means the militant defense of one's reputation against any supposed slights—not a quality in itself but rather just the often empty assertion of it through superior swordplay. Of course, the word "honor" is a favorite target of eighteenth-century writers, for its diverse meanings epitomize the ongoing debate between an intrinsic system of values and a system of values proved by external signs, as we see, for example, in the debates between Pamela and Mr. B. in Richardson's text. Fielding himself had played with the word before in *Tom Jones*, making Sophia's self-serving maid Honour a glaring representative of the disjunction between signified and signifier.

Through the various verbal contests in *Amelia*, Fielding highlights the competing forces working against the unambiguous meanings of words—of words' essential, irresolvable heteroglossia.[58] Such heteroglossia works against any authoritative discourse, including presumably the very text that highlights it. Dr. Harrison, Fielding's spokesman, may assert the "true meanings" of words, but Col. Bath's definitions have equal force in the play of the text.

Various dialogues within the text also highlight the inability of authoritative discourse to sustain itself as such. Booth's sentimental history of his courtship of Amelia is accompanied by Miss Mathews's running commentary—a commentary that undermines the idyllic picture he paints. When Booth describes how Amelia's innocence keeps her from recognizing deceit (a notion common to both Fielding's fiction and his nonfiction), Miss Mathews responds: "It is highly generous and good in you . . . to impute to Honesty what others would perhaps call Credulity" (*Am* 71). When Booth paints a tender picture of Amelia's nervous distress after caring for his wound, Miss Mathews cries, "A Man had better be plagued with all the Curses of Egypt than with a vapourish Wife" (120). Booth's intended glorification of his beloved wife is recontextualized by the catty commentary of his jealous would-be mistress. And although Fielding presumably wishes to cast no shadows on Amelia but merely to highlight Miss Mathews's maliciousness, his inclusion of the commentary nevertheless makes us regard Amelia as somewhat credulous, vapourish, and so forth. Again, the inspirational story has the diametrically opposed effect from what it should presumably have; our own possibly skeptical responses to panegyric are anticipated by Miss Mathews. The didactic commentary of the primary narrator is itself implicated in the process of recontextualization.

The same sort of recontextualization also occurs with Dr. Harrison's epistle on adultery. The letter is presented as a viable instrument of moral reform—a rightfully authoritative text. But discarded by Col. James at the masquerade, it winds up in the hands of several "Bucks," one of whom proceeds to read it aloud to a mocking assembly. With his running commentary on the text, the orator attempts to turn the serious into the merely pompous. The reading of the letter, too, is an instance of what Mikhail Bakhtin calls "reported speech," and as such it highlights the conflict between various meanings and undermines the letter's authority. For, by reporting the Doctor's words to an audience that the Doctor had not intended, the orator brings competing contexts to bear upon them. As Bakhtin explains, "reported utterance . . . has the capacity of entering on its own, so to speak, into speech, into its syntactic makeup, as an integral unit of the construction," and the competing context works against the one in which the speech was originally framed: "The reporting context strives to break down the self-contained compactness of the reported speech, to resolve it, to obliterate its boundaries."[59] Fielding may have intended the scene as a satire on the irreligious bucks of the age, but he implicitly calls Dr. Harrison's authority into question by putting his words in their mouths. What is perhaps intended as the text's most sincere expression of Fielding's moral vision is undermined by the context in which it appears.

The fate of the Doctor's letter might, in fact, provide a cynical comment on the fate of all texts. Unaddressed and unsigned, it makes its rounds among the characters, and rather than serving as an inspiration to its intended recipient, it serves as a source of confusion to all involved. It provokes jealousy in Booth, a situation it was meant to deflect, and nearly brings Col. James and Col. Bath to blows. The letter thus serves as a catalyst for various actions, but it does not fulfill its intended function. Its lack of salutation and signature may enable it to have a general application—to address itself to all would-be adulterers—but this same lack deprives it of any meaningful context. And even when its author is acknowledged, the letter is still appropriated by others for diverse purposes. Its fate points to the uncontrollability of all texts, the undermining of all authority.

The Booths' troubles stem in part from a misappropriated text, Mrs. Harris's will. After the death of Mrs. Harris, Amelia's sister Betty and the lawyer Murphy make a new will that essentially disinherits Amelia, depriving the Booths of the funds that might have enabled them to avoid the pecuniary difficulties they face throughout the novel. Although Amelia is restored to her rightful estate, the forgery incident indicates that even the most sacred documents are subject to self-interested revision. In Fielding's England, documents relating to property could not be considered as stolen property in themselves, as the good magistrate who clears up the inheritance problem makes clear: "He said Title Deeds savoured of the Realty, and it was not Felony to steal them" (*Am* 523). The law seems implicitly to acknowledge that texts cannot belong to anyone. The Doctor's exasperated response might sum up Fielding's own attitude on the subject: "'Savour of the Realty! savour of the Fartalty,' said the Doctor. 'I never heard such incomprehensible Nonsense. This is impudent, as well as childish trifling with the Lives and Property of Men'" (523). One cannot depend on a text to carry out one's "will," for it is always subject to appropriation, revision, and subversion.

The conversion of Booth and the providential ending may optimistically assert that literature can exert an authority to bring about change and that moral authority can be restored to its rightful position. But such conclusions seem imposed or unearned, precisely because the evidence against them is so overwhelming. Traditionally, critics have regarded the unassimilated, disruptive elements of *Amelia* as a sign of its aesthetic deficiency. But I would argue that the very problems we have with *Amelia* stem from Fielding's attempt to impose order on cultural material that resists it. As Felicity Nussbaum and Laura Brown point out, the eighteenth century has often been put forward as a time of stability and order:

> the prominence of political analysis in modern historiography has continued to support the stereotype of pervasive and long-term stability in the period, a political stability linked to an image of equivalent social and cultural coherence, to a sense of an unchallenged class hierarchy represented and perpetuated in a literary culture where aesthetics, ethics, and politics perfectly mesh.[60]

Fielding's text demonstrates that there is no such mesh. *Amelia* is indeed a "problem" novel, although not quite in the usual sense, for it shows us a world where exemplars go unrecognized and perhaps cannot even exist, where society is caught up in a positive feedback loop of vice, where the possibilities for reform are slim at best, and where both textual authority and moral authority are undermined by forces too pervasive to resist. Despite his claims for the text's epic status, Fielding lacks a clear sense of just what sort of relationship it has with its literary forebears and just what sort of offspring might follow. The text's so-called aesthetic deficiencies are, in reality, a sign of the ideological conflicts that Fielding found himself unable to resolve in this, his final novel.

CHAPTER SIX

Mansfield Park

Dismantling Pemberley

The heroine's friendship to be sought after by a young Woman in the same Neighbourhood, of Talents & Shrewdness, with light eyes & a fair skin, but having a considerable degree of Wit, Heroine shall shrink from the acquaintance.
—Jane Austen, "Plan of a Novel" *(MW 429)*

The woman who has only been taught to please will soon find that her charms are oblique sunbeams, and that they cannot have much effect on her husband's heart when they are seen every day, when the summer is passed and gone. Will she then have sufficient native energy to look into herself for comfort, and cultivate her dormant faculties? or is it not more rational to expect that she will try to please other men, and, in the emotions raised by the experience of new conquests, endeavour to forget the mortifications her love or pride has received?
—Mary Wollstonecraft, *Vindication of the Rights of Woman*

If, indeed, women were mere outside form and face only, and if mind made up no part of her composition, it would follow that a ball-room was quite as appropriate a place for choosing a wife, as an exhibition room for choosing a picture. . . .
—Hannah More, *Stricture on the Modern System of Female Education*

IN *THE OPPOSING SELF,* Lionel Trilling points out that "Fielding's *Amelia* . . . may be said to bear the same relation to *Tom Jones* that *Mansfield Park* bears to *Pride and Prejudice*."[1] Trilling's statement anticipates the intra-canonic, trans-gendered, trans-generational connections that I have been making throughout. I would add that *Mansfield Park* not only serves as the dark counterpoint to *Pride and Prejudice* but also revises many of the themes and motifs of *Amelia.* It explores the implications of the conduct-book heroine ideal that Fielding's final novel helped promulgate, addresses the issue of adultery from a woman's perspective, and problematizes the issue of moral and literary authority in a patriarchal society.

Tom Jones and *Amelia,* its contrapuntal sequel, test various ways of reviving a moribund social structure, each with varying degrees of success. Seemingly subversive in both content and presentation, *Tom Jones* comes to argue for the recuperability of traditional forms through the incorporation of something new—the bastard Tom or the novel form. With its exemplary heroine and its didactic tone, *Amelia* ostensibly puts forth a conservative agenda, but this conservatism is straining at the seams.

Pride and Prejudice and *Mansfield Park* have a similar obverse relationship. Like *Tom Jones, Pride and Prejudice* attempts to solve the problem of societal decline through seemingly subversive means—the insertion of a woman into the patriarchal plot of the reconstitution of the estate. But, as with Fielding's novel, Austen's also falls back on the old verities; traditional forms may require the introduction of a new element but they are intrinsically good. To a certain extent, just as *Amelia* appears at first as a sort of sequel to *Tom Jones,* the opening setup in *Mansfield Park* speaks back to the conclusion of *Pride and Prejudice.* Claudia Johnson notes that "The Bertrams end where Darcy begins—with the family circle which Austen's more attractive patricians learn to outgrow."[2] But we might also say that the Bertrams begin where Darcy ends—with the marriage of a proud and wealthy gentleman to a woman of inferior social standing. Lady Bertram may not be an older avatar of Elizabeth Bennet; but Sir Thomas Bertram, like Darcy, is the quintessential patriarch—sober, authoritative, responsible—and Mansfield Park, like Pemberley, is the repository of traditional values. The manor, in fact, provides the model for proper social behavior, as Fanny Price's wistful assessment makes clear: "At Mansfield, no sounds of contention, no raised voices, no abrupt bursts, no tread of violence was ever heard; all proceeded in a regular course of cheerful orderliness; every body had their due importance; every body's feelings were consulted" (*MP* 391–92). The "cheerful orderliness," the "due importance" of everyone, the consultation of everyone's feelings—such a description suggests that this is a well-regulated world, its hierarchical structure balanced with an almost democratic consideration of the wishes of all its members. But Fanny deludes herself, seemingly forgetting the miserable experiences she has so recently undergone there. As we see, the inhabitants of Mansfield Park often pervert or ignore such values. Whereas *Pride and Prejudice* holds forth hope for a renewal—an improvement—of the estate, *Mansfield Park* implicitly qualifies such hope, calling such values into question even as it attempts to assert their soundness.

The predominant features of Mansfield Park explicitly support traditional values. Fanny Price is an exemplary heroine, faithful to a hero who is momentarily deflected from her steadfast love but finally cognizant of her perfections. The resolution of the plot—wherein the constant Fanny gets her man and the instigators of change are banished from Mansfield—validates the argument for supporting the status quo.

However, the surface polemic of Austen's novel is disturbed by an underlying countercurrent of skepticism. Austen may explicitly sanction Fanny's good behavior, but as Fanny's story shows, female exemplarity is an insidious notion. The attributes of the exemplary woman—obedience to authority, self-effacement, and silence—actually disable her from fulfilling her function of providing proper moral guidance. The plot may resolve itself in a conventionally happy ending, but such happiness is built upon an underlying foundation of misery. The very things that promise social reformation highlight the fissures in society, fissures that have an implicit connection with the overarching values of Austen's time. Like *Amelia*, *Mansfield Park* reworks, recontextualizes, and refutes the easy solutions of an earlier text.[3]

Yet *Mansfield Park* also calls into question several of the assumptions underlying *Amelia*. Drawing on the motif of the beleaguered heroine, each text attempts to revise the status quo and testifies to the difficulty of so doing. Yet although *Amelia* demonstrates Fielding's increasing doubt that society can return to traditional values, it never questions the appropriateness of such a return. By reworking Fielding's material Austen calls such values into question, however. She shows us the underside of Amelia-like exemplarity and faults the overarching patriarchal structure that implicitly encourages behavior leading to social breakdown.

Excellent Woman

From the outset, nobody has known what to make of Fanny Price. Austen's earliest readers were divided on the subject; one of her nieces, for example, was "delighted with Fanny" while another "could not bear" her ("Opinions of *Mansfield Park*," *MW* 431, 432). Our own assessments of *Mansfield Park* are, in fact, integrally related to our assessments of Fanny.

Her perverse integrity and her unprepossessing virtues prompt the ambivalence and dissatisfaction we feel in regard to the text as a whole. Nina Auerbach subtitles an essay on *Mansfield Park* "Feeling as One Ought about Fanny Price"—a title suggestive of the quandary in which we find ourselves when confronted with Austen's least engaging heroine.[4] Fanny's sickliness, her voicelessness, her rectitude put us off, especially in that she is wedged between Austen's two most lively heroines, Elizabeth Bennet and Emma Woodhouse. Although Tony Tanner notes that "nobody falls in love with Fanny Price," he joins with Lionel Trilling in defending her, arguing that she is a typical Christian heroine, thus subject to unwarranted antipathy on the part of the more secular modern-day reader.[5] Auerbach, on the other hand, seems to regard Fanny's connection with otherworldly realms as tending toward the demonic rather than the angelic: Fanny is "a blighter of ceremonies and a divider of families," a vampire figure who "feasts secretly upon human vitality in the dark."[6] Yet the problem lies not so much with Fanny's conduct-book character, off-putting as that may sometimes be. Rather, it lies with the fact that Fanny's story shows us how little is to be gained by maintaining such a character.

Although the conduct-book heroine had thrived in the half-century since Richardson and Fielding put forward their paragons, Jane Austen generally mocked it. Austen's most memorable protagonists are not of the conduct-book type but instead are lively, somewhat wrong-headed characters capable of change and growth. They consistently transgress, or at least stretch, the bounds of what is considered proper behavior for women. The texts we have tended to favor, such as *Pride and Prejudice*, follow a bildungsroman structure; the protagonist errs, faces up to her faults (generally at the instigation of the male mentor), and undergoes a certain amount of development. Violations of what is strictly proper lead in part to chastisement and self-recognition, certainly, but such violations also bring about positive outcomes—for example, Elizabeth's sassing of Lady Catherine makes Darcy aware of her love for him. Furthermore, although each heroine may renounce a propensity toward imaginative flights, none evidences a newfound desire to become a model woman.[7] Elizabeth Bennet persists in "her lively, sportive manner" of talking to Darcy (*PP* 387–88); and Mr. Knightly marries Emma in part, we are to assume, because she is "faultless in spite of her faults" (*Em* 433), that is, because her very faults make her attractive in his eyes.

Fanny may not be Austen's only conduct-book protagonist, but she is the most insistently so. With her strict adherence to duty Elinor Dashwood has affinities to the model, but she also has an acerbic, domineering quality that keeps her out of the ranks of exemplary womanhood; her sister, Marianne, has gotten all the allotment of tenderness that is essential for ideality. Anne Eliot, although she has often been regarded as an older version of Fanny, explicitly questions the implications and consequences of her own dutifulness, which thus enables Austen to engage in a deliberate self-conscious assessment of conduct-book behavior.

Fanny, however, is consistently exemplary, the text validating her as the epitome of womanhood. She just about fulfills Edmund Bertram's prescription for "the perfect model of a woman" (*MP* 347)—and he only holds back his full praise because he lacks the insight that has been granted his gentle cousin. Henry Crawford describes her in terms that elevate her above the common run of womankind: "She is exactly the woman to do away every prejudice of such a man as the Admiral, for she is exactly such a woman as he thinks does not exist in the world. She is the very impossibility he would describe" (293). Such panegyrics come not only from Edmund and Henry but also from the Austen narrator, the narrative voice thus lending authority to a definition of womanhood that, because of our prior acquaintance with Austen, we might otherwise suspect. The narrator continually sings Fanny's praises; she has "heroism of principle" (265) and a "delicacy of taste, of mind, of feeling" (81) that we are told Mary Crawford lacks. Despite Mary's attractiveness to readers, in the contest between her and Fanny the narrator always weighs in on Fanny's side, encouraging us to champion her, as is evidenced by the epithet "my Fanny" (461), the phrase marking a brief, uncharacteristic return to the overtly authorial stance. Constant in her affections and her principles, combining a melting tenderness with an adherence to what is right, Fanny is represented as the most gendered of her gender according to contemporary notions of femininity.

Fanny comes from a long line of model heroines, and by comparing her with some of these we can begin to see how Austen attenuates the tradition. Fanny's forebears include not only Fielding's happy homemaker Amelia, but also the angelic martyr Clarissa and the noble-minded name-dropper Cecilia. Like them Fanny is gentle and pious; she is the only one of Austen's heroines for whom a place of worship clearly means more than a gathering place for village society, although Anne Eliot's concern for her cousin's traveling on Sunday might indicate that she is equally pious. It is likely that when we picture Fanny, we think of her in her virginal white dress—"A woman can never be too fine while she is all in white," says Edmund (*MP* 222)—and her amber cross, as if she were a little nun.

With regard to the piety of conduct-book heroines, we might reverse the old cliché and say that behind every great woman is a great man. Often, the exemplary heroine owes her moral authority to a male mentor who is a man of the cloth. Amelia has her Dr. Harrison, Clarissa has her Dr. Lewen, Cecilia her Dean, and Matilda (the heroine of the second half of Elizabeth Inchbald's A *Simple Story*) her priest Sandford. This configuration of church-sanctioned female exemplarity is suggestive of what Jacques Donzelot calls the "ancient complicity" operating "between the system of matrimonial exchanges—the key to the old familial order—and the religious apparatus."[8] In effect, by having the female exemplar authorized/authored by the clergy, the novels can provide a transcendental imperative for her behavior and thus mask how well it serves secular interests. And Fanny is no exception. As with her sister heroines, her mind has been "formed" by a clergyman (in this case, an aspiring one): Edmund "recommended the books which charmed her leisure hours, he encouraged her taste, and corrected her judgment; he made reading useful by talking to her of what she had read, and heightened its attraction by judicious praise" (*MP* 22). Fanny indeed outdoes her mentor, standing firm against Henry Crawford while Edmund succumbs to the temptation of Crawford's sister.[9] Overall, Austen locates the source of Fanny's moral authority firmly in a patriarchal structure.

To a certain extent, Fanny outdoes her sister heroines in exemplarity. Lionel Trilling points out that, in creating her frail heroine, Austen was following "the tradition which affirmed the peculiar sanctity of the sick, the weak, and the dying."[10] Fanny must be on her way to sainthood—we hear a litany of her ills, from headache to exhaustion to excessive sensitivity to noise. Clarissa, after all, is fairly robust up until the time of the rape, and Amelia seems to bounce back from her fainting fits with renewed vigor. We should bear in mind that, as Mary Wollstonecraft had pointed out fifteen years earlier, conduct books advise a woman to hide the fact that "she can take more exercise than another" and that "she has a sound constitution."[11] Fanny's illness thus goes hand in hand with ultra-femininity. Whereas Amelia and Cecilia properly disdain putting themselves forward, Fanny effaces herself to the point of disappearing altogether. She is not just quiet-spoken ("an excellent thing in woman"), she is practically voiceless—the sentence "Fanny coloured, and said nothing" (*MP* 225) epitomizes her behavior. When Sir Thomas attempts to gauge Fanny's feelings toward Henry Crawford, he realizes that she is a cipher to him: "She was always so gentle and retiring, that her emotions were beyond his discrimination" (366). Pamela, Clarissa, Amelia, and Cecilia make a few missteps, Clarissa indeed stepping fatally outside her father's walls and into the arms of her ravisher. But Fanny makes no false moves. She understands the pernicious nature of the theatricals, she correctly assesses the true character of the Crawfords, and so forth. Overall, she is hyper-exemplary.

Yet, as the text demonstrates, pushed to its logical conclusion the notion of the exemplary woman will show signs of strain, on the levels of both symbol and plot. Clarissa's physical disintegration after the rape symbolizes her gradual transcendence to a higher plane where she will leave earthly woes behind and, presumably, take her place among the angels. Fanny's illness, on the other hand, tends toward no heavenly elevation; it leaves us instead with an idea of chronic enervation, suggestive of the enervation of exemplars. If Fanny represents enduring values, such values are sickened.

The implicit connection between Fanny and Lady Bertram bears out this notion. I would not go so far as Gilbert and Gubar, who argue that Fanny is "destined to become the next Lady Bertram, following the example of Sir Thomas's corpselike wife."[12] But there certainly are similarities between the two. Fanny prefers Lady Bertram for female companionship: "She talked to her, listened to her, read to her; and the tranquillity of such evenings, her perfect security in such a *tête-à-tête* from any sounds of unkindness, was unspeakably welcome to a mind which had seldom known a pause in its alarms or embarrassments" (*MP* 35). Both Fanny and Lady Bertram depend on others to articulate for them, although Fanny (unlike her indolent aunt) actually has a thought or two to articulate. Both are fixed—Lady Bertram on her couch, Fanny in her opinions. Fanny, of course, has a core of moral fiber that Lady Bertram lacks, but the outward appearance is the same. Rather than considering Fanny as the replacement for Lady Bertram, we might consider Lady Bertram as the replacement for Fanny, a bloodless doppelgänger with the form—though not substance—of the proper lady. This connection is suggestive of the fact that hyper-exemplarity and hyper-insipidity can be easily confused.

Fanny's gentleness points to another area of strain in the notion of exemplary womanhood. She cannot make herself understood. Henry Crawford persists in his suit in part because Fanny is too ladylike in her refusals: "Her manner was incurably gentle, and she was not aware of how much it concealed the sternness of her purpose. Her diffidence, gratitude, and softness, made every expression of indifference seem almost an effort of self-denial; seem at least, to be giving nearly as much pain to herself as to him" (*MP* 327). The very sweetness "which makes so essential a part of every woman's worth in the judgment of man" (294) renders her own judgment incapable of being considered.

We have one anomalous instance of Fanny's voicing opposition to the match between herself and Crawford. In *Pride and Prejudice* Elizabeth's rejection of Mr. Collins's proposal provided Austen with an opportunity to expose the plight of women forced to hear out the addresses of men they do not like. Yet Austen leaves it to the generally taciturn Fanny rather than the loquacious Elizabeth to articulate most fervently this plight. Fanny's speech to Edmund to this effect is, in fact, her longest speech in the text. Herein she protests against the assumption that a woman must find a man acceptable because he has found her so: "Let him have all the perfections in the world, I think it ought not to be set down as certain, that a man must be acceptable to every woman he may happen to like himself" (*MP* 353). She questions a code of sexual conduct that both prohibits a woman from having feelings for a man until he has made clear he has feelings for her and then requires that the woman reciprocate in kind: "How then was I to be—to be in love with him the moment he said he was with me?" (353). Fanny may generally conform to conduct-book behavior, but she herein voices a sharp critique of the behavioral absurdities to which women are expected to accede, a critique Austen seems to agree with.[13] It is significant that Edmund just does not get it: "My dear, dear Fanny," he tells her, "now I have the truth. . . . the very circumstance of the novelty of Crawford's addresses was against him" (353–54). He lays claim to "the truth"—but by seizing on the notion of novelty he ignores Fanny's truth, that she does not and cannot love Henry. Fanny's statement that "we think very different of the nature of women" points to a rift between female and male assessments of woman's nature that even the seemingly enlightened Edmund cannot bridge and that the text brings to the fore with its portrait of the conflicted Fanny.

Generally, however, Fanny "properly" lacks assertion and rhetorical force, and as a consequence she is unacknowledged. When paragons undergo trials, they usually have the dubious satisfaction of having their perfections recognized. As Anna Howe writes Clarissa, in the first letter of the novel, "Every eye, in short, is upon you with the expectation of an example."[14] Cecilia's excellencies are known far and wide, prompting the male paragon Delvile to seek her out. Even the rivalrous Miss Mathews acknowledges that Amelia is "a much better Woman" than herself, and Amelia's husband, Booth, talks of "the general Admiration which . . . pursued her, the Respect paid her by Persons of the highest Rank" (*Am* 38, 66). Few sing Fanny's praises, however. Edmund and (later) Henry Crawford recognize her virtues, certainly, and by the end of the novel her importance to the Mansfield residents has been acknowledged. But no one says of her, as Anna Howe says of Clarissa, "She was a wonderful creature from her *infancy*."[15] People are much more likely to point out, as Mrs. Norris does, that her behavior "is very stupid indeed, and shows a great want of genius and emulation" (*MP* 19). And although Edmund discovers her virtues early on, not until he has undergone disappointment and heartbreak does he "learn to prefer soft light eyes to sparkling dark ones" (470). Sir Thomas eventually realizes that she is "the daughter that he wanted" (472), but it is only his actual daughters' transgressions that throw his niece's virtues into relief. Henry's love is an odd one, spurred perhaps as much by his desire for the unattainable as his recognition of Fanny's excellencies. Neither Mrs. Norris nor the Bertram daughters nor Fanny's parents ever recognize that they have a little paragon in their midst, and in the concluding pages Lady Bertram, after some initial resistance, soon comes to substitute Susan for Fanny, even coming to find her "the most beloved of the two" (472–73). So much for Fanny's importance to Lady Bertram!

Readers themselves may have a hard time recognizing Fanny's importance. Like Amelia, Fanny is somewhat of a hidden heroine. Granted, we are in her mind pretty much from the outset of the novel. But, as the other characters are active rather than passive, they take over the action and thus the interest of the story. They often take over the narrative focus as well. In each of her novels Austen shifts the focalization at times from her main character to various subsidiary ones. In no other, however, does she so consistently explore the motives and feelings of the other characters or give us so much access to the minds of her villains. We receive vivid, emotionally charged accounts of Mary Crawford's fondness for Edmund and her disappointed hopes, of Julia's jealousy of her sister, of Maria's humiliation at Henry's defection. We end up feeling that the other stories have potential. Mary certainly threatens to supplant Fanny in the readers' affections just as she supplants her in Edmund's. As has often been noted, she has the liveliness that makes Elizabeth Bennet so endearing; "with her lively dark eye, clear brown complexion, and general prettiness" (*MP* 44), Mary bears more than a passing resemblance to Elizabeth, whose "fine eyes" first attract Darcy and whose tanned complexion later prompts his defense of her to Caroline Bingley. Fanny's closest analogues in Austen's novels (besides Anne Eliot, who is a deepened, matured, more self-aware version) are the shadowy secondary characters that occur in the texts written before and after *Mansfield Park*—the two Janes, Bennet and Fairfax. Both are sweet girls, forced to bear in silence a lover's apparent defection. With Fanny it is as if Austen tries to bring forward the kind of character she is generally content to leave in the background—and then runs up against the problem that a Rosencrantz can never have the impact of a Hamlet.

Ignored and unrecognized for what she is, Fanny virtually has no impact. Richardson's Pamela almost single-handedly reforms a corrupt squirarchy; Clarissa is highly influential in life and death; Cecilia's noble example prompts noble action on the part of others. Although Amelia cannot single-handedly reform the corrupt society that surrounds her (Fielding also acknowledging the fading power of exemplars, though for different purposes), she does manage to provide important instruction to her children and, ultimately, to inspire Booth and a small circle of friends.

Moreover, throughout the text that bears her name, Amelia functions consistently as the emblem for good to which Booth must aspire. But Fanny is granted little or no capacity for influence. She is unable to stop Maria Bertram from slipping around the iron gate with Mr. Crawford, to bring order to the Portsmouth house, or to dissuade Edmund from participating in the play and falling in love with the improper Mary. The only significant influence she has is over her sister, Susan, and rather than attempting to reform the Portsmouth residents the two sisters retreat up the stairs to avoid "a great deal of the disturbance of the house" (*MP* 398), just as the Mansfield residents retreat from the rest of society at the end of the novel.

Fanny's most significant failure is with Henry Crawford. Austen clearly sets up a story that is meant to remind us of the "rake reformed" theme of *Pamela*. Henry sets out a net for Fanny, but he is caught in it himself. He seems to be on the road to reformation—he recognizes her superiority to other women, and he takes on the squirarchical duties he had previously neglected. But, as Frank Bradbrook suggests, there is more than a little of a Laclos influence in *Mansfield Park*, and Henry may be more of a Valmont than a Mr. B., mouthing a reformation that has only partially taken hold.[16] If Fanny is indeed "the woman whom he had rationally, as well as passionately loved" (*MP* 469), we must wonder at a passion that can be deflected by seeming whim, and all the narrator's explanations as to the faultiness of Henry's education do little to satisfy us. To a certain extent Henry's love for Fanny seems to have less to do with his growing appreciation of her virtues than with her indifference to his suit: "it was a love which . . . made her affection appear of greater consequence because it was withheld, and determined him to have the glory, as well as the felicity, of forcing her to love him" (326). Henry thus regards Fanny not so much as a person to be valued than as an object to be conquered, and he pursues a course similar to that of the Noble Lord in *Amelia*, who abandons a woman once he has seduced her. It is significant that Henry turns his attention to the less-than-exemplary Maria when she seems to offer greater resistance: "He must exert himself to subdue so proud a display of resentment" (468). By thwarting our expectations that Fanny will reform Henry and become his bride, Austen drives home the inadequacy of the exemplary woman/reformed rake paradigm.

She seems here to have borrowed a leaf from Hannah More's book. Fifteen years prior More had scoffed at "that fatal and most indelicate, nay gross maxim, that a reformed rake makes the best husband," arguing that it goes on the "preposterous supposition . . . that habitual vice creates rectitude of character, and that sin produces happiness."[17] In undermining the maxim herself, Austen reinforces our sense of Fanny's negligible capacity for influence.

Indeed, whatever reformation occurs in *Mansfield Park* results not from Fanny's influence but from the bad experiences the characters undergo. Fanny essentially wins Edmund's affections by default, Mary's weaknesses rather than Fanny's virtues leading him to transfer his affections to his gentle cousin. Sir Thomas recognizes his folly only after Maria's elopement. And it takes a brush with death to make Tom Bertram a better man.

Not only is Fanny incapable of influencing the characters within the text, but the representation of her is probably incapable of influencing those who read the text. As Nancy Armstrong argues in *Desire and Domestic Fiction*, the rising novel enabled a social agenda whereby "the female relinquishes political control to the male in order to acquire exclusive authority over domestic life, emotions, taste, and morality."[18] In effect, the versions of female exemplarity that novels put forth were intended to provide a model for feminine authority and to carve out its particular realm of influence—the inculcation of values within the domestic sphere. Samuel Richardson, for instance, made no bones about his didactic purposes. After listing Pamela's manifold virtues at the conclusion of the novel, he points out that they "Are all so many signal instances of the excellency of her mind, which may make her character worthy of the *imitation* of her sex" (*Pam* 509, emphasis mine). More grandly, in his postscript to *Clarissa*, he explains that he intended the novel to "inculcate upon the human mind, under the guise of an amusement, the great lessons of Christianity," specifically through making the reader desire to emulate his saintly heroine: "And who that are in earnest in their profession of Christianity but will rather envy than regret the triumphant death of CLARISSA, whose piety from her early childhood, whose diffusive charity; whose steady virtue; whose Christian humility; whose forgiving spirit; whose meekness, whose resignation, HEAVEN only could reward?"[19] Fielding's and Burney's heroines are also put forth as worthy of emulation. How worthwhile can it be to emulate Fanny, however, if such emulation leads to naught? Imitating Fanny would not give one the capacity to lead others to virtue, or so *Mansfield Park* implies.

Moreover, imitating Fanny would mean resigning oneself to a painful existence. Stories such as those of Pamela, Clarissa, Amelia, Miss Sidney Biddulph, and Cecilia show us that the lot of the model woman is to suffer. After all, if the protagonist's exemplary character is fixed, the novel's action cannot depend upon self-revelation and internal growth but must instead depend upon the external events that beset the heroine—preferably, events that enable her exemplarity to shine forth. Fanny ostensibly goes through no more than her sisters in ideality.

Or does she? Her sister heroines at least can pride themselves on their consciousness of their own virtue, but Fanny has no such salve. Pamela and Clarissa, for example, know that they are right to resist the importunities of their would-be seducers. Cecilia, in renouncing a secret marriage with Delvile, takes consolation in her own virtue, as the following passage indicates:

> notwithstanding the sorrow she felt in apparently injuring the man whom, in the whole world, she most wished to oblige, she yet found a satisfaction in the sacrifice she had made, that recompensed her for much of her sufferings and soothed her into something like tranquillity; the true power of virtue she had scarce experienced before, for she found it a resource against the cruelest dejection, and a supporter in the bitterest disappointment.[20]

Compare the above with Austen's description of Fanny's feelings after she has told Sir Thomas she cannot marry Henry Crawford:

> Her mind was all disorder. The past, present, future, every thing was terrible. But her uncle's anger gave her the severest pain of all. Selfish and ungrateful! to have appeared so to him! She was miserable for ever. She had no one to take her part, to counsel, or speak for her. Her only friend was absent. He might have softened his father; but all, perhaps all, would think her selfish and ungrateful. She might have to endure the reproach again and again; she might hear it, or see it, or know it to exist for ever in every connection about her. She could not but feel some resentment against Mr. Crawford; yet, if he really loved her, and were unhappy too!—it was all wretchedness together. (*MP* 321)

Fanny is damned if she does and damned if she does not. She cannot act without violating some prescription of proper feminine behavior. She may see more clearly than Sir Thomas, but she may not derive consolation from this fact.

The changes Austen rings on the term "duty" underscore the double bind in which the model woman finds herself. For Fanny, duty consists of sticking to her principles, as she acknowledges resignedly after that dreadful interview with Sir Thomas: "she believed she had no right to wonder at the line of conduct he pursued. He who had married a daughter to Mr. Rushworth. Romantic delicacy was certainly not to be expected from him. She must do her duty, and trust that time might make her duty easier than it now was" (*MP* 331). But only a few pages later Lady Bertram puts forward a different definition of duty with her reiteration of Sir Thomas's view that Fanny has an obligation to accept Henry: "And you must be aware, Fanny, that it is every young woman's duty to accept such a very unexceptionable offer" (333). We have, of course, encountered a similar notion of female duty in an earlier passage—and we might recall what fatal results attend it:

> Being now in her twenty-first year, Maria Bertram was beginning to think matrimony a duty; and as a marriage with Mr. Rushworth would give her the enjoyment of a larger income than her father's, as well as ensure her the house in town, which was now a prime object, it became, by the same rule of moral obligation, her evident duty to marry Mr. Rushworth if she could. (38–39)

The contested meanings of "duty" underscore Austen's point that the model woman often must attempt to align what may be mutually exclusive aims—the preservation of moral integrity and the attainment of wealth and standing. Here we have no happy resolution as in *Pride and Prejudice,* wherein Elizabeth manages to preserve her integrity and marry a man with ten thousand pounds a year. (Charlotte Lucas's situation, of course, hints at the dilemma faced by Fanny.) Fanny's conception of her "moral obligation" is directly at odds with the Bertrams'.

By the end of the text the Bertrams will come to redefine duty, learning that Fanny's conception of it really serves the family's interests after all, but in the meantime we are made privy to Fanny's suffering as she struggles with impossible demands. Indeed, she is unable to find a Cecilia-like tranquillity until the end of the volume. Overall, few moments of pleasure relieve the long scenes of torture that Fanny undergoes. Even her pleasures are riddled with painful sensations: as she prepares for the ball given in her honor she worries about whether to wear Mary's or Edmund's necklace and sighs over Edmund's profession of love for Mary; the welcome news of William's promotion is followed by Henry's unwelcome proposal. Austen makes clear the connection between Fanny's feelings of oppression and her conduct-book behavior. After refusing Henry's proposal, Fanny dreads an encounter with Mary, rightly fearing that Mary will bring up distressing issues. But Mary need only appeal to Fanny's notion of proper behavior:

> She was determined to see Fanny alone, and therefore said to her tolerably soon, in a low voice, "I must speak to you for a few minutes somewhere;" words that Fanny felt all over her, in all her pulses, and all her nerves. Denial was impossible. Her habits of ready submission, on the contrary, made her almost instantly rise and lead the way out of the room. She did it with wretched feelings, but it was inevitable. (*MP* 357)

The intensity of Fanny's emotions is played off against her almost automaton-like behavior. As in the scene after her interview with Sir Thomas,

Fanny's sense of propriety renders her miserable. No wonder that the text gives us such oxymorons as "painful gratitude" (322); to be an exemplary woman means to be beset with contradictory impulses.

Austen's final disposition of her conduct-book protagonist is ambivalent. Fanny does get the requisite happy ending that would seem to validate her "womanly" behavior: she is married to Edmund; William is on his way to naval glory; and Susan has supplanted her as Lady Bertram's companion, thus freeing Fanny of the guilt she might feel at not being able to make all of the people happy all of the time. But we might bear in mind that Austen rewards all her protagonists with a happy ending, and she gives us no indication that Elizabeth will stop teasing Darcy or that the imperious Emma will be satisfied with any but "the best treatment." Austen's improper ladies may briefly pay penance for their sins. The scene wherein Emma reproaches herself after insulting Miss Bates, for example, may be one of the most emotionally charged in the Austen canon. The proper Fanny, however, continually pays penance for sins she does not commit, essentially serving as a scapegoat for society's failures to regulate itself correctly. At one time, she evokes a Griselda-figure, willing to humble herself for the sins of others: "Sir Thomas's look implied, 'On your judgment, Edmund, I depended; what have you been about?'—She knelt in spirit to her uncle, and her bosom swelled to utter, 'Oh! not to *him*. Look so to all the others, but not to *him*'" (*MP* 185). We must assume that only Fanny's habitual self-effacement keeps her from kneeling in actuality. And, despite the uncharacteristic emphasis on religion, Austen offers us no more suggestion that a heavenly reward awaits Fanny than she does in regard to her other protagonists.

When Mrs. Norris—that mouthpiece for all that is awry in the social structure—tells Fanny that she "must be the lowest and the last" (*MP* 221), she may indeed be voicing the implicit agenda of a society that depends on female submission. For the behavior that it prescribes for rendering women "womanly" is that which calls for their obedience, their dependence, their sense of their own inferiority. We might consider Fanny as exemplary to the second power—as the exemplary case of the exemplary woman, allowing us to see the consequences of the concept. The character of Fanny may stem from Austen's internalizations of society's "should-be's," but the plot in which she is inscribed may stem from Austen's concurrent resistance to the plot of feminizing women.

THE FALL OF THE HOUSE OF MANSFIELD

As in *Amelia*, the resolution of the plot overtly champions conservative values but simultaneously problematizes them by the evidence put forward in their support. Maria's adulterous liaison with Henry flies in the face of such values, but it also is the inevitable offshoot of an extreme version of them. The reestablishment of spiritual principles in Mansfield, represented by Fanny's new role there, serves as an ostensible solution to the problems besetting the estate, but Austen implicitly demonstrates that the solution works on only a limited scale.[21]

Soon after the Crawfords arrive in the Mansfield neighborhood, Mrs. Grant optimistically predicts that "Mansfield shall cure you both—and without any taking in. Stay with us and we will cure you" (*MP* 47). In a world wherein Mansfield had maintained its emblematic significance as a center of moral authority, such an outcome might be possible. Henry would marry Fanny, renouncing his libertine ways and taking his squirarchical duties seriously. Mary would marry Edmund, learning like Elizabeth Bennet to use her wit as a corrective rather than destructive force. Maria Bertram would console herself with high society. Aunt Norris, after her initial resentment had passed, would take credit for Fanny's match, becoming as obnoxious in her attentions to Fanny as she had been in her snubs. Henry himself offers a view of an ideal community that might, in other circumstances, have served Austen as a final line for the novel: "'Mansfield, Sotherton, Thornton Lacey,' he continued, 'what a society will be comprised in those houses! And at Michaelmas, perhaps, a fourth may be added, some small hunting-box in the vicinity of every thing so dear'" (405). Such an outcome does not occur, of course, and the contrast between Henry's vision and the actual conclusion throws into relief the fissures running through the seemingly solid edifice of Mansfield Park.

Rather than finding a cure at Mansfield, the Crawfords infect—or at least lower—the Bertrams' resistance to disease. Although the taint of city living may give the Crawfords a certain outsider status, essentially they are insiders, members of the same class as the Bertrams and certainly more acceptable socially than the child of a lieutenant of Marines. Henry is, after all, a landowner, responsible for the well-being of his tenants. In effect, the threat to the gentry comes from within the gentry.

Such a threat has all the more force in that it cannot be easily discerned. Despite Henry's fears of being "taken in," it is the Bertrams who are taken in, blinded to the Crawfords' moral bankruptcy by their attractiveness. Sir Thomas regards both Crawfords as suitable matches for his own children; the connection he envisions ends up, ironically, an illicit one. We might expect Edmund—the only one of Austen's clergymen with an actual vocation (with the possible exception of Edward Ferrars)—to have the surest sense of the threat posed by the Crawfords, but he becomes the particular friend of both. Only Fanny, the silent observer, can assess the true implications of their apparently innocent high-spirited behavior, and she has no voice with which to alert the others.

The characterization of the Crawfords also blinds us—or at least destabilizes our expectations. In *Amelia* Fielding eschews his usual practice of succinctly summing up the characters when he introduces them, thus often leaving us uncertain as to characters' motives and dependent on further revelations. Austen similarly keeps us off-balance. The Crawfords are initially attractive to us as well as to the characters within the novel, and for the most part Austen forgoes the sort of commentary that might give us clear indications as to how we are to read them.[22] If, as Q. D. Leavis has argued, *Mansfield Park* is a revised version of Austen's epistolary "Lady Susan," it subtilizes the blatant character revelations of the earlier work, in which Lady Susan's letters to Mrs. Johnson provide a clear illustration of her character, and Mrs. Vernon's suspicions of her seem fairly disinterested.[23] In *Mansfield Park*, however, our main clues come from the Crawfords' speech and actions and Fanny's unvoiced assessments. But we may be inclined to read the Crawfords' speech and actions as evidence of a proper lack of control rather than of villainy, and we may consider Fanny's assessments, when unseconded by the narrator's validation, as somewhat skewed, especially in light of her evident jealousy of Mary. Furthermore, the Crawfords' genuinely kind acts mitigate their improprieties. Mary pays marked attention to Fanny after one of Mrs. Norris's particularly virulent barbs, and Henry envisions that in making Fanny his wife he can elevate her from her "dependent, helpless, friendless, neglected, forgotten" condition (*MP* 297). Granted, their behavior (particularly Henry's) often verges on the improper, but the Crawfords appear redeemable.

After giving us an instance of misbehavior on the Crawfords' part, Austen generally juxtaposes an instance of kindness. It is only in the very last chapters of the novel that the scales tip irrevocably toward the bad. Mary's mercenary desire for Tom Bertram's death, expressed in a self-serving letter to Fanny, reveals a cold-bloodedness that is inexcusable according to Austen's worldview. Henry's elopement with Maria Bertram is an egregious social transgression, indicative of his overweening selfishness and heartless lack of concern for consequences. But it may be that up until these particular occurrences, we expect—perhaps even hope—that Austen will allow each Crawford an epiphanic moment of self-revelation and a subsequent reformation. Unlike Austen's other novels, wherein we can predict the eventual partners if not what will bring them together, *Mansfield Park* offers several possible plot paths, and the hypothetical resolution envisioned by Henry does not seem to be completely out of the question.

The elopement of Henry and Maria marks the point at which characters in the novel and readers of the novel must have done with the Crawfords. The man who "so requited hospitality, so injured family peace" (*MP*

469) no longer has a place in the Mansfield world. Despite Edmund's high-mindedness, we might expect (as Fanny does) that his feelings for Mary would win out over his elevated sense of propriety and that she at least would not have the gates of Mansfield forever barred to her. But her plan to persuade Henry to marry Maria implicates her in Henry's crime, at least in Edmund's eyes, as he makes clear to Fanny:

> but the manner in which she spoke of the crime itself, giving it every reproach but the right, considering its ill consequences only as they were to be braved or overborne by a deficiency of decency and impudence in wrong; and, last of all, and above all, recommending to us a compliance, a compromise, an acquiescence, in the continuance of a sin, on the chance of a marriage which, thinking as I now thought of her brother, should rather be prevented than sought—all this together most grievously convinced me that I had never understood her before. (458)

Mary's attempt to unite the two transgressors in marriage might seem to have a certain affinity to Darcy's engineering of the wedding of Lydia and Wickham. But an adulterous liaison is not recuperable, and there is no grateful Elizabeth Bennet to thank Mary for her pains. Instead, Edmund regards the suggestion as evidence of Mary's duplicity: "How have I been deceived! Equally in brother and sister deceived!" (495). To Edmund the woman who can speak lightly of adultery is as culpable as the adulterer. Clearly, a proper lady must condemn adultery, and Fanny's "shudderings of horror" (41) mark the correct response.

The Henry-and-Maria elopement marks both the point beyond which the Crawfords can no longer be part of the Mansfield world and the point beyond which the Mansfield family unit cannot survive as a whole. In *Pride and Prejudice* Mr. Bennet receives the unrepentant Lydia Wickham back into the family circle. Sir Thomas, however, refuses to receive the abandoned Maria, offering the following justification: "Maria had destroyed her own character, and he would not by a vain attempt to restore what never could be restored, be affording his sanction to vice, or in seeking to lessen its disgrace, be anywise accessary to introducing such misery in another man's family, as he had known himself" (*MP* 465). No one, except the silly Mr. Collins, frets that Lydia's bad example may cause others to emulate her. Maria's dissimilar fate enables Austen to demonstrate that adultery signals an unassimilable infraction of the social code.

Although almost all of Austen's novels touch on some sort of illicit sexuality, none of these situations has the disruptive force—both within the story and as a symbolic element—of the Henry-and-Maria elopement. Maria's marriage to Rushworth links the grand estate of Mansfield with "one of the largest estates and finest places in the country" (*MP* 38); it is "a connection exactly of the right sort; in the same country, and the same interest" (40). If it does not have the symbolic resonance of, say, Tom Jones's marriage to Sophia Western, the Bertram-Rushworth marriage nonetheless signifies a consolidation of squirarchical power, property, and wealth, and it reaffirms the continuation of the status quo through propagation. Maria and Henry's transgression flies directly in the face of such values, for it essentially disregards Rushworth's rights to his own "property." The potential threat of bastardy lies at the margins of the text, symbolically reinforced by the fact that Maria plays an unwed mother in *Lover's Vows*. As in *Amelia* adultery undermines the values that preserve the status quo, and adulterers cannot be reabsorbed into the society that they threaten.[24]

By drawing on the adultery motif Austen introduces an undermining element not only into Mansfield Park but into *Mansfield Park*. Once adultery has entered the world of the text, there can be no return to prior assumptions about the appropriateness of the status quo, despite the text's effort to establish this very point. As Tony Tanner suggests in *Adultery in the Novel*, adultery is a disruptive force for the novel genre itself: "In confronting the problems of marriage and adultery, the bourgeois novel finally has to confront not only the provisionality of social laws and rules and structures but the provisionality of its own procedures and assumptions"[25] This text's focus on adultery is much more limited than that of the bourgeois novels Tanner discusses or even that of *Amelia*, wherein adultery serves as the central problem addressed. After all, the Henry-and-Maria elopement takes place only within the last three chapters. Yet it is the crucial action of the novel, effecting the final disposition of all the major characters. Too, as with the bourgeois novels Tanner studies, the adultery motif in *Mansfield* implicitly undermines the surety of the values the text expresses.

As in *Amelia* adultery serves as both cause and effect of social breakdown, a positive feedback loop dismantling traditional values. Sir Thomas is the archetypal patriarch, perhaps the most formidable authority figure in the Austen canon. In a novel ostensibly pushing traditional values, we might expect that he would be their most staunch supporter. After all, despite his overabundance of pride, Darcy fulfills his patriarchal duties: he saves both Georgiana and Lydia from ruin, essentially preserving two households. Sir Thomas, however, enables or encourages the tendencies that lead to the destruction of the household. Sir Thomas errs throughout in valuing appearance over essence. Because his daughters have been educated in the surface accomplishments he is satisfied: "the Miss Bertrams continued to exercise their memories, practise their duets, and grow tall and womanly; and their father saw them becoming in person, manner, and accomplishments, every thing that could satisfy his anxiety" (*MP* 20). However, as Sir Thomas discovers too late, "with all the cost and care of an anxious and expensive education, he had brought up his daughters, without their understanding their first duties, or his being acquainted with their character and temper" (464–65). Making no attempt to delve below appearance, Sir Thomas is willing to accept Maria's feigned professions of respect for Rushworth. Prizing a blind obedience to the dictates of authority over a considered attempt to formulate right values, he browbeats Fanny in order to make her accept Henry Crawford. His manner authoritarian rather than authoritative, he prompts both Maria and Julia to flee from the restrictions he imposes.[26]

Granted, by the final chapter, Sir Thomas realizes his errors, and we must assume that he will be a better baronet in the future. But what is significant is that, unlike Darcy, the highest representative of social order in the novel facilitates, rather than quells, disorder. Nor do we have a sense that his children can do much better. Sir Thomas's heir has become, by the close of the novel, "useful to his father, steady and quiet" (*MP* 462), but we are given no instances of model behavior on Tom Bertram's part. Edmund, the guardian of Mansfield's spiritual values, gets no opportunity actively to enforce them. We have here no Darcy or Knightley to reassure us that, though flawed, the patriarch will ultimately put things to rights.

The critique of patriarchal values in *Mansfield Park* at times echoes Mary Wollstonecraft's radical *Vindication*. In the following passage, Wollstonecraft might as well be discussing Sir Thomas's confusion of external accomplishments with internal virtues, epitomized in the education he provides his daughters: "Manners and morals are so nearly allied that they have often been confounded; but, although the former should only be the natural reflection of the latter, yet when various causes have produced factitious and corrupt manners, which are very early caught, morality becomes an empty name."[27] When Wollstonecraft describes how woman's lack of real power "gives birth to cunning," we may recall how the Bertram daughters learn "to repress their spirits in [Sir Thomas's] presence" (*MP* 463), their powerlessness before their authoritarian father occasioning duplicity.[28] Even Fanny, exemplary in her powerlessness as well as in her virtue, may possess some share of this quality; we can certainly see in her some evidence of the contemporary manifestation of cunning—passive aggressive behavior. When things are not going as she would like, she tends to fall ill or assume a martyr role, as in the following passage wherein Fanny sulks at Edmund's absence: "she thought it a very bad exchange, and if Edmund were not there to mix the wine and water for her, would rather go without it than not" (66). Finally, as the epigraph at the outset of this chapter indicates, Wollstonecraft suggests that adultery itself results from a system of female education that teaches women their only object is to render themselves pleasing to men. Once trained in the art of attracting men, women will continue to do so even after they are married, a hypothesis confirmed by Maria's actions. In *Mansfield Park* Austen gives concrete representation to some of the arguments that Wollstonecraft makes in *Vindication*.

But Austen is not here subjecting patriarchal values to a radical critique à la Wollstonecraft. Some of the same sorts of concerns that Wollstonecraft addresses are addressed by Hannah More in her *Strictures* on female education. She too deals with the matrimonial difficulties of a woman who has been taught only to attract and please: she will "escape to the exhibition room" and put herself on display once more; she will be "exposed to the two-fold temptation of being at once neglected by her husband, and exhibited as an object of attraction to other men."[29] Thus, although Austen's text has affinities to Wollstonecraft's, it has affinities to More's as well, and although it is tempting to regard Austen as putting forward a feminist agenda, we can just as likely regard her as putting forward a *feminine* one—one wherein women's improvement is put in service of patriarchal values. The elevation of morals over manners would sustain, rather than undermine, the authority of the Sir Thomas Bertrams of the land. Overall, Austen advocates not that traditional values be overthrown but that they be strengthened or revived—thus seemingly taking the same sort of conservative stance that we saw Fielding take in *Amelia*.

For all its conservatism, however, *Mansfield Park* unlike *Amelia* implicitly links societal breakdown to an overarching patriarchal structure. Through the fates meted out to its female characters, the text exposes the underside of a system that constrains and undermines women. Fielding gives us the exemplary Amelia, cheerful and supportive in the face of her husband's adultery, unfounded accusations, and improvidence. He also gives us transgressive female characters, such as Miss Mathews and Mrs. Atkinson, who are subject to ridicule and shown as deserving the fates they get. Austen, on the other hand, shows us that the fate of the exemplary woman is to suffer silently as she experiences the defection of the man she loves and faces conflicting demands. Even Austen's transgressive women are presented sympathetically. We are made aware that, however misguided they are, Mary Crawford, Maria Bertram, and Julia Bertram have feelings that may be wounded and manipulated. Mary does indeed care for Edmund, and when all intercourse has come to an end between them she finds herself "in need of the true kindness of her sister's heart" (*MP* 469). Maria succumbs to Henry's "animated perseverance" (468) of her, and although his pursuit of her is prompted by mere vanity, she is in love with him, hoping that he will marry her. Maria's act of adultery irrevocably destroys her reputation, necessitating her banishment from England, but Henry's will be forgiven, as Austen dryly acknowledges: "That punishment, the public punishment of disgrace, should in a just measure attend his share of the offence, is, we know, not one of the barriers, which society gives to virtue" (468). The text demonstrates the psychic toll that a patriarchal structure takes on women even as it overtly argues in favor of its soundness.

In order for traditional values to be revived and sustained, Austen—like Fielding in *Amelia*—emphasizes the important role played by religion. We might recall that one of the first acts performed by the reformed Mr. B. in *Pamela* is the reconsecration of the family chapel—a reconsecration symbolic of Pamela's accession to spiritual authority in Mr. B.'s household. Austen, too, gives symbolic resonance to the motif of the family chapel, making an implicit connection between the degeneration of the Rushworth family and the unused chapel at Sotherton. Fanny considers the custom of family prayers a vital part of the regulation of a great estate: "It was a valuable part of former times. There is something in a chapel and chaplain so much in character with a great house, with one's ideas of what such a household should be!" (*MP* 85). We are left with the sense that the continuance of such a custom may have made Rushworth less foolish and his mother less vain. We are told too that paying attention to religion might have saved the Bertram daughters from disgrace: "they had never been properly taught to govern their inclinations and tempers by that sense of duty which alone can suffice. They had been instructed theoretically in their religion, but never required to bring it into daily practice" (463). Religion it seems might provide the missing element that would keep society on track.

As the clergyman son of a noble family Edmund would appear to provide a hope for the future. Attempting to justify his choice of profession to Mary Crawford he prescribes the proper function of a clergyman, a prescription to which he will no doubt adhere:

> And with regard to their influencing public manners, Miss Crawford must not misunderstand me, or suppose I mean to call them the arbiters of good breeding, the regulators of refinement and courtesy, the masters of the ceremonies of life. The *manners* I speak of might rather be called *conduct*, perhaps, the result of good principles; the effect, in short, of those doctrines which it is their duty to teach and recommend; and it will, I believe, be every where found, that as the clergy are, or are not what they ought to be, so are the rest of the nation. (*MP* 93)

The proper clergyman as Edmund defines him could supply what is wanting in the Bertram daughters, in the Crawfords, in the household at Sotherton, in society at large.

Although the text gives us an optimistic glimpse of what that revitalized society might be, it concurrently undermines the likelihood of such a society occurring. In the world of Mansfield, Mary's succinct comment that "A clergyman is nothing" (*MP* 92) seems more apt. During the discussion of the Sotherton chapel, Mary offers an astute—if tactless—rejoinder to Fanny's notion about the importance and efficacy of family prayers: "It must do the heads of the family a great deal of good to force all the poor housemaids and footmen to leave business and pleasure, and say their prayers here twice a day, while they are inventing excuses themselves for staying away" (86–87). Fanny and Edmund take umbrage at Mary's remarks, Austen nudging us to identify with their values. Yet the dialogic interchange undermines our surety that religion ever did or could have the sort of regulatory power with which Edmund and Fanny invest it. Mary's high-spirited comment that "The young Mrs. Eleanors and Mrs. Bridgets" had their "heads full of something very different—especially if the poor chaplain were not worth looking at" compels us to consider that reinstituting family prayers may simply lead to false piety (87).

Rather than influencing others to do well, Edmund tends to be influenced by others to go against his principles. Granted, when he gives in to the others over the play, he is not yet ordained, but he clearly knows it is his duty to dissuade, not succumb. Although by the close of the novel Edmund has presumably become a proper shepherd to his flock, the only instance we have of his pastoral influence is the guidance he gives Fanny during her youth—and by the time of the actual story, teacher and pupil seem to have changed places. The only other clergyman in the novel is Dr. Grant, who, as Mary indecorously but accurately says, is "an indolent selfish bon vivant, who must have his palate consulted in every thing, who will not stir a finger for the convenience of any one, and who, moreover, if the cook makes a blunder, is out of humour with his excellent wife" (*MP* 111). With Dr. Grant, Austen gives us a picture of a bad clergyman in the tradition of Mr. Collins and Mr. Elton, and we are compelled to wonder whether this picture is not more apt than the one she gives us of Edmund Bertram. In any case, Austen does not reassure us as to the corrective influence of the clergy.

Because Austen gives neither Crawford an internal moment of self-revelation, we are left with the feeling that they will continue their thoughtless ways. Certainly, we are told that they regret their past actions. Mary, after all, is "long in finding" someone who can "put Edmund Bertram sufficiently out of her head" (*MP* 469). But she nonetheless is "perfectly resolved against ever attaching herself to a younger brother again"—a sign that she has not renounced the mercenary interests that made her wish for Tom Bertram's death. Henry, we are told, ends up with "no small portion of vexation and regret" (468). But as we get this information only in summary, we are divorced from any emotional involvement; we do not get a sense of the potency of Henry's pain as we get, for example, from Willoughby's anguished confession to Elinor in *Sense and Sensibility*. In forgiving Henry, society will enable if not encourage him to follow the course he has always followed.

Mansfield Park ends on an apparently happy note, like *Amelia*, but this conclusion—similar to that of Fielding's text—offers us little hope of societal reformation. In the final pages we are told that Tom Bertram has become "useful" and "steady"; Lady Bertram has found Susan to be an indispensable companion; Sir Thomas has discovered "the daughter he wanted"; and most important, Fanny and Edmund have been united in marriage. Tanner regards this marriage as a positive outcome: "a marriage it is, and a celebratory one, symbolising or suggesting more far-reaching reconciliations and restorations; a paradigmatic marriage for society in a larger sense, which transcends personal gratifications."[30] But the conclusion of *Mansfield Park* is suggestive of alienation and exclusion rather than of celebration and reconciliation. The effects of adultery, like those of a stone thrown in a pond, spread beyond the original incident, leaving havoc in their wake. Henry and Maria must be expelled from the world of Mansfield because their action threatens social breakdown. Despite their expulsion, however, social breakdown nevertheless occurs. The adultery divides Edmund from Mary, the Grants and the Rushworths from the Bertrams, and the Bertrams from one another. Whereas the ending of *Pride and Prejudice* allows all to join in the final celebration, this is not the case with *Mansfield Park*. Even Lady Catherine, with all her arrogance and bossiness, can finally be readmitted to Pemberley; Aunt Norris, on the other hand, must die in exile.

Too, although clearly put forward as a happy event, the marriage of Edmund and Fanny is nevertheless suggestive of social regression. Several recent discussions of *Mansfield Park* have dealt with the troubling "incest" motif in the novel, and I think that we cannot ignore its symbolic import.[31] Cousin marriage, though legally sanctioned, still manages to invoke the old incest taboo. By continually referring to the consanguineous connection between Fanny and Edmund, Austen ensures that we keep this thought before us. At the end of the novel Fanny and Edmund are not "the married couple" but "the married cousins" (*MP* 473), their kinship relationship seemingly more important than their marital one. In his study of the connection between the incest taboo and social structure, Talcott

Parsons suggests that the taboo enables the proper functioning of society: "it is essential that persons should be capable of assuming roles which contribute to functions which no nuclear family is able to perform, which involve the assumption of non-familial roles. Only if such non-familial roles can be adequately staffed can a society function." Without the incest taboo there can be no "formation and maintenance of supra-familial bonds on which major economic, political and religious functions of the society are dependent."[32] The happy ending for Fanny and Edmund is paradigmatic of the ending of social intercourse. Mansfield may have its emblematic function restored, but this function will not extend beyond its grounds. We might playfully extend Austen's story and envision a marriage between Susan—"the stationary niece"—and the other Bertram son.[33]

What happens with the triangular romantic configurations in the novel reinforces the motif of Mansfield Park closing in on itself. In Volume 1 (wherein Fanny is not "out") we have Mary Crawford and the two Bertram brothers and Henry Crawford and the two Bertram sisters. Once Fanny has entered the game the configurations shift, and their elements are reduced; the triangles now consist of Mary-Edmund-Fanny and Edmund-Fanny-Henry. By the novel's conclusion only the two elements both triangles have in common—the cousins Fanny and Edmund—remain.

The final centering of Edmund and Fanny within the household does indeed make clear that moral values have been restored to Mansfield Park. As Tony Tanner points out, Fanny is "the true inheritor of Mansfield Park."[34] Although Tom Bertram is the actual heir, Fanny and Edmund—installed in the living on the estate—presumably inherit Sir Thomas's moral authority and hold out the promise that Mansfield Park may attain the ideal that Fanny envisioned while exiled to Portsmouth.[35] As a good conduct-book heroine, of course, Fanny will work behind the scenes in her domestic realm, leaving to clergyman Edmund the active enforcement and modeling of morality.

But such moral revitalization is achieved at what cost? The first line of the final chapter has often been marked as signaling Austen's desire to hurry through the process of tying things up. What has not often been marked is the statement's irony. When Austen proclaims, "Let other pens dwell on guilt and misery" (*MP* 461), we expect that she intends to have done with such subjects. But rather than abandoning them she revels in them. The happy ending is offset by language hammering us with reminders of the unhappy events that have taken place, as the following somber litany, culled from the final chapter, demonstrates:

> guilt misery odious melancholy suffering disappointment regret sorry sorrow misery self-reproach anguish evil grievous bitterly wretchedly disappoint-

> ment wretchedness hatred punishment misery despised disappointments punishment punishment guilt mortified unhappy reproach melancholy destroyed misery punishment evil bitter danger evil irritation tormenting hurtful disappointment bitterness dread horrors selfish guilt folly ruined cold-blooded coldness repulsive mortified anger regretting punishment punishment vexation regret vexation self-reproach regret wretchedness wound alienate distressing regret disappointment apoplexy death regretting anxious doubting sick poor hardship struggle death painful alarm.

No wonder we have trouble with Austen's claim that "the happiness of the married cousins must appear as secure as earthly happiness can be" (473). Such a positive statement lays but a thin veneer over the negative terms embedded within the chapter. In order "to complete the picture of good" (the accession of Fanny and Edmund to the Mansfield living), "the death of Dr. Grant" must occur, the happiness of the principles thus dependent upon the misfortune of others (473).

This is not to say that we can ignore the strong argument in favor of traditional values that is presented in the novel. The happy ending that rewards Fanny and Edmund ratifies the values they espouse. Although the Mansfield community ends up reorganized in part, it nevertheless revolves around most of its original members, the return to the status quo confirming the soundness of things as they are. Moreover, the argument of *Mansfield* is quite in keeping with views Austen expresses in a letter, which appeared soon after the publication of the text, in which she gives her niece Fanny Knight advice about a suitor:

> And as to there being any objection from his *Goodness*, from the danger of his becoming even Evangelical, I cannot admit *that*. I am by no means convinced that we ought not all to be Evangelicals, & am at least persuaded that they who are so from Reason and Feeling, must be happiest & safest.— Do not be frightened from the connection by your Brothers having most wit. Wisdom is better than Wit, & in the long run will certainly have the laugh on her side; & don't be frightened by the idea of his acting more strictly up to the precepts of the New Testament than others. (Letter 103, *LSC* 410)

Wisdom does indeed seem to have the laugh on her side as Austen banishes the Crawfords from the sacrosanct grounds of Mansfield and installs Fanny and Edmund as guardians of the Old World order.

We, on the other hand, do not laugh. Not (as sometimes has been argued) because we are uncomfortable with an Austen who validates the status quo. After all, she does pretty much the same thing in the beloved

Pride and Prejudice when she lets super-patriarch Darcy save the day. We are uncomfortable with an Austen who puts forward an argument in favor of tradition but who presents evidence that makes another case entirely.

Mansfield Park (as does *Amelia*) poses a problem to its readers in that the ideological conflicts are never satisfactorily resolved. Austen here embraces the traditional conduct-book heroine, a figure she had earlier ridiculed; in doing so she ostensibly embraces the conduct-book novel. There is not, as in the first inheritance plot in *Pride and Prejudice*, a direct confrontation with the patriarchal system of estate settlement, nor is there any sense that the nontraditional woman may revitalize the estate. Whatever revitalization Mansfield Park undergoes occurs because Fanny adheres to tradition, seeing more clearly than the patriarch how she can best serve him. If we regard *Mansfield Park* simply as an exemplary conduct-book novel, then we can say that Austen puts her authorial vocation in the service of a patriarchal literary tradition, creating a model version of feminine behavior.

Like *Amelia*, however, *Mansfield Park* works against its own ostensible aims. Austen speaks with a double voice, as she does in *Pride and Prejudice*, and she subtly interweaves her championing of traditional values with her critique of patriarchal institutions that define and deny women. Like Fanny, Austen generally is eminently ladylike and proper in expressing her sentiments here. Yet, also like Fanny, she draws our attention to the vexed position in which the exemplary woman finds herself. When Fanny, discussing Henry's proposal with Edmund, attempts to articulate the truth of a woman's experience she mirrors her creator, turning a perceptive eye to the ambiguities of lived experience for women in her society. Austen may try her hand at the conduct-book novel of her predecessors, but she problematizes its didactic tendencies and reveals, perhaps unwittingly, that this particular literary lineage has come to an end.

Afterword

I do not think my Child is entirely free from Faults. I know nothing human that is so; but surely she doth not deserve the Rancour with which she hath been treated by the Public. However, it is not my Intention, at present, to make my Defence; but shall submit to a Compromise, which hath been always allowed in this Court in all Prosecutions for Dulness. I do, therefore, solemnly declare to you Mr. Censor, that I will trouble the World no more with any Children of mine by the same Muse. —Fielding's defense of *Amelia* (CGJ 65–66)

I return to you the "Quarterly Review" with many thanks. The Authoress of "Emma" has no reason, I think, to complain of her treatment in it, except in the total omission of "Mansfield Park." I cannot but be sorry that so clever a man as the Reviewer of "Emma" should consider it as unworthy of being noticed. —Jane Austen, *Letters* (453)

PAIRING THE NOVELS of Fielding with those of Austen enables us to see not only how the writers are confronting similar problems as they attempt to establish the novel genre, but also how they diverge as they contend with gender issues. Fielding takes for granted the masculinist basis of the novel and asserts its patrilineage. Austen on the other hand contends with the masculinist basis, questions it, and struggles to feminize the novel without trivializing it. In several of her major novels she revises Fielding's canonical texts, decentering their implicitly masculine set of values. Although she has difficulties placing herself outside a patriarchal system of representation, she nonetheless manages to canonize the female text, as is demonstrated in that, up until recently, we considered her the first noteworthy female writer.

To some extent I have presupposed—even imposed—comparable career paths on the part of Fielding and Austen: a movement from parody, through mastery of the novel genre, to a questioning of its authoritative premises. Of course, this scheme of like trajectories breaks down once we go beyond *Amelia* and *Mansfield Park*. After *Amelia* Fielding publicly renounced his novelistic vocation, implicitly acknowledging that the text's failure to maintain and enforce literary authority was indicative of the genre as a whole. On the other hand after *Mansfield Park* Austen discovered new means to define and refine the novel genre. Whether she was aware of the conflicted nature of her only true conduct-book novel, we cannot know. But the following two novels and fragment mark a departure from the conduct-book formula, indicating Austen's willingness to explore different ways of conveying female experience. Clearly, for Austen, the novel remained a viable form.

With *Amelia* more than with his previous texts Fielding had attempted to make the entertaining story serve a serious moral purpose. Yet the text succeeded as neither entertainment nor instruction, and its negative reception must have surprised and disappointed Fielding.[1] In *The Covent-Garden Journal* of January 25 and 28, 1752, Fielding responded to the critical attacks on *Amelia* by having the book up before the "Court of Censorial Enquiry" on a charge of "Dulness" (*CGJ* 57). Fielding drew on actual complaints about the book in order to skewer his critics. Resorting to the genealogical tropes he had invoked in *Tom Jones*, he also made clear his emotional investment in *Amelia:* "If you, Mr. Censor, are yourself a Parent, you will view me with Compassion when I declare I am the Father of this poor Girl the Prisoner at the Bar; nay when I go farther, and avow, that of all my Offspring she is my favorite Child" (65). Yet despite his affection for "this poor Girl"—or perhaps because of it—he concluded with a resolution to "trouble the World no more with any Children of mine by the same Muse" (66).

Fielding stuck to his resolution. The attacks on *Amelia*, his increasing responsibility as magistrate, and his declining health may all have contributed to the cessation of further literary offspring "by the same Muse." Yet there are indications, too, that Fielding began to lose faith in the efficacy and authority of the novel genre he had so fervently championed, that he perhaps even lost interest in the perpetuation of the line. He turned his literary talents to other genres. For nearly a year he produced twice-weekly editions of the *Covent-Garden Journal*, a journal that is, as the Battestins point out, "colored throughout by the graver moral purpose that characterizes all of Fielding's writings of these last years."[2] In 1753 he published the ambitious—and ambitiously titled—*Proposal for making an Effectual Provision for the Poor, for Amending their Morals, and for Rendering them useful Members of the Society*. Clearly Fielding no longer regarded the novel genre as capable of implementing the moral reforms he envisioned.

In his final piece of prose, the posthumously published *The Journal of a Voyage to Lisbon*, Fielding indeed questions the epistemological authority of the novel, seemingly turning round on himself as he argues against the fictional narratives he had earlier extolled as models for his own novels:

> But, in reality, the Odyssey, the Telemachus, and all of that kind, are to the voyage-writing I here intend, what romance is to true history, the former being the confounder and corrupter of the latter. I am far from supposing Homer, Hesiod, and the other antient poets and mythologists, had any settled design to pervert and confuse the records of antiquity; but it is certain they have effected it; and for my part I must confess I should have honored and loved Homer more had he written a true history of his own times in humble prose, than those noble poems that have so justly collected the praise of all ages. (*JVL* 189)

In *Joseph Andrews* and *Tom Jones* the designation "true history" referred to the novels themselves. It is significant that he here applies it to a nonfictional, traditionally "historical" kind of writing. According to his classifications, his own fictions apparently would now be classed under the disparaging term "romance."

Fielding cannot entirely rid himself of his notion that the good fiction writer achieves a certain "truth"; speaking of the classical poets, he claims, "They are not, indeed, so properly said to turn reality into fiction, as fiction into reality" (*JVL* 189). Too, he formulates a poetics for his travel writing that is strikingly similar to the one he formulated for the novels. As he had in *Tom Jones*, he calls for a judicious selection of incidents: "it is better to be hungry than surfeited; and to miss your dessert at the table of a man whose gardens abound with the choicest fruits, than to have your taste affronted with every sort of trash that can be picked up at the green-stall or the wheelbarrow" (187). He notes the importance of the narrator being "an agreeable as well as an instructive companion" (187). Somewhat paradoxically he even justifies a certain fictionalizing of truth: "Some few embellishments must be allowed to every historian; for we are not to conceive that the speeches in Livy, Sallust, or Thucydides, were literally spoken in the very words in which we now read them. It is sufficient that every fact hath its foundation in truth, as I do seriously aver is the case in the ensuing pages" (193). Although he may draw on devices that he drew on for his novels, Fielding makes quite clear that *The Voyage* is another kind of writing entirely. He discovers greater epistemological authority in a nonfiction based on actual experiences than in a fiction based on the truth of human nature.

Austen, however, continued to draw on the novel as a means for elucidating various truths about human (particularly women's) experience, testing out new fictional approaches to the problems of moral and epistemological authority that she had dealt with in her earlier texts. Despite her disappointment that *Mansfield Park* was not reviewed she went on to write two very different novels after it, one of which was indeed reviewed, and by no less an authority than Sir Walter Scott.[3] In her later work, however, we do see a shift. Austen seems less certain about the possibility of social renewal under existing guidelines. We can trace a gradual erosion of the optimistic assertion that things are intrinsically sound as they are. Moreover, we can observe Austen confidently breaking new ground, eschewing tried-and-true formulas in favor of more experimental fiction.

To some extent, *Emma* deliberately reacts to the conduct-book tendency of *Mansfield Park*. Austen in fact acknowledged that those who had enjoyed *Mansfield Park* would find *Emma* "very inferior in good sense" (Letter 120, *LSC* 443). Rather than giving us a modest, passive heroine such as Fanny Price, Austen boldly sketched "a heroine whom no one but myself will much like"—a meddler and a snob—and returned to the bildungsroman structure of *Pride and Prejudice*. Yet Emma is not simply charmingly influenced by her pride and prejudice, as Elizabeth Bennet is. Her interference in the lives of others occasions wounded pride, discomfort, and genuine pain. Her gossip about Jane Fairfax has potentially disastrous consequences. And her mockery of Miss Bates rivals the rude behavior of any of Austen's most boorish villains. Overall, Emma's faults are more egregious than Elizabeth's, her humiliation is more complete, and her male counterpart more knightly than Darcy. Ostensibly, the text presents Emma as a negative exemplar, thereby making a persuasive case for proper female conduct. Emma is, after all, rewarded with Knightley once she has learned the faultiness of her own judgment and has resolved to defer to his. Critics, however, have debated whether this outcome is positive—or what lesson Emma actually learns.[4] More than any of Austen's other texts *Emma* makes clear the stultifying nature of female existence, even (perhaps even especially) for Emma, Austen's only well-off heroine. By doing so the text complicates our understanding of Emma's experience. Emma may indeed be put in her place, but Austen unsettles us as to the appropriateness of her final disposition.

Moral issues are not as clear-cut as they initially appear. The text consistently foregrounds cultural assumptions about gender and class, showing that such assumptions are necessary for things to run smoothly in Highbury society. It also highlights the complex motives underlying human behavior. Emma's efforts to raise Harriet's social standing are ultimately proved wrongheaded, and in her arguments with Mr. Knightley she does indeed often end up "abusing the reason" she has (*Em* 64). Nevertheless her observations are often canny, even astute, as when she points out to Mr. Knightley why she expects Harriet will make a good match: "till it appears that men are much more philosophic on the subject of beauty than they are generally supposed; till they do fall in love with well-informed minds instead of handsome faces, a girl, with such loveliness as Harriet, has a certainty of being admired and sought after" (63). Mr. Knightley's name is for the most part put forward unironically, but even this exemplary figure manifests jealousy, bad temper, and autocratic behavior, believing as complacently in the correctness of his own opinions as Emma does in hers.

The conclusion of the text further complicates our perception that *Emma* takes a clear moral stance. We might expect that Emma will be carried off by her knight to Donwell Abbey, that ideal estate that is, after all, "just what it ought to be" (*Em* 358). Yet it is Mr. Knightley who takes up residence at Hartfield, deferring to Mr. Woodhouse's fidgets and fusses. Are we to read the scene as yet another instance of Mr. Knightley's perfectly gentlemanlike behavior? An instance of good nature deferring to selfishness? An instance of Emma finally getting her own way? In any case, the moral ideal of Donwell Abbey is never achieved, and this motif of deferral is reinforced by the narrator's observations on Emma's engagement to Mr. Knightley: "Seldom, very seldom, does complete truth belong to any human disclosure; seldom can it happen that something is not a little disguised, or a little mistaken" (3, 18).[5] More than in any of her prior texts Austen deals with the moral ambiguities of social existence.

Although *Mansfield Park* had firmly anchored itself in the tradition of the conduct-book novel, *Emma* breaks new ground. Granted, it draws upon prior texts, including Austen's own. With her wittiness and willfulness, Emma has certain affinities to Miss Milner, the erring heroine of Elizabeth Inchbald's *A Simple Story*. Her incorrect readings of others link her with Charlotte Lennox's female Quixote and Austen's own Catherine Morland, although her portrait is far more subtly drawn than are those of the parody heroines. The text relies finally on a marriage plot as conventional as the plot of *Pride and Prejudice*, yet there is an unexpectedness throughout. Excursions and events are planned, but they never quite come off; when they do, they end up with a very different function from the one we were expecting. Emma keeps forgetting the lessons she has learned, falling back into mistakes. Although Mr. Knightley correctly rebukes her for her insult of Miss Bates, he is never apprised of her other, more consequential faults—her malicious gossip about Jane Fairfax and her further attempt to get Harriet married above her station. It is interesting that he marries her because she is "faultless in spite of all her faults" (*Em* 3, 13). The ostensible bildungsroman structure is slightly off-kilter, the causal connections fuzzy. *Emma* may serve as Austen's attempt to play against narrativity, especially to resist its moralizing tendencies.[6]

Although Austen's last completed novel, *Persuasion*, breaks new ground, it returns to some of the same locales as *Northanger Abbey* and refers back to the other novels as well. Like *Pride and Prejudice* it deals with an estate that is entailed away from the daughters in the family. Of more significance, it features—like *Mansfield Park*—a faulty representative of patriarchal tradition and an intelligent, virtuous heroine. In fact, Anne Eliot might be considered a more mature version of Fanny Price. Although Anne also appears to be a conduct-book heroine, her story does have anti-conduct-book tendencies. Essentially, Anne's story is a sequel to an unwritten prior novel—one in which the proper Anne dutifully took the advice of her friends and family and gave up her engagement to the dashing but financially insecure Wentworth. Now, if such a novel had been written by, say, Fanny Burney or the Austen of *Mansfield Park*, Anne's adherence to duty would have been vindicated by the conclusion. But that prior story drew to a close without such a vindication occurring. Eight years of pain and regret fill the interval between Anne's early history and the "sequel." Much, if not most, of *Persuasion* is devoted to Anne's inner dialogue about the consequences of her dutiful behavior:

> She did not blame Lady Russell, she did not blame herself for having been guided by her; but she felt that were any young person, in similar circumstances, to apply to her for counsel, they would never receive any of such certain immediate wretchedness, such uncertain future good.—She was persuaded that under every disadvantage of disapprobation at home, and every anxiety attending his profession, all their probable fears, delays, and disappointments, she should yet have been a happier woman in maintaining the engagement, than she had been in the sacrifice of it. (*Per* 1, 4)

With Fanny Price, Austen shows us the self-division women face when they try to behave as proper ladies, but she ultimately makes the case that proper feminine behavior will be appreciated and rewarded. With Anne Eliot, on the other hand, Austen begins through Anne's inner dialogue to show us that such behavior may wrong women too much. Anne does not finally urge women to resist their guardian's advice, but she does leave open the possibility. *Persuasion* thus stands as a long rumination on the implications of woman's dutifulness, Anne giving (inner) voice to the questions that Fanny Price and her creator could not articulate in *Mansfield Park.*

Unlike Austen's earlier texts *Persuasion* argues for the renovation of a tradition-based society but for the rejection of it—a rejection made significantly on both gender and class grounds. It points toward the creation of an entirely new sort of society, making a case for the integral part of the female and the self-made man in the creation of a new order. The landed estate is abandoned as the repository of moral values.[7] The vain and silly Sir Walter Eliot will be succeeded by his self-serving and calculating nephew, while Anne and Wentworth form an essential part of that circle of good-hearted, generous naval families that congregate throughout the novel.

In conjunction with Austen's increasing cynicism about traditional authority in society, we find an increasing cynicism about the textual forms supporting this position. In her final completed novel, through Anne, Austen makes a sustained argument about the veracity—or, more accurately, lack of it—of authorial tradition: "Men have had every advantage of us in telling their own story. Education has been theirs in so much higher a degree: the pen has been in their hands. I will not allow books to prove anything" (*Per* 234). Austen's ability to envision a new society, one whose values are to a great extent upheld by women and other previously marginalized figures, marks a rejection of the patriarchal plots to which she subscribed in her earlier texts.

Although but a fragment, *Sanditon* gives us a glimpse of Austen in a modern mode. We do not have quite enough of it to see exactly where it is going, but it marks a real departure for Austen. She has moved from the grand estates and sleepy villages of her earlier texts to a newfangled spa, and she seems intent on addressing the problems of modernity. What sorts of solutions she would discover we can only guess.[8]

After writing her problem novel Austen followed a very different trajectory than Fielding had. On the heels of the comparative failure of *Amelia,* Fielding turned against the very genre he had helped establish, replacing factual fictions with fictionalized fact. Austen, however, drew new inspiration from the very elements we find problematic in *Mansfield Park,* reassessing both the conduct-book heroine and conduct-book sentiments and thereby taking the novel in exciting new directions.

The dialogue that I have set up between Fielding and Austen enables us to discover their common ground as they address problems of moral and literary authority and to see, too, the line of demarcation that runs through it, a line drawn up on the basis of gender. Perhaps, however, dialogue is an inapt designation, for there are not two main participants here but three; the third participant has with authorial fiat turned authors into characters, characters who serve the purpose of her own narrative. However, although Fielding and Austen cannot speak, they continue to speak—through the texts that inspired this one. My authorial manipulation must, like theirs, be subject to the countervailing forces that work against any authoritative rendering of some ultimate narrative truth or ultimate truth of narrative. What Fielding and Austen do in their text—what I do in mine—is engage in a conversation. It is a conversation that stretches across lines of genre, gender, and time; a conversation that is retrospective and progressive; a conversation that others will enter in an effort to come to terms with that most flexible, that most modern, of genres—the reactionary, revolutionary novel.

Ultimately, throughout their novelistic careers, neither Fielding nor Austen adequately resolved the vexed question of moral and literary inheritance. But it is not the purpose of novels to resolve issues. Instead, they serve as matrices that enable us to fathom the competing forces that make such totalizing resolutions impossible.

NOTES

INTRODUCTION

1. In "Archimedes and the Paradox of Feminist Criticism," a critique of Elaine Showalter's *A Literature of Their Own*, Myra Jehlen argues for going beyond "the circumscribed world of women writers": "Without knowing the surrounding geography, how are we to evaluate this woman's estate, whose bordering peaks we have measured anyway, not by any internal dimensions, but according to those of Mount Saint Dickens and craggy Hardy? Still less can one envision the circumscribed province as becoming independently global—hence probably the visionary vagueness of Showalter's ending. Instead of a territorial metaphor, her analysis of the world of women as a subculture suggests to me a more fluid imagery of interacting juxtapositions the point of which would be to represent not so much the territory as its defining borders" ("Archimedes," 582). With regard to eighteenth-century texts, Patricia Meyer Spacks suggests, "The tension between meanings perceived by men and by women, between assumptions associated with one sex and the other, informs and invigorates the century's fiction" (*Desire and Truth: Functions of Plot in Eighteenth-Century Novels*, 3).

2. I use "misprision" in the sense that Annette Kolodny does. She discusses women writers' "misprision" of male texts in her essay "A Map for Rereading: Gender and the Interpretation of Literary Texts." In the essay Kolodny, criticizing the inherent gender-bias in Harold Bloom's *A Map of Misreading*, argues that female, as well as male writers, "misread" the texts of their literary forefathers.

3. The phrases come from J. M. S. Tompkins, *The Popular Novel in England, 1770–1800*, v, 1. Tompkins argues that there were "four great novelists" in the eighteenth century—Fielding, Richardson, Sterne, and Smollett—and that after the death of Smollett, no work of significant artistic merit occurred until Austen and Scott began writing. A. Walton Litz puts forth a similar, although more overtly gender-based, argument about the decline of the novel in *Jane Austen: A Study of Her Artistic Development*: "During the fifty years from 1740 to 1790 the annual production of works of fiction increased from approximately twenty to over eighty, and this accelerated production was matched by a decline in quality. As the reading audience rapidly widened, the influence of the few intelligent commentators waned, and popular taste fell under the control of those readers (mainly women) who patronized the sentimental fiction of the circulating libraries" (5).

4. Ian Watt, *The Rise of the Novel: Studies in Defoe, Richardson, and Fielding*.

5. Michael McKeon, *The Origins of the English Novel, 1600–1740*. Stimulating as McKeon's study is, at times it tends toward a certain ahistoricism and blurs

the lines between the various categories it puts forward. For a critical appraisal of McKeon's work, see Homer Obed Brown's review essay "Of the Title to Things Real: Conflicting Stories."

6. Lennard J. Davis also focuses on Defoe, Richardson, and Fielding in *Factual Fictions: The Origins of the English Novel.*

7. Throughout this text, I use the term "feminocentric" to include not only novels written by women but novels that focus on feminine concerns, as they were defined by the particular sociohistorical circumstances of the late eighteenth century. I am indebted to Laura Runge for drawing my attention to the appropriateness of this term.

8. Jane Spencer, *The Rise of the Woman Novelist: From Aphra Behn to Jane Austen;* Janet Todd, *The Sign of Angellica: Women, Writing, and Fiction, 1660–1800;* Nancy Armstrong, *Desire and Domestic Fiction: A Political History of the Novel;* Patricia Meyer Spacks, *Desire and Truth;* Susan Sniader Lanser, *Fictions of Authority: Women Writers and Narrative Voice*. The approaches of the revisionary critics are certainly not uniform. For example, both Spacks and Lanser have important disagreements with Armstrong. Spacks argues that eighteenth-century novels go beyond merely expressing power relations in their society; they not only "contain their society's myths" but also "modify the meanings of those myths" (*Desire and Truth*, 6). Lanser questions Armstrong's use of *Pamela*, a male-authored text, to support her argument about the rise of female authority in the novel (*Fictions of Authority*, 38).

9. Armstrong, *Desire and Domestic Fiction*, 7. For a different take on the tendency to regard the novel as a modern, primarily male, British institution, see Margaret Anne Doody's ambitious *The True Story of the Novel.* By examining texts stretching back to 400 B.C., Doody attempts to demonstrate that "the Novel as a form of literature in the West has a continuous history of about two thousand years" (1), a history that most scholars of the novel have ignored.

10. In addition to Watt's argument that Austen joins Fielding's "realism of assessment" with Richardson's "realism of presentation" (*Rise of the Novel*, 296–99), we have the statement by F. R. Leavis in *The Great Tradition: George Eliot, Henry James, Joseph Conrad* that, although "Fielding made Jane Austen possible by opening the central tradition of English fiction," Richardson "is a major fact in the background of Jane Austen" (3, 4).

11. See, for example, Jocelyn Harris's *Jane Austen's Art of Memory*. Harris argues that Austen was drawn back to Richardson's novels, which she had earlier parodied, after reading Anna Laetitia Barbauld's 1804 edition of his correspondence and that the Richardsonian influence is especially evident in *Sense and Sensibility*, *Pride and Prejudice*, and *Mansfield Park*. Gerard A. Barker's *Grandison's Heirs: The Paragon's Progress in the Late Eighteenth-Century English Novel* traces the Grandisonian hero through to Darcy. In *Jane Austen and Her Predecessors*, Frank Bradbrook acknowledges the influence of both Fielding and Richardson on Austen, but he finds a greater connection to the Richardsonian line through the women writers such as Fanny Burney to whom Austen was closely indebted. In analyzing Austen's work critics are more apt to point out allusions to Richardson's novels than Fielding's, as we see with Kenneth L. Moler's *Jane Austen's Art of Allusion* and Tony Tanner's *Jane Austen.*

12. The "Biographical Notice of the Author" appears at the outset of Chapman's edition of *Northanger Abbey* and *Persuasion*, 7. In *Jane Austen, Her Life and Letters: A Family Record*, William Austen-Leigh and Richard Arthur Austen-Leigh echo Henry Austen's assessment (237).

13. See Margaret Kirkham, *Jane Austen: Feminism and Fiction*, 53–60. John Halperin's biography, *The Life of Jane Austen*, challenges the traditional notion of Austen as a retiring, serene spinster. Although Fay Weldon states that *Grandison* was one of Austen's favorite books, she is skeptical of Austen's criticism of Fielding: "Had Austen known that a light remark of hers about Fielding—possibly uttered to suit the occasion and keep the social wheels running smoothly—was to stand as her one, true, lasting opinion of Fielding through the centuries, she might well have phrased it differently" (*Letters to Alice on First Reading Jane Austen*, 74–75).

14. In a letter to Cassandra dated January 9, 1796, Austen mentions a mutual friend, Tom Lefroy, thus: "he has but one fault which time will, I trust, entirely remove—it is that his morning coat is a great deal too light. He is a very great admirer of Tom Jones, and therefore wears the same coloured clothes, I imagine, which he did when he was wounded" (Letter 1, *LSC* 3). The passage takes on a particular resonance if we consider that, as Park Honan suggests in his biography of Austen, she may well have been in love with Lefroy. See the chapter "Love," in *Jane Austen: Her Life*, 95–111.

15. Although praising Austen in her 1953 analysis of *Pride and Prejudice*, Dorothy van Ghent notes Austen's limitations: "if we expect artistic mastery of limited materials, we shall not be disappointed" (*The English Novel: Form and Function*, 99). Despite his admiration for Austen, Ian Watt remarks that the limited vision of her works anticipates a narrowing of scope in the novel tradition: "In Jane Austen, Fanny Burney, and George Eliot, the advantages of the feminine point of view outweigh the restrictions of the social horizon which have until recently been associated with it. At the same time it is surely true that the dominance of women readers in the public for the novel is connected with the characteristic weakness and unreality to which the form is liable—its tendency to restrict the field on which its psychological and intellectual discriminations operate to a small and arbitrary selection of human situations, a restriction which, since Fielding, has affected all but a very few English novels with a certain narrowing of the framework of experience and permitted attitude" (*Rise of the Novel*, 299). Litz also discusses the limitations of Austen's subject matter (*Artistic Development*, 24). Recent studies, such as those by Armstrong, Spencer, Todd, and Lanser, have begun to counter the notion of limitation, seeing in the courtship plot itself a reflection of one of the major circumstances of female existence. For related arguments see Todd's *Women's Friendship in Literature* and Deborah Kaplan's *Jane Austen among Women*. See also Honan's chapter "Prelude: Frank Austen's Ride," a prologue of sorts to the biography, which cleverly demonstrates how much Jane Austen must have known of the harsh realities of British life in the early nineteenth century. Honan notes that Austen's keeping explicit references to politics out of her novels was, in fact, a sign that "she was politically astute" in good Tory fashion by "[s]upporting the king" and remaining "outwardly unpolitical" (*Her Life*, 58).

16. McKeon, *Origins*, 150. In *The Rise of the Novel*, because Watt argues

that the novel relies on realism and individualism rather than the idealizing abstractions of romance, he finds himself compelled to downplay the significance of texts that do not fit neatly under the rubric of "formal realism." McKeon regards his own work as an attempt to extend Watt's, and in his introduction he provides an incisive critique of Watt's position (*Origins*, esp. 1–4). For a Watt-like argument, see also Lennard Davis's claim that "the romance is not usefully seen as a forebear of, a relative of, or an influence on the novel" (*Factual Fictions*, 25)

17. In Chapter 3, I explore in detail the suggestive implications of the bastard motif. I am indebted to Homer Brown for drawing my attention to the emblematic function of Tom's bastardy. See "*Tom Jones*: The 'Bastard' of History." The essay has been reprinted in Brown's *Institutions of the English Novel: From Defoe to Scott*, 82–115.

18. Lanser, *Fictions of Authority*, 18.

19. For a recent discussion of the significance of gender in the critical acceptance of the novel, see Laura Runge, "Gendered Strategies in the Criticism of Early Fiction," 365.

20. McKeon, *Origins*, 20. McKeon notes, "Questions of truth and questions of virtue concern different realms of human experience, and they are likely to be raised in very different contexts." Nevertheless, each deals with similar questions: "What kind of authority or evidence is required of narrative to permit it to signify truth to its readers? What kind of social existence or behavior signifies an individual's virtue to others?" Although McKeon's aims are far more comprehensive than my own, his linking of moral authority and epistemological authority, which I herein restrict to literary authority, is important to my own project.

21. Franco Moretti, *The Way of the World: The Bildungsroman in European Culture*, 205. Although his insights are sharp, Moretti tends to dismiss the English bildungsroman too easily, as the following passage shows: "One enjoys oneself, without ever being carried away; one finds plenty of certainties, but no way of addressing problems" (213). Moretti argues that the "juridical frame of mind" common to the English novel resulted in "the worst novel of the West" (214). As I argue, the inheritance plot attempts to provide a solution to problems. That solution may perhaps be an uncomfortable one, but therein lies its merit.

22. Donald Greene, *The Age of Exuberance: Backgrounds to Eighteenth-Century English Literature*, 67.

23. J. G. A. Pocock, *The Ancient Constitution and the Feudal Law: A Study of English Historical Thought in the Seventeenth Century*, 49. Pocock expands upon this point throughout the text.

24. Pocock deals with the issue of authority in his essay "Authority and Property: The Question of Liberal Origins." McKeon's *Origins* provides a detailed discussion of the conflicts concerning authority that give birth to the novel genre.

25. J. G. A. Pocock, "Virtues, Rights, and Manners: A Model for Historians of Political Thought." In this essay and in "Authority and Property," Pocock discusses the complex history of the conflict over real and mobile property. He argues that the initial basis of the conflict was the corrupting force of patronage. After the 1690s, "there was created a new class of investors great and small . . . who had lent government capital that vastly stabilized and enlarged it, and henceforth

lived off their expectations of a return (sometimes a marketable one) on their investments. The landed classes, and still more their ideologues to the right and left, saw in this process a revolutionary expansion less of a trading and manufacturing market, than of a system of parliamentary patronage" ("Authority and Property," 68). Such a conflict has bearing on a text such as *Amelia*, wherein the land-poor Booth is confronted by the corruptions of a pervasive system of patronage.

26. Lanser points out that the novel was "one of the few accepted means for women to intervene in public life" (*Fictions of Authority*, 17).

27. Marilyn Butler discusses the effect of the French Revolution and the resultant 1793 war against France on people of Austen's class: "A host of conservative politicians, some of the most effective of whom were churchmen, gave the war a convincing rationale by representing it as the defense of religion, the family, and the gentry way of life. The upper and middle orders were given a coherent if idealized self-image, which has been the basis of British Toryism ever since: a personal ideal compounded of independence, honor, decency, patriotism, public service, chivalry to women, and civility to inferiors" ("History, Politics, and Religion," 204). In *Romantics, Rebels, and Reactionaries: English Literature and Its Background, 1760–1830*, Butler notes that Austen would have been particularly influenced by public opinion during her writing apprenticeship: "Jane Austen was of an age . . . to be peculiarly susceptible to the extremes of the counter-revolution, the hysterical reaction of 1796–98" (97).

28. David Spring, "Interpreters of Jane Austen's Social World: Literary Critics and Historians," 60. Spring points out that Austen's novels "celebrated" the rise of the pseudo-gentry (63).

29. Butler, "History, Politics, and Religion," 204.

30. Certainly, Richardson also is concerned with inheritance. Pamela's Cinderella-like elevation by the squire who recognizes her worth is similar to what happens to Elizabeth Bennet and Fanny Price. Clarissa's inheritance of her grandfather's estate helps to precipitate the ensuing tragedy. Nevertheless, Austen's work more closely and consistently follows the particular recognition-inheritance pattern that we find in Fielding.

31. See Moretti on the fairy-tale aspects of the inheritance plot (*Way of the World*, 205). For a psychoanalytic discussion of the "primal fantasy" nature of such plots, see Christine van Boheemen, *The Novel as Family Romance: Language, Gender, and Authority from Fielding to Joyce*. Northrop Frye, in *Anatomy of Criticism: Four Essays*, provides a useful discussion of the archetypal forms informing all plot structures.

32. In their first letter to their daughter in Richardson's sequel, Pamela's parents write: "For, I don't know how it is, but though you are our daughter, and are so far from being lifted up by your high condition, that we see no difference in your behaviour to us, your poor parents; yet, when we look upon you as the lady of so fine a gentleman, we cannot forbear having a kind of respect, and—I don't know what to call it—that lays a little restraint upon us" (*Pamela, or Virtue Rewarded*, 2:308).

33. Moretti, *Way of the World*, 205.

34. In *The British Novel, Defoe to Austen: A Critical History*, 90–109, when discussing *The Castle of Otranto*, John Allen Stevenson demonstrates the way in

which issues of inheritance took on a particularly ambivalent character in an age wherein the attempt to establish the legitimacy of the Hanoverian succession was countered by Jacobite claims. We see such ambivalence in the inheritance plots of Fielding and Austen, wherein the apparent outsider becomes an instrument for reinforcing the continuity of tradition. In *Anatomy of Criticism*, Frye speaks of comedy's support of the status quo: "the hero's society is a Saturnalia, a reversal of social standards which recalls a golden age in the past before the main action of the play begins. Thus we have a stable and harmonious order disrupted by folly, obsession, forgetfulness, 'pride and prejudice,' or events not understood by the characters themselves, and then restored" (171). Comedy's subversive impulse is thus put in service of traditional values.

35. I enter an ongoing debate about the relation of Jane Austen to her society. Critics such as D. W. Harding have argued for the subversive nature of her novels; see "Regulated Hatred: An Aspect of the Work of Jane Austen," 166–79. More recently, Claudia Johnson has discussed Austen's challenges to the status quo in *Jane Austen: Women, Politics, and the Novel*. On the other hand, critics such as Alistair Duckworth, in *The Improvement of the Estate: A Study of Jane Austen's Novels*, and Marilyn Butler, in *Jane Austen and the War of Ideas*, have argued for her essential conservatism.

36. Peter Brooks, *Reading for the Plot: Design and Intention in Narrative*, 11–12.

37. See Wayne C. Booth, *The Rhetoric of Fiction*.

38. Michel Foucault, "What Is an Author?" 124.

39. Of relevance is the distinction made by David Saunders and Ian Hunter: "we can distinguish the attributes of the authorial persona—as an ensemble of instituted virtues, rights, liabilities, capacities—from the individual who writes" ("Lessons from the 'Literatory': How to Historicise Authorship," 483).

40. For a provocative, if at times problematic, argument about Fielding's ambivalence toward traditionally masculine forms of power, see Jill Campbell's *Natural Masques: Gender and Identity in Fielding's Plays and Novels*. Although I find insightful Campbell's remarks about certain gender ambiguities in Fielding's texts, I think Fielding nevertheless adheres overall to a masculine set of values.

41. Spacks, *Desire and Truth*, 84.

42. Mikhail Bakhtin has made one of the most cogent cases for the subversive force of the novel in *The Dialogic Imagination: Four Essays*. Although I find the novel less subversive than Bakhtin would have it, I agree with his notion that its incorporation of diverse genres and language systems precludes it from being an authoritative discourse. Bakhtin at times is too uncritical when he points to the intentional double-voicedness of the novel. On the other hand, in *Desire and Domestic Fiction*, Armstrong argues for the novel's prescriptive nature, but she does not take into account the element of "play" that is the adjunct of fictional discourse.

1. Discovering Homer's Heir

1. In his essay "Of the Title to Things Real," Homer Obed Brown discusses the freighted value of the term "novel," arguing that our use of it is governed by a

complex of institutional procedures unavailable to writers of the mid–eighteenth century.

2. With the name Joseph, of course, Fielding self-consciously makes allusion to the biblical character. We may find out Joseph's true surname by the end of the novel, but we do not find out his actual given name. Although the title is a cheat, the protagonist never quite loses his identity as Joseph Andrews.

3. In their biography of Fielding, Martin Battestin and Ruthe Battestin point out that, despite its publication date of 1743, *Jonathan Wild* was probably originally composed between 1737 and 1741–1742 (*Henry Fielding: A Life*, 281, 655 n. 37). According to the Battestins, the gap between the date of composition and the date of publication may have occurred because "Walpole paid [Fielding] to suppress it" (282).

4. Although *Jonathan Wild* is often called a novel, I would imagine that this is for the sake of convenience as much as anything else. Robert Alter offers a succinct argument against its being classified as such in *Fielding and the Nature of the Novel*: "it belongs instead with *Gulliver's Travels*, *Candide*, *Rasselas*, and the other satiric or philosophic fables of the eighteenth century, which are ingenious fictional schematizations of experience in the service of ideas rather than attempts to create through fiction a convincing illusion of life in contemporary society" (viii–ix). But, for a recent argument that places *Jonathan Wild* with Fielding's novels, see John Bender's *Imagining the Penitentiary: Fiction and the Architecture of Mind in Eighteenth-Century England*, 138–63. Bender argues that "Fielding's novels record a struggle for control of narrative resources that is characteristic of early metropolitan society in London" (155); in *Jonathan Wild*, "the moral warfare between Wild and Heartfree" is "a combat between variant novelistic accounts of material circumstances" (157). Ronald Paulson provides a useful distinction between the satiric mode and the novel genre in *Satire and the Novel in Eighteenth-Century England*.

5. I mention only some of the more obvious influences that may have inspired Fielding to attempt a work that was, according to his own claims, unique in its combination of structure and matter. For extended discussions of the various social and aesthetic contexts of *Joseph Andrews*, see Martin C. Battestin, *The Moral Basis of Fielding's Art: A Study of "Joseph Andrews"*; Homer Goldberg, *The Art of "Joseph Andrews"*; and J. Paul Hunter, "Some Contexts for *Joseph Andrews*." The Battestins give a detailed account of how the Licensing Act was a deliberate attempt to muzzle Fielding and how it kept him from fulfilling his ambition (*Henry Fielding*, 217–34). As they point out, "Fielding had only just completed his apprenticeship in the theatre and was dreaming of greater triumphs to come" (233).

6. Battestin and Battestin, *Henry Fielding*, 302.

7. Hunter elaborates upon several other targets of Fielding's attack—including the pamphlet war between the followers of George Whitefield and those of Dr. Joseph Trapp; Colley Cibber's *Apology*; and Dr. Conyers Middleton's dedication to Lord Hervey in *Life of Cicero*—noting that the text is "the best book report on 1740" (*Occasional Form*, 77); see his chapter "Historical Registers for the Year 1740," in *Occasional Form*, 77–93. The Battestins argue that Robert Walpole was also one of Fielding's targets; *Shamela* "opens by deriding the morals and virility of

the Prime Minister and his lieutenant Hervey," and it closes with Parson Williams "very much Walpole's man in the name of 'Pollitrick'" (*Henry Fielding*, 307).

8. This discrepancy between words and actions is a persistent concern for Fielding, developed at length in "An Essay on the Knowledge of the Characters of Men" and vividly illustrated in his novels. Methodism, with its doctrine of grace over works, comes under particular attack from Fielding, and Shamela's Methodistic leanings are emblematic of her hypocrisy.

9. Henry Fielding, "Preface to *Familiar Letters on David Simple*," 132.

10. Goldberg, *Art of "Joseph Andrews,"* 7; and see also 3–24 for a detailed argument about Fielding's claims in the preface.

11. Watt, *Rise of the Novel*, 254.

12. Doody notes that one assumption about the eighteenth-century novel was that it replaced a feminized type of writing: "One way of looking at prose fiction before the eighteenth century is to assume that it is an old-fashioned, feudal, and feminine thing, which it is necessary to turn into an appropriately modern and manly thing. Such an assumption is apparently behind Henry Fielding's *Joseph Andrews* (1742). In the fable of the babies swapped in their cradle, Joseph, 'a poor sickly Boy,' substituted for the former occupant, a girl, 'a fat thriving Child,' seems a figure for Fielding's new novel, which is to replace the old one" (*True Story*, 274). Doody leaves implicit what masculine infirmity might signify with regard to the novel.

13. Wolfgang Iser discusses the way in which Fielding draws on familiar generic categories in order to arouse expectations from which the novel will diverge; see "The Role of the Reader in *Joseph Andrews* and *Tom Jones*," in *The Implied Reader: Patterns of Communication in Prose Fiction from Bunyan to Beckett*, 31–46.

14. See Goldberg's discussion of Fielding's indebtedness to not only *Don Quixote* but other Continental prototypes, including Scarron, *Le Roman comique;* Lesage, *Gil Blas;* and Marivaux, *La Vie de Marianne* and *Le Paysan parvenu* (*Art of "Joseph Andrews,"* 25–72). Goldberg argues that by drawing on these works Fielding learned to mingle comic action with romantic ingredients.

15. Daniel Defoe, *The Life and Strange Surprizing Adventures of Robinson Crusoe*, 1.

16. McKeon develops his argument throughout the section "Questions of Truth," in *Origins*, 24–128, esp. 89, 95, 109.

17. Campbell, in *Natural Masques*, argues that through his portrayal of the various characters in *Joseph Andrews* Fielding calls into question and refines contemporary notions of masculinity. Campbell's point about the ambiguous gendering of the characters is provocative and often convincing. The masculinity of the author figure, however, appears in no way ambivalent or compromised.

18. During his successful but short-lived career as a playwright Fielding had also experimented with an apparent characterized author figure. In both *The Author's Farce* and *Pasquin*, an ostensible author comments upon his play as it is being performed. The difference with the plays is that it is not the actual play that is being discussed, but a play-within-the-play; what we get is thus not so much an embedded poetics but a satire on the contemporary theater scene.

19. Raymond Williams analyzes the various permutations of meaning undergone by the term "literature" in his *Keywords: A Vocabulary of Culture and Society*, 183–88. Williams argues that a change occurred after the eighteenth century wherein "literature" shifted from referring to all books and writing to referring almost exclusively to creative or imaginative writing. He also discusses the recent challenges to this usage. See also Michel Foucault's discussion of how the word "literature" came to stand for imaginative writing in *The Order of Things: An Archaeology of the Human Sciences*, 229–300.

20. Leo Braudy regards Fielding's novels as stages in the development of a theory about the relation of the novel to history; see *Narrative Form in History and Fiction: Hume, Fielding, and Gibbon*, 7.

21. Battestin, *Moral Basis*, 116. For a discussion of the rhetorical effect of the chastity theme, see also Hunter's "Some Contexts for *Joseph Andrews*." Sir Leslie Stephen was unable to take the chastity theme seriously: "The doctrine of male chastity, expounded in *Pamela*, struck [Fielding] as simply ridiculous" (*History of English Thought in the Eighteenth Century*, 2:321).

22. Hunter contrasts Fielding's "more limited uses of journey in *Joseph Andrews*" with his "syncretism of traditions and conflations of experiential myths" in *Tom Jones*, arguing that whereas "Joseph's journey is a progress" Tom's is simultaneously pilgrimage, progress, and quest (*Occasional Form*, 148–49).

23. Campbell, *Natural Masques*, 69.

24. McKeon argues that "Joseph is Pamela as she should have been," that he "masters both his sexual and social appetites" (*Origins*, 399).

25. In *Occasional Form*, Hunter points out that Fielding does not generally rely on positive exemplars, but instead on "negative exemplars, cautionary figures placed on our path for evitation rather than imitation" (86).

26. Campbell provides one of the most detailed discussions of how *Joseph Andrews* brings gender issues to the fore, claiming that "Fielding's construction of a compromised gender identity for his title character becomes . . . a vehicle for an imaginative negotiation between opposite allegiances traditionally systematized by gender" (*Natural Masques*, 110). Although I find the claim somewhat overstated, Campbell persuasively demonstrates that Fielding's response to traditional notions of gender roles is more complicated than has heretofore been discussed.

27. Campbell examines how the text also reveals the asymmetry between class and gender hierarchies: Joseph's "disentitlement as a servant limits his power to act on his own virtue while his sexual entitlement as a man limits the dramatic *authority* of his power to do so" (ibid., 68).

28. Rather than regarding Fielding's purpose for Adams as inconsistent, Goldberg maintains that Fielding makes Adams less engaging as the novel progresses so as to shift the reader's interest from Adams to Andrews: "he would guide the reader to a progressively more sympathetic view of Joseph and a somewhat less appealing impression of his old teacher. In the middle of the novel he would shift the emphasis of Adams' comedy from his endearing natural simplicity to his vanity, from his misestimates of individual character to his mistaken beliefs and misapplied doctrines" (*Art of "Joseph Andrews,"* 90). However, Adams's virtues and weaknesses appear concurrently throughout, resulting from Fielding's uncertain aims.

29. Hunter suggests, for example, that Joseph "becomes a wiser and better man" ("Some Contexts for *Joseph Andrews*," 107; for the full argument see 107–114).

30. Ibid., 113.

31. Battestin, *Moral Basis*, 119. For an opposing position, however, see Hunter's argument that the tale works against the thrust of the novel itself, its main function being to demonstrate where rhetoric goes wrong (*Occasional Form*, 151–57).

32. As Marie Maclean points out, "To men in our culture, the name of the father is an irrevocable identity" ("The Performance of Illegitimacy: Signing the Matronym," 99). Christine van Boheemen also discusses the way in which meaning derives from the child's relationship to the father (*The Novel as Family Romance*, 7). But see Campbell for the argument that Joseph's identity depends on his link with his mother (*Natural Masques*, 123–30).

33. Brian McCrea argues that Fielding substitutes the birth-mystery plot for the chastity plot of *Pamela* in order to clear up "the confusion about rank" left open in Richardson's text: "Fielding takes the 'popular' and socially subversive achievement of Richardson and attempts to render it 'polite'" ("Rewriting *Pamela*: Social Change and Religious Faith in *Joseph Andrews*," 138).

34. Hunter points out that the "fullness of *Tom Jones* can be glimpsed in *Joseph Andrews*, but only at moments or in diluted forms or as a corollary to something else" (*Occasional Form*, 161).

2. Written by "A Lady"

1. The note is reproduced in *Minor Works*, facing p. 242. Cassandra Austen states that *First Impressions* was begun in 1796 and finished in 1797. In his introductory note to *Pride and Prejudice*, R. W. Chapman indicates that *First Impressions* was actually offered for publication at that time, but that the manuscript was rejected (*PP* xi). Cassandra also states that *Sense and Sensibility* was begun in 1797, following the earlier *Elinor and Marianne*.

2. R. W. Chapman argues that *Pride and Prejudice* "was constructed on the calendar year of 1811–12, and was not merely rewritten, but very largely recast, in the year preceding publication" (*Jane Austen: Facts and Problems*, 79). A. Walton Litz notes that "There is no reason to believe that *Northanger Abbey* underwent extensive revision" after 1803 and that "the late revisions [of *Pride and Prejudice*] were radical ones" ("Chronology of Composition," 49, 51). On the other hand, John Halperin argues that Austen made few significant revisions to *Pride and Prejudice* after 1797 (*Life*, 65–69). As I show in the following pages, however, we are right to regard *Northanger Abbey* as the less mature work.

Why *Susan*, the original version of *Northanger Abbey*, was not published in 1803 remains a matter for conjecture. Park Honan suggests that the publisher may have found the subject matter incompatible with its agenda: "*Susan*, if it resembled *Northanger Abbey* in having a flippant attitude to parental advice, might have subverted their campaign to publish morally approved novels. But *Susan* surely had run counter to Crosby's interests in seeming to be a lightsome, laughing attack on a pillar of English fiction, Crosby's own Radcliffe" (*Her Life*, 384).

3. Lanser in *Fictions of Authority*, 67, makes a similar connection between *Joseph Andrews* and *Northanger Abbey*.

4. Ian Watt suggests that the novel was established by midcentury (*Rise of the Novel*). But for an argument that it was still in the process of becoming see Homer Brown, "Of the Title to Things Real."

5. Watt, for example, notes the quantitative contribution of female writers, but he undermines any qualitative contribution: "The majority of eighteenth-century novels were actually written by women, but this has long remained a purely quantitative assertion of dominance" (*Rise of the Novel*, 298). As Laura Runge points out in her perceptive analysis of the gender values inherent in eighteenth-century literary criticism, the sort of "gendered literary hierarchy" as practiced by Watt may be traced to the eighteenth-century devaluation of women's novels: "certain practices developed in the criticism of the eighteenth-century enabled literary historians of later generations to ignore or diminish the prolific achievements of the early female authors" ("Gendered Strategies," 365). According to Kirkham the influence of Sir Walter Scott also contributed to the later devaluation of woman's fiction: "For a period of around thirty years women produced a great variety of interesting and memorable fiction, and, but for the intervention of Scott, they would also be seen as having dominated the development of the novel in English throughout the whole of this period" (*Feminism and Fiction*, 33).

6. For checklists of prose fiction, see William Harlin McBurney, *A Check List of English Prose Fiction, 1700–1739*; Leonard Orr, *A Catalogue Checklist of English Prose Fiction, 1750–1800*; and James Raven, *British Fiction, 1750–1770: A Chronological Check-List of Prose Fiction Printed in Britain and Ireland*. Orr cites *Edward and Sophia* (96); Raven cites *Miss Pittborough* (274). We have no way of knowing whether such novels were actually written by women. As Raven points out, some of the "unattributed works 'by a Lady,' . . . as well as some with women's names on the title pages, were actually written by male hacks" (18). The checklists reveal, too, that even such figures as Sterne and Goldsmith published anonymously. Nevertheless, in the checklists we see that novels dealing with what appears to be a feminine realm of values generally tend to be anonymous.

7. "A Whimsical Writing Lady Displayed," 462.

8. Spencer, *Rise of the Woman Novelist*, 21.

9. Armstrong in *Desire and Domestic Fiction* demonstrates the complementary function of novels and conduct books in shaping a realm of feminine authority.

10. Runge, "Gendered Strategies," 375. Doody makes a similar point: "Whenever the Novel is freshly masculinized, women are warned to keep off. Women writers of the eighteenth and nineteenth century were . . . supposed to keep to the 'private sphere,' and the approved way to do that in novel-writing, if one must write, was to write only 'domestic novels'" (*True Story*, 291).

11. Hannah More, *Strictures on the Modern System of Female Education*, 1:157, 158.

12. Ibid., 159–60.

13. Ibid., 169–70.

14. Ibid., 171, 172. Presumably, such condemnation did not apply when More herself later wrote *Coelebs in Search of a Wife*. Lanser points out that More's novel, unsurprisingly, pushes a patriarchal agenda: "the best-selling novel by a woman was then Hannah More's *Coelebs in Search of a Wife* (1808), in which, if I may put it crassly, a male narrator tells women how to please men" (*Fictions of Authority*, 71).

15. More, *Strictures*, 1:164.

16. In "The Dream of a Common Language: Hannah More and Mary Wollstonecraft," Harriet Guest demonstrates that, despite their political differences, More and Wollstonecraft share similar notions about feminine corruption.

17. Mary Wollstonecraft, *A Vindication of the Rights of Woman*, 306.

18. Mary Wollstonecraft, *Maria, or The Wrongs of Woman*, 80, 78. Like *Northanger Abbey*, *Maria* itself serves as a counterfiction, using the novel form to criticize sentimental novels and recontextualize gothic ones.

19. Wollstonecraft, *Vindication*, 306, 308, 308–9.

20. Lanser remarks upon the "marvelous doubleness" of Austen's phrase "mother tongue," regarding it as Austen's positioning of herself in a "female-centered space" (*Fictions of Authority*, 70–71). Jocelyn Harris even argues that "in light of Mrs Barbauld's derisive account of Richardson's pedant Brand . . . [Austen's] meekness suddenly looks like a wicked attack on the oblivious Mr. Clarke" (*Art of Memory*, 47).

21. Clarke, incidentally, with remarkably single-minded obtuseness, persisted in his attempts to supply Austen with subject matter, entreating in one letter that she take a clergyman as her hero and in another that she venture beyond her national terrain and historical period: "Perhaps when you again appear in print you may chuse to dedicate your volumes to Prince Leopold: any historical romance, illustrative of the history of the august House of Cobourg, would just now be very interesting" (Letters 120a, 126a, *LSC* 444–45, 451). In the satirical pastiche "Plan of a Novel" (*MW* 428–30), Austen has fun at Clarke's expense, slyly modeling her "exemplary Parish Priest" on the autobiographical information he gave her.

22. Sandra M. Gilbert and Susan Gubar, *The Madwoman in the Attic: The Woman Writer and the Nineteenth-Century Literary Imagination*, 117. The argument appears throughout the chapter "Shut Up in Prose: Gender and Genre in Austen's Juvenilia" (107–45).

23. Alison Sulloway, *Jane Austen and the Province of Womanhood*, xvi.

24. See Ismay Barwell, "Feminine Perspectives and Narrative Points of View," 96–97.

25. George Levine, in *The Realistic Imagination: English Fiction from Frankenstein to Lady Chatterley*, provides an insightful discussion of the complicated relation between *Northanger Abbey* and its parodic targets. As he points out, "The relation of *Northanger Abbey* to the novels it parodies is complex, not necessarily self-contradictory" (65). Levine, however, does not address the question of how much this complex response may be attributable to Austen's reluctance to undermine too strongly the feminocentric novel.

26. Harris marks an interesting correspondence between Austen's defense and the defense of the novel that Anna Laetitia Barbauld put forward in her 1804 edition of Richardson's correspondence (*Art of Memory*, 40).

27. Alan D. McKillop, "Critical Realism in *Northanger Abbey*," 60.

28. After Arabella fancies that an ex-servant is trying to abduct her, her would-be lover, Glanville, "silently curse[s] his ill Fate, to make him in Love with a Woman so ridiculous" (Charlotte Lennox, *The Female Quixote, or The Adventures of Arabella*, 155).

29. Homer Brown in "Institutions of the Imaginary: *Northanger Abbey*" provides an in-depth analysis of the contest over different ways of representing experience that occurs during the conversation between Catherine and the Tilneys.

30. Gilbert and Gubar, *Madwoman in the Attic*, 135.

31. Ibid. As they point out, Catherine's suspicions of the General spring from her own sense of victimization at his hands: "Feeling confined and constrained in the General's house, but not understanding why, Catherine projects her own feelings of victimization into her imaginings of the General's wife" (ibid., 141).

32. As Homer Brown comments, "the implication is that artifice or convention precedes and controls, shapes—textualizes—experience or perception" ("Institutions of the Imaginary," 20).

33. Gilbert and Gubar, *Madwoman in the Attic*, 132. Levine argues that the unconvincing comic resolution derives from the nature of parody itself: "The texture of parody is normally comic, while the object of parody is normally a literature allowing too easy triumphs for hero or heroine, that is, literature in a comic form. The logic of rejection would entail (as in *Northanger Abbey* itself) an unhappy ending. But a comic texture tends to imply a comic form so that to be true to its content, parody would likely be untrue to its form" (*Realistic Imagination*, 72).

34. Gilbert and Gubar, *Madwoman in the Attic*, 145.

35. Marvin Mudrick, "Irony Versus Gothicism," 82.

36. Ibid., 84.

37. See, for example, Gilbert and Gubar, *Madwoman in the Attic*, 138–45.

38. Carol Gilligan, *In a Different Voice: Psychological Theory and Women's Development*, 6.

39. Lanser, *Fictions of Authority*, 80, 72.

3. *Tom Jones*

1. Although I am indebted to Homer Brown's essay "*Tom Jones*" for drawing my attention to the connection Fielding makes between text and hero, my emphasis in the following pages diverges from Brown's. Whereas Brown stresses the way in which the text functions as bastardized history, I focus on the text's illegitimacy with regard to traditional literary genres.

2. One need only think of the varied quality of Tony Richardson's film versions of the two novels; *Tom Jones* is a delightful romp, capturing the spirit (if not quite the philosophical bent) of Fielding's original, whereas *Joseph Andrews* is dull and flat, an embarrassment lacking in energy and indeed point.

3. Ronald Paulson discusses the connection between the "novel" as an aesthetic category and the novel genre, regarding the latter as the prose fiction embodiment of the former: "The works I categorize under the Novel and Strange were given other names by their authors, working terms that corresponded to practical rather than aesthetic categories (e.g., 'modern moral subject,' 'comic history-painting,' 'comic epic in prose'). . . . The generic term 'novel' applied to the form written by Fielding and Sterne, as well as Richardson, did not have more than occasional usage until the 1770s. So far as I knew it has never been used in the way I use it to join Addison's aesthetics, Hogarth's theory, and the emerging forms of prose fiction" (*The Beautiful, Novel, and Strange: Aesthetics and Heterodoxy*, xv).

4. After I had completed an earlier version of this chapter my attention was brought to Robert L. Chibka's essay "Taking 'The Serious' Seriously: The Introductory Chapters of *Tom Jones*." Like myself, Chibka argues that there are "suggestive juxtapositions" (28) between Tom's story and the introductory chapters. Chibka's purpose, however, is to establish that Fielding's "self-conscious artifice," rather than separating "theory and practice," actually demonstrates that "learning to live and learning to read are finally one and the same process" (38–39). My own purpose is to show how the thematic reverberations and Tom's story further a plot of authorship.

5. Doody provocatively argues that the critical dialogue within prefaces was replaced by book reviews: "Novel reviewing serves as a kind of gatekeeper for the *civitas*. It is official and responsible. Its rise in importance noticeably if subtly diminished the importance of novels' prefatory material" (*True Story*, 277).

6. The introductory chapters to *Charlotte Summers* are reproduced in Ronald Paulson and Thomas Lockwood, eds., *Henry Fielding: The Critical Heritage*, 219–22. Wilbur L. Cross also discusses this imitative text in his biography of Fielding, *The History of Henry Fielding*, 2:133–36. Several of the prefaces to *Henry* are reproduced in Claude Rawson, ed., *Henry Fielding: A Critical Anthology*, 192–93.

7. I discuss Sterne's exploration and demonstration of narrative structure in "Spiraling down 'the Gutter of Time': *Tristram Shandy* and the Strange Attractor of Death."

8. Judith Frank examines the aesthetic principles advanced in the prefaces to *Joseph Andrews*. She does not, however, rigorously analyze how these portions of the text detract from or contribute to textual unity, as we see in discussions of the prefaces in *Tom Jones*. See Judith Frank, "The Comic Novel and the Poor: Fielding's Preface to *Joseph Andrews*."

9. Pierre Antoine de la Place, Letter, 1750, in Paulson and Lockwood, *The Critical Heritage*, 224; Lord Monboddo, *Of the Origin and Progress of Language* (1776), 3:296–98, reprinted in Rawson, *A Critical Anthology*, 177–78. De la Place's practice, incidentally, is by no means completely attributable either to his era or to his milieu, for during this century Somerset Maugham performed a similar dismemberment when he brought out his edition of *Tom Jones*.

10. Watt, *Rise of the Novel*, 277; Booth, *Rhetoric of Fiction*, 216–19; Michael Bliss, "Fielding's Bill of Fare in *Tom Jones*"; Patricia Meyer Spacks, *Imagining a Self: Autobiography and Novel in Eighteenth-Century England*, 230, 254; Alter, *Fielding*,

34. To Booth the prefatory matter actually functions as a sort of subplot of the increasing intimacy between "the implied author" and the readers. Yet even in this century, the prefaces have continued to be regarded as ad hoc additions to the text. In the 1930s Ethel Thornbury in *Henry Fielding's Theory of the Comic Prose Epic* argued that the prefaces were irrelevant conventional insertions that Fielding probably wrote after the novel was in the hands of the publisher. More recently Martin Battestin has suggested that the prefaces were composed later than the story (general introduction, *Tom* 1:xxxvii).

11. Fred Kaplan, "Fielding's Novel about Novels: The 'Prefaces' and the 'Plot' of *Tom Jones*." In his useful study of trends in *Tom Jones* criticism, H. George Hahn points out that, with Kaplan's essay, "The critically inevitable had occurred: the expository had become narrative" ("Main Lines of Criticism of Fielding's *Tom Jones*, 1900–1978," 18). For an interesting inversion of the prefaces/story argument see Thomas Lockwood, "Matter and Reflection in *Tom Jones*." Lockwood argues that Fielding's "talk" (both the prefatory chapters and his intra-narrative comments) is basically a long eighteenth-century essay and that the narrative functions as an illustrative story. Rather than making the prefaces part of the fiction Lockwood essentially makes the fiction part of the essays.

12. The term comes from Jacques Derrida, "Outwork," 44–45.

13. I make a distinction between this textual construct and Fielding the historical personage. Yet the identification between the two persists in contemporary criticism. For example, see Henry Knight Miller, "The Voices of Henry Fielding: Style in *Tom Jones*." Miller assumes that Fielding—not a narrative persona but the historical personage himself—is the hero of the novel. Battestin, too, discovers Fielding himself in the novel: "More than any other novelist of the period, Fielding—or, if one prefers, that heightened and idealized projection of him which has been called his 'second self'—is immanent in his book. His themes and characters, his episodes and opinions, reveal the pressure of his personal circumstances and the climate of life and thought in which he wrote" (general introduction, *Tom* 1:xxxiv). The experiences and attitudes of Fielding the writer appear in the text, granted, but they cannot be separated from the textualized version of self that reflects and promotes a particular ideological agenda—a very different version than that which appears in *Amelia*.

14. Stevenson discusses Tom's state as a "free-floating signifier" in *The British Novel*, 56.

15. With regard to Fielding's latitudinarianism and his rejection of the notion of absolute reprobation, see Battestin's discussion of John Tillotson's influence over Fielding (*Tom* 1:79–80 n. 4). Battestin cites Tillotson's sermon "The goodness of God": "God is infinitely better than the best of men, and yet none can possibly think that man a good man, who should absolutely resolve to disinherit and destroy his children, without the foresight and consideration of any fault to be committed by them." I generally agree with Battestin as to the latitudinarian bent of *Tom Jones*. For a more qualified view of Fielding's latitudinarianism, however, see Paulson, *Beautiful, Novel, and Strange*, 98–135.

16. See Alter, *Fielding*, 41–42, for a sharp analysis of the passages regarding Bridget and the Captain.

17. One of the delights of *Tom Jones* is that, like any good mystery, it provides many clues to Tom's parentage from the outset. Yet Fielding cheats in his duty as a good mystery writer with regard to Summer; we do not get any hint as to Summer's existence until the end of the tale. For an interesting, if not entirely convincing, attempt to make Bridget a psychologically motivated, sympathetic character, see Sheridan Baker's "Bridget Allworthy: The Creative Pressure of Fielding's Plot."

18. In *Illegitimacy: An Examination of Bastardy*, Jenny Teichman points out that "Roman law, the law of Christendom (canon law) and English common law all adhere rigidly to the rule that the only children born legitimate are those who are born in wedlock, those who are conceived in wedlock and those who are both conceived and born in wedlock" (28).

19. Pocock, "Authority and Property," 55.

20. McKeon, *Origins*, 195. McKeon develops this argument in detail throughout the chapter "The Destabilization of Social Categories," 131–75.

21. Pocock, "Virtues, Rights, and Manners," 48. See also Pocock, "Authority and Property" and "The Mobility of Property and the Rise of Eighteenth-Century Sociology" for further discussion of the connection made between virtue and property. In the latter essay Pocock notes, "Property and power are the prerequisites of authority and virtue" (106).

22. For a persuasive argument that Fielding consistently ironizes Allworthy, see Alter, *Fielding*, esp. 84–87.

23. Stevenson points out that "the real struggle for Tom throughout the novel is to make his identity and his character coincide" (*The British Novel*, 59).

24. Spacks's comments on character in the eighteenth-century novel are relevant here: "Eighteenth-century novelistic characters, although a great deal happens to them, testify their stability far more eloquently than their flexibility. . . . identity, far from problematic, remains solid against all external pressure, the substantiality of their being in itself suggesting their virtue" (*Imagining a Self*, 8).

25. For an analysis of the changes Fielding rings on the word "prudence" see Martin C. Battestin, "Fielding's Definition of Wisdom: Some Functions of Ambiguity and Emblem in *Tom Jones*." See also Stevenson's argument that prudence "functions as a kind of language" (*The British Novel*, 63–64).

26. Brown, "*Tom Jones*," 202–4.

27. Samuel Richardson, *Clarissa, or The History of a Young Lady*, 614.

28. Christine van Boheemen points out that the family-romance structure of *Tom Jones* erases the significance of the mother, thus abetting the patriarchal agenda of the novel genre (*The Novel as Family Romance*, esp. 6–7, 31–32, 86).

29. Maclean discusses the subversive potential of bastardy in "The Performance of Illegitimacy." As my argument shows, Fielding ultimately defuses this potential. Campbell in *Natural Masques* questions the facile identification of Fielding with a masculine tradition of the novel. Although Campbell convincingly demonstrates that Fielding's exploration of gender roles within his characters is complex and fluid, she avoids addressing Fielding's masculinist assumptions about the authorial enterprise.

30. Brown, "*Tom Jones*," 224–25.

31. Bakhtin, *The Dialogic Imagination*. See, in particular, the essays "Epic and Novel" (3–40) and "Discourse in the Novel" (259–422).

32. Ernst Curtius traces the valorization of "the book of nature" back to the Middle Ages: "In a disputation the layman proves superior to the scholar, because he had acquired his knowledge not from the books of the schools but 'from God's books,' which He 'has written with His own finger'" (*European Literature and the Latin Middle Ages*, 321). For the full argument see the section "The Book of Nature," 319–26.

33. Lennard Davis examines the prevalence during the early eighteenth century of what he terms "news/novel discourse" in *Factual Fictions*. Davis argues that the novel originated as a bifurcation from this discourse. Braudy deals extensively with the interplay between fictional and historical narrative during the period in *Narrative Form*.

34. James Boswell, *Boswell's Life of Johnson*, 1:455.

35. See Battestin, "Fielding's Definition of Wisdom."

36. Braudy observes, "Cut off from cause, Tom is unfortunately the perfect receptacle for the causes imposed by others" (*Narrative Form*, 180).

37. Paulson observes, "Fielding's masterpiece is about the fictions people create in order to live in the world, variations on the larger fiction of Fielding's novel itself" (*Beautiful, Novel, and Strange*, 119). Susan McNamera analyzes the self-referential function of the characters' fictionalizing in "Mirrors of Fiction within *Tom Jones*." Homer Brown discusses the significance of anonymous gossip within *Tom Jones* in "The Errant Letter and the Whispering Gallery."

38. The phrase comes from Jacques Derrida, "Plato's Pharmacy," in *Dissemination*, 150, 149. See the entire chapter (63–171) and in particular the section "The Heritage of the Pharmakon: Family Scene" (142–55).

39. The preface to Sarah Fielding, *The Adventures of David Simple: Containing an Account of His Travels through the Cities of London and Westminster in the Search of a Real Friend*, 4.

40. Letters, dated January 22, 1749–1750, and January 21, 1750–1751, in Paulson and Lockwood, *The Critical Heritage*, 215, 238.

41. Paulson discusses the traditional bastard status of the picaro in *Satire and the Novel*, 24.

42. Brown, "*Tom Jones*," 204.

43. See Brooks, *Reading for the Plot*, 93–94. See also the chapter "Reading for the Plot" (3–36) for a discussion of the dynamic of narrative movement.

44. Homer Brown observes that letters within texts "are almost always supplementary and repeat in one way or another information found elsewhere in the novel" ("The Errant Letter," 589).

45. As Homer Brown remarks, this particular letter "is never actually delivered" (ibid., 590).

46. "Outwork," esp. 9. See, too, J. Hillis Miller's discussion of the liminal nature of the preface in his self-reflexive introduction, "Preface: Between Theory and Practice," xiii–xxi.

47. "Outwork," 44–45.

48. Curtius notes, "Theognis stamps his name on his verses as a 'seal' . . . to

prevent them from being stolen; this was imitated later" (*European Literature*, 515).

49. Pocock, "Mobility of Property," 107.

50. Pocock deals with the appeal to an immemorial fundamental law in *The Ancient Constitution*. He notes that although the notion of "immemorial custom" was "in decay" in the eighteenth century, "to the end of their *grand siècle* the Whigs—and all Englishmen who took their stand on the principles of 1688—clung to the habit of appealing to a supposedly actual English past not less and perhaps more than to abstract principles of government" (*The Ancient Constitution*, 239, 231).

51. Pocock proposes in a later text that "the legitimation of *de facto* authority" necessitated by the revolution of 1688 was based on the argument that the change occurring in the governing structure actually reinforced tradition: "The central point, of course, is that the apologists preferred to argue that the government was not dissolved, that traditional institutions retained their authority, and that the actions taken and being taken were to be justified by reference to known law." See "The Varieties of Whiggism from Exclusion to Reform: A History of Ideology and Discourse," in *Virtue, Commerce, and History*, 223, 224. In "*Tom Jones*," Brown also discusses the connections between Tom's bastardy and the issues raised by the 1688 revolution.

52. Claude Rawson, *Henry Fielding and the Augustan Ideal under Stress: "Nature's Dance of Death" and Other Studies*, 7. Samuel Richardson's complaint typifies the reaction against Fielding's unorthodox proceeding: "What Reason has he to make his Tom illegitimate, in an age where Keeping is become a Fashion?" See Letter, August 4, 1749, in Paulson and Lockwood, *The Critical Heritage*, 174.

53. In contrast, consider Stevenson's argument about impotence and dynastic succession that appears in his chapter on *The Castle of Otranto* in *The British Novel:* "A dynasty . . . suggests both an escape from reproduction, in that its legitimizing principle is unchanging and immortal, and an extraordinary reproductive imperative, since the body politic must always have someplace to call home" (97). Allworthy himself does not reproduce, yet curiously he does reproduce *himself*—in the person of his heir, Tom Jones.

54. Teichman, *Illegitimacy*, 103.

55. McKeon, *Origins*, 418.

56. Edward Said, *Beginnings: Intention and Method*, xiii.

57. Teichman discusses this practice in *Illegitimacy*, 103.

58. Said, *Beginnings*, 83, 84.

59. Campbell argues that Sophia encapsulates two opposing notions of femininity—the Whig "new woman" who is modest and passive, and the spirited, passionate woman who is associated "with an old economic and political order." See her chapter "'Tom Jones,' Jacobitism, and Gender" in *Natural Masques*, 160–181, esp. 170–74. Although Sophia is much more spirited than the Richardsonian conduct-book heroine, Fielding consistently makes it clear that learned, assertive females are contrary to his ideal of femininity.

60. Battestin maintains that the passage directly expresses Fielding's aim in the novel: "What Fielding has here done—and what he intended throughout *Tom Jones* to be the basic point and symbol of the novel—is to invert the terms of a fa-

miliar analogy, as old at least as Plotinus: God is to his creation as the poet to his poem" ("*Tom Jones:* The Argument of Design," 289–319).

61. Michel Foucault, "The Discourse on Language."

4. *Pride and Prejudice*

1. Walter Scott, review of *Emma*, in *Quarterly Review* 14 (1815–1816); reprinted in *Sir Walter Scott on Novelists and Fiction*, 225–26.

2. Lanser, *Fictions of Authority*, 71, 72.

3. See, for example, Pocock's argument about the connection traditionally made between property and moral authority in "Authority and Property."

4. Critics have often remarked how Austen balances pragmatism and romance in the marriage of Darcy and Elizabeth. In *English Novel*, Dorothy van Ghent regards the marriage as a reconciliation of "utility and morality" (104). Murray Krieger, in *The Classic Vision: The Retreat from Extremity*, points out that the union enables Elizabeth "to join inclination and convenience" (239). Austen thus allows her heroine to avoid having to make a choice that might highlight problem areas in society. Johnson remarks on how the conclusion cancels out conflict: "it happily averts a showdown between survival and self-respect, or love and friendship, for the two principal marriages at the end settle potentially competing claims without conflict or sacrifice" (*Women, Politics, and the Novel*, 92).

5. Edward Copeland discusses the common late eighteenth-century motif of the "economic wanderer" that appears in Austen's early work in his *Women Writing about Money: Women's Fiction in England, 1790–1820*, 56–60. Although Elizabeth Bennet's plight is not as dire as that of various other characters in Austen's texts (or that of many eighteenth-century heroines), it nevertheless makes her a wanderer. As Copeland notes, "Austen's early novels partake of the economic turmoil of the 1790s with an unselfconscious acceptance of its baleful promise for women" (57).

6. Chapman discusses the disparity between parents and offspring in *Facts and Problems*, 186–87. Daniel Cottom describes "Austen's children" as "changelings, their connection to parents and siblings as much a matter of chance and circumstance as their connections to persons outside of the family," in "The Novels of Jane Austen: Attachments and Supplements."

7. In his chapter "The General Calamity: The Want of Money" Copeland provides a useful guide to the relative spending power of contemporary incomes. He points out that an income between £1,000 and £3,000 typifies that of the squires, between £3,000 and £5,000 typifies that of the wealthy gentry (*Women Writing about Money*, 32).

8. Gilbert and Gubar point out that Austen's heroines are dependent "on the whim of wealthier family or friends" in order "to experience the wider world outside their parents' province" (*Madwoman in the Attic*, 122).

9. In his chapter "Fictions of Employment: Female Accomplishments" Copeland discusses the lack of genteel occupations for middle-class women: "Female employment looms as an especially nettling matter for the genteel heroine,

who, when she seeks employment, unavoidably betrays her own class and all its urgent aspirations for station" (*Women Writing about Money*, 161).

10. Duckworth discusses the social degradation that threatens many of Austen's heroines (*Improvement of the Estate*, esp. 2). Lillian Robinson points out that in the world Austen depicts, "Earning her own living, even were that possible, would be degrading for a woman like Elizabeth or for Charlotte" ("Why Marry Mr. Collins?" 189). The situation that threatens the Bennet daughters was similar to that which overtook the Austen daughters. After Mr. Austen's death Mrs. Austen, Cassandra, and Jane had little upon which to live and were forced to depend upon the Austen sons for excursions and extras; one wonders whether Mrs. Austen ever told Jane, "I shall not be able to keep you—."

11. Barbara English and John Saville, *Strict Settlement: A Guide for Historians*, 23.

12. Lawrence Stone, *The Family, Sex and Marriage in England, 1500–1800*, 79; Weldon, *Letters to Alice*, 30. Stone points out that childbirth was a leading cause of death for a certain segment of the population: "Because of this high mortality from childbirth, at all periods from the sixteenth to the nineteenth century, in three out of four cases of all first marriages among the squirarchy that were broken by death within ten years, the cause was the death of the wife" (*Family, Sex and Marriage*, 79–80). We must assume that rates were even higher further down the social scale.

13. Austen herself had experienced the dreadful consequences of excessive childbearing. On October 10, 1808, Elizabeth Austen, wife of Austen's brother Edward, died, "ten days after the birth of her eleventh child in fifteen years, and worn down by an especially arduous confinement" (Halperin, *Life*, 165).

14. Weldon, *Letters to Alice*, 76. Happily for Mrs. Bennet, she does get all her daughters married off eventually—if not in the novel itself, then in Austen's imaginative extension of it. William Austen-Leigh and Richard Arthur Austen-Leigh tell us that Austen envisioned Kitty as marrying a clergyman near Pemberley and Mary as marrying one of Uncle Phillip's clerks (*Life and Letters*, 264).

15. Chapman's careful chronology in his edition of the novel (*Facts and Problems*, 400–408) gives us an idea of the rapidity with which Mr. Collins transfers his affection from one young lady to another. Such a motif is common in Austen. In the early story "The Three Sisters" a Collins-like suitor, rebuffed by one sister, immediately shifts his attentions to another. In *Emma*, we have Mr. Elton's rapid shift from Emma to Augusta Hawkins and Harriet's transfer of affection from Mr. Martin to Mr. Elton to Mr. Knightley and back to Mr. Martin. But even the more sensible of Austen's characters have a tendency to rapid shifts in affection; Cottom points out that Austen's fickle characters "serve to demonstrate that all attachments are fragile and subject to displacement" ("Novels of Jane Austen," 153).

16. Lawrence Stone and Jeanne C. Fawtier Stone, *An Open Elite? England, 1540–1880*, 74. See also pages 69–82 for a good discussion of the convention of patrilineal descent.

17. English and Saville, *Strict Settlement*, 24, 23. The authors point out in the glossary that in theory in tail female "was a possible interest" that "in practice did not occur" (139).

18. See their discussion of the evolution of the strict settlement (13–17). In some sense, the strict settlement worked precisely because it was designed to be broken in the interest of preserving primogeniture. As the Stones suggest in *An Open Elite?* it was not so much the legal strictures but a particular mind-set that sustained the long-term interests of the family: "The settlement was thus broken every generation, new debts were charged upon the estate, and some land was sold or mortgaged or conveyed to trustees to pay off debts and obligations. Thus it was not the strict settlement which preserved family properties intact, but the mind-set which allowed father and son to act in collusion to break it, and in most cases kept them working in the best long-term interests of the family" (*An Open Elite?* 77). Breaking the settlement depended on such a collusion between father and son, a situation that the Bennets had hoped would occur. After breaking the settlement a father and son could draw up a new settlement that would ensure the family's solvency. This new settlement would usually continue the practice of primogeniture.

19. In the "Advertisement by the Author" at the end of his completion of *The Watsons*, John Coates asks, "can anyone tell me how Mr. Bennet's estate was entailed on a Mr. Collins without, of course, introducing a change of surname which should surely have been mentioned if it had occurred?" (*The Watsons*, 313). Upon marriage a Bennet daughter would, of course, change her surname unless, under some *Cecilia*-like settlement, her husband were required to change his.

20. For the discussion of the "angry dowagers," see Gilbert and Gubar, *Madwoman in the Attic*, 170–74. Although Elizabeth resembles Lady Catherine in her outspokenness, she also, unlike Lady Catherine, generally demonstrates good sense and good humor. Gilbert and Gubar explain the unsympathetic portrait of Lady Catherine as "the vilification always allotted by the author to the representatives of matriarchal power" (172).

21. Ibid., 136. See also Copeland's discussion of women's economic vulnerability in his chapter "The General Calamity" in *Women Writing about Money*.

22. Gilbert and Gubar, *Madwoman in the Attic*, 137.

23. Paulson, "Jane Austen: Pride and Prejudice," in *Satire and the Novel*, 300. Paulson regards the true satirist as one who attempts to cure social ills through satire.

24. Sulloway provides a useful distinction between male and female satire of the eighteenth century, arguing that whereas "Women satirists . . . tend to pay other women the compliment that the female sex is as various as the male," male satirists, epitomized by the Augustans, "tended to make women as an entire sex a target for their wit" (*Province of Womanhood*, xv).

25. Butler, *War of Ideas*, 216.

26. Paulson, *Satire and the Novel*, 300. Spacks observes that Elizabeth learns how to laugh correctly: "It is apparently too late for Mr. Bennet really to change, but not too late for Elizabeth. Her growth in self-knowledge and in sensitive awareness of others manifests itself partly in her new relation to laughter" ("Austen's Laughter," 73).

27. Donald Greene in "The Original of Pemberley" argues that the model for Pemberley is "the great country seat of the Cavendishes, Dukes of Devonshire,

Chatsworth House" (2). The sixth duke of Devonshire—Austen's contemporary—was, "like Darcy, a young, handsome, intelligent, sensitive man in his twenties," with a sister named Georgiana (16). The duke, however, epitomized what Greene calls the "grand Whiggery" of Austen's time, holding "social and political eminence" yet indulging in "scandalous exploits" (18). Greene suggests that Austen's connecting of Pemberley with Chatsworth and its owner with the duke may have been intended as a criticism of the wealthy Whigs: "Disgusted at the dissoluteness and irresponsibility of the class which had inherited the control of the wealth and destiny of England, a class to which she herself was related, she perhaps decided to promote the hero of *First Impressions* from merely an upper-middle-class gentleman to 'one of the most illustrious personages of the land,' and to give him the vigour, virtue, and sense of responsibility she thought the new owner of Chatsworth would have" (22). See also Greene's argument that *Pride and Prejudice* serves as a satire of Whiggism, in his article "Jane Austen and the Peerage."

28. Harris makes the case that Austen's characters have counterparts in Samuel Richardson's *Sir Charles Grandison*. See her chapter on *Pride and Prejudice* in *Art of Memory* (84–129). Although Austen's characters indeed have affinities with Richardson's, their configuration in the plot is closer to the setup in Fielding's text.

29. Krieger, *The Classic Vision*, 236–37.

30. Ibid., 229–30.

31. Frances Burney, *Evelina*, 35.

32. David Monaghan notes that breaches of manners have ramifications beyond a personal slight and that the discourtesy between Elizabeth and Darcy undermines more than their relationship: "Repeated displays of bad manners by both parties serve only to widen the gap between them and, symbolically, to create a rift between the aristocracy and the gentry-middle-class which threatens the structure of English society." Bad manners can lead to social chaos ("Jane Austen and the Position of Women," 116). Johnson also discusses the far-reaching implications of failures in politeness (*Women, Politics, and the Novel*, 82–83).

33. Samuel Kliger, "Jane Austen's *Pride and Prejudice* in the Eighteenth-Century Mode," 56–57.

34. Greene, "Jane Austen and the Peerage," 160, 162. See also "The Original of Pemberley" for a gloss on his argument about the Whig critique. Butler points out that gentry families such as Austen's "were naturally suspicious of the values of the established upper classes" ("History, Politics, and Religion," 193).

35. Lawrence Stone points out that the Reformation lifted the incest taboos to the extent that "Even first cousins could now marry" (*Family, Sex, and Marriage*, 139). Such unions were not uncommon among the higher ranks.

36. David Spring suggests that "Jane Austen's social vocabulary . . . is something different from the modern (largely nineteenth-century) language of class" ("Interpreters of Jane Austen's Social World," 55).

37. Greene, "Jane Austen and the Peerage," 162.

38. The term comes from Spring. He notes that Austen's novels deal not so much with the rise of the middle class as with "the rise of the pseudo-gentry"—those who have no landed property but who have gentry aspirations ("Interpreters

of Jane Austen's Social World," 63). Mr. Bennet, of course, does have landed property, but his descendants apparently will not.

39. Robinson, "Why Marry Mr. Collins?" 183.

40. Copeland notes, "In all, women's fiction of the late eighteenth and early nineteenth centuries negotiates an unsteady balance between rank and gender as it confronts the economy" (*Women Writing about Money*, 13).

41. Armstrong, *Desire and Domestic Fiction*, 51. Armstrong argues that "the domestic ideal helped create the fiction of horizontal affiliations that only a century later could be said to have materialized as an economic reality" (65).

42. Gender and class are not separable categories, as Lillian Robinson reminds us: "Women differ from each other by race, by ethnicity, by sexual orientation, and by class. Each of these contributes its historic specificity to social conditions and to the destiny and consciousness of individual women" ("Feminist Criticism: How Do We Know When We've Won?" 146). The feminist agenda of Austen and many of her sister writers tends, perhaps understandably, to encompass only members of their own class.

43. Armstrong, *Desire and Domestic Fiction*, 50, 51.

44. Kirkham, *Feminism and Fiction*, 84.

45. Nina Auerbach, "Jane Austen and Romantic Imprisonment," 25. Auerbach argues, "Jane Austen . . . casts upon her protecting patriarchs a relentless double vision, though she is so deft an artist that she may lead us to think our own vision is slightly out of focus" (22).

46. Duckworth observes, "Elizabeth's final location within the park of Pemberley is also the self's limitation of its power to define its own essence, the heroine's recognition of moral and social limits within which she must live" (*Improvement of the Estate*, 140). Although Austen implicitly validates such limitation, Duckworth's "must" gives us a sense of the lack of alternative visions in Austen's society. Gilbert and Gubar, *Madwoman in the Attic*, and Auerbach, "Romantic Imprisonment," are also useful on this point.

47. Reuben Brower, "Light and Bright and Sparkling," 71.

48. It is interesting that, despite Elizabeth's belief in her newfound objectivity, we are left wondering if getting at the truth can ever be divorced from subjective wishes. After all, Elizabeth hears Wickham's story after she has been flattered by his attentions and slighted by Darcy's comment on her looks; she hears Darcy's after Darcy has flattered her by an offer of marriage and Wickham has slighted her by transferring his affections to Mary King. The "truth" of the letter's truthfulness lies in subsequent events, which indeed vindicate Darcy.

49. Gilbert and Gubar, *Madwoman in the Attic*, 154.

50. Deborah Kaplan, "Achieving Authority: Jane Austen's First Published Novel," 546.

51. In an enlightening reassessment of the novel genre (a genre that "has always had a close tie with the feminine") Christine van Boheemen sums up its intrinsically patriarchal nature: "The final effect of the fiction is the reconfirmation of the supremacy of the symbolic order in which woman cannot be given autonomous subjectivity. Her speech and authority derive from patriarchy, as each narrative enactment confirms. In short, the law of the genre—the ineluctable

modality to which it conforms, which it imposes, and to which it lends reality—is the supremacy of the father. The novel is the instrument of patriarchy, giving presence to its predominance in the act of utterance" (*The Novel as Family Romance*, 32–33).

52. One of the most thorough readings is probably that of van Ghent (*English Novel*, 105). For an interesting more recent analysis see also Rachel Brownstein, "Jane Austen: Irony and Authority," 64.

53. Wayne A. Booth, *A Rhetoric of Irony*, 184.

54. Spacks notes that in a play production of *Pride and Prejudice*, Austen's opening line was assigned to Mr. Bennet ("Austen's Laughter," 71). In her adaptation of the novel for the BBC, Fay Weldon assigned it to an appropriately ironic Elizabeth—a more fitting speaker to my mind (*Pride and Prejudice, or First Impressions*). The different assignations point to the problems of interpretation inherent in the line.

5. *Amelia*

1. For a discussion of the sequels and imitations of *Tom Jones*, see Cross, *The History of Henry Fielding*, 2:133–34.

2. Ibid., 330. For the connection between Amelia and Charlotte Cradock, see also Martin Battestin's introduction to *Amelia*, ix–xx; and Pat Rogers, *Henry Fielding: A Biography*, 76.

3. Samuel Richardson, letter, February 22, 1752, in Paulson and Lockwood, *The Critical Heritage*, 335.

4. Rawson regards Booth as "an older Tom Jones" (*Augustan Ideal under Stress*, 71).

5. Tanner, *Jane Austen*, 55.

6. Battestin refers to this passage in "The Problem of *Amelia*," 147 n. 2. Some critics argue that the threats in *Amelia* may be too insignificant to drive the novel forward. Spacks notes that Amelia's "history, in essence, records stasis, as does Booth's" (*Imagining a Self*, 281). Tanner regards Amelia as a "non-novel" because of the sedentary nature of its heroine: "There is simply not enough alteration in *Amelia* to make it a memorable or successful novel" (*Jane Austen*, 55).

7. Eric Rothstein claims, "Booth has won Miss Matthews' 'heart' by letting her imagine herself an Amelia" (*Systems of Order and Inquiry in Later Eighteenth-Century Fiction*, 174). Peter LePage discusses at length the motif of broken bonds in "The Prison and the Dark Beauty of *Amelia*." He argues that all the different plot strands of the novel "imitate one action, to destroy the *Copula* through imprisonment or ensnarement in an illicit love affair" (350).

8. Campbell similarly marks a resemblance between the Booth narrator/narrative and the Fielding narrator/narrative: "In this way, however, [Booth] is not so different from the narrator of *Amelia* himself, who frequently offers incompatible descriptions of characters or accounts of events in succession, seeming to hold himself responsible for local coherence but not for a sustained and total vision of the novelistic world he describes" (*Natural Masques*, 206). I agree with Campbell,

who sees the problematic narration as a result of ideological conflict, although her argument gives greater emphasis to the conflicting notions of gender roles.

9. Campbell regards Amelia as "a kind of proleptic cultural dream" (ibid., 204). Although Amelia indeed anticipates—and helps inaugurate—the conduct-book heroine so popular in the latter half of the eighteenth century, her role as emblem links her to an earlier, romantic tradition.

10. Paulson notes that "structurally, Amelia is not in the Sophia position but in the Tom position—misread and misrepresented in one way or another by all the characters" (*Beautiful, Novel, and Strange*, 151).

11. If we compare Fielding's treatment of Amelia with Thackeray's treatment of her namesake in *Vanity Fair,* we are struck by the sincerity of Fielding's portrait. Although Thackeray's Amelia, like Fielding's, reflects an idealized, sentimental version of womanhood, her portrait is rendered ironic by such phrases as "tender little parasite." She is not, like Fielding's Amelia, rewarded with the happily-ever-after that might signal authorial approval of her, for she ends up displaced in the affections of her husband by her daughter.

12. For an analysis of the influence of *Clarissa* on *Amelia*, see T. C. Duncan Eaves, "Amelia and Clarissa."

13. J. Paul Hunter, "The Lesson of *Amelia*."

14. According to Hester Lynch Piozzi, "[Johnson's] attention to veracity was without equal or example: and when I mentioned Clarissa as a perfect character; 'On the contrary (said he), you may observe there is always something which she prefers to truth. Fielding's Amelia was the most pleasing heroine of all the romances." See *Anecdotes of the Late Samuel Johnson, LL.D.* (1786); rpt. in *Johnsonian Miscellanies*, ed. G. B. Hill (1897) 1: 297; in Paulson and Lockwood, *The Critical Heritage*, 445.

15. Terry Castle provides a detailed and provocative analysis of the masquerade episode in *Masquerade and Civilization*. Regarding the masquerade topos as "a master trope of destabilization in contemporary fiction," Castle argues that in *Amelia* it is "a figure for ambiguous authorial intentions" (117, 126); the masquerade episode thwarts rather than supports its ostensible didactic purpose.

16. Although Mrs. Atkinson is referred to as Mrs. Bennet before her marriage to Sgt. Atkinson, I am sticking with her married name throughout in order to avoid confusion. Castle analyzes the shift in appellations and the ambiguous nature of Mrs. Atkinson in *Masquerade and Civilization*, 220–22.

17. Ibid., 179.

18. The flawed nose, of course, gave Fielding's early critics a field day. Cross notes, "Though the novel would have failed for other reasons, it was poor Amelia's nose more than all else that did the business" (*History of Henry Fielding*, 338–39). The wags of the time attributed the heroine's noselessness to the same cause as Moll's. For a sample of this "nose" criticism, see ibid., 338–341. Fielding himself gave many of his critics their ammunition by neglecting to have his heroine's nose repaired in the first edition. The historical collation in Battestin's edition enables us to see the "cosmetic surgery" Fielding performed on the nose in subsequent printings (app. 6, 565–82). See Paulson's argument that the flawed nose serves as "a basis of redefining the Beautiful" as mixed (*Beautiful, Novel, and*

Strange, 144–46). See also Braudy's argument that the disfigured nose lends a comic element to her characterization that serves (or should serve) to warn us away from idealizing her too much" (*Narrative Form*, 200). Campbell argues that, although the damaged nose symbolizes Amelia's "singular and distinctly feminine heroism," it can "easily collapse back into a sign either of woman's absurdly inadequate impersonation of male identity or of her own threatening qualities of unruliness and passion within an older model of female nature" (*Natural Masques*, 211).

19. The *Oxford English Dictionary* lists the first usage of this definition as 1697.

20. Paulson, *Beautiful, Novel, and Strange*, 152.

21. Mary Poovey in *The Proper Lady and the Woman Writer: Ideology as Style in the Works of Mary Wollstonecraft, Mary Shelley, and Jane Austen* argues that the changing conception of woman throughout the eighteenth century—"From metaphorical agent of damnation to literal agent of salvation"—enables a prescriptive harnessing of female desires in the service of patriarchal imperatives (esp. 9).

22. See Martin C. Battestin, "Henry Fielding, Sarah Fielding, and 'the Dreadful Sin of Incest.'"

23. J. G. A. Pocock, "Modes of Political and Historical Time in Early Eighteenth-Century England," in *Virtue, Commerce, and History*, 97. For a related discussion of the way in which property is seen as ensuring against corruption, see Pocock, "Authority and Property."

24. Lyall Powers, "The Influence of the *Aeneid* on Fielding's *Amelia*," 334–35; Alter, *Fielding*, 145. Both Powers and Alter regard the Virgil influence as ennobling *Amelia*, but the arguments seem somewhat strained. Although Booth does refrain from a second duel, as Powers points out, he does not know about it and thus has no opportunity to make clear that he has embraced Christian principles. Nor does Booth clearly demonstrate the heroism Alter ascribes to him. For a discussion of the epic qualities in the text see also George Sherburn, "Fielding's *Amelia*: An Interpretation."

25. Paulson regards Booth's treatment of Amelia as "peculiarly sadistic" (*Beautiful, Novel, and Strange*, 147).

26. Samuel Richardson, letter, February 23, 1752, in Paulson and Lockwood, *The Critical Heritage*, 336.

27. Powers, "Influence of the *Aeneid*," 335.

28. Richard Steele, "On Duelling," *Tatler* 25, June 7, 1709, reprinted in *Essays of Richard Steele*, 219.

29. In Bakhtin, *The Dialogic Imagination*, 13, 15.

30. Ibid., 15.

31. Sherburn, "Fielding's *Amelia*," 4.

32. Battestin, "The Problem of *Amelia*," 619. LePage regards the prison as symbolic of the individual's subjection to passion ("The Prison and the Dark Beauty," 342–43).

33. Both Martin Battestin and D. S. Thomas point out that Hobbes and Hume advance similar arguments about the passions. See Battestin, "The Problem of *Amelia*"; also D. S. Thomas's "Fortune and the Passions in Fielding's

Amelia." Eric Rothstein notes an essential difference between Robinson's and Booth's philosophical outlooks: "Robinson's fatalism asserts an order that precludes inquiry, since he cannot isolate causes. Booth offers causes (motives) after a fashion—the hazard of the passions—but cannot assert an order" (*Systems of Order*, 170).

34. Battestin draws our attention to the curious fact that, during the debate, Dr. Harrison ends up aligning himself with Humean philosophy when he states that he believes men act from their passions ("The Problem of *Amelia*," 634).

35. D. S. Thomas, for example, points out how the narrator's opening argument that fortune should not be held responsible for people's failures and successes is undercut by continual—and seemingly un-ironic—references to fortune's power. The text ultimately demonstrates that neither Stoicism nor the doctrine of predominant passions "provides the answer to the uncertainties of human life," yet at the same time the text does not reject either philosophical position, deferring the discussions that might clarify Fielding's position ("Fortune and the Passions," 185, 187). Battestin demonstrates that the doctrine Booth renounces most accurately explains the characters' motivations, for again and again we see those characters acting precisely on the basis of their predominant passions ("The Problem of *Amelia*," esp. 633–37). Both Spacks and John Coolidge find that, rather than mastering the art of life as the novel's opening chapter suggests will happen, the Booths are more or less mastered by it. See Spacks, *Imagining a Self*, 292; and Coolidge, "Fielding and the 'Conservation of Character,'" 258. Sheridan Baker in "Fielding's *Amelia* and the Materials of Romance" also argues that Fielding does not demonstrate his apparent thesis (448).

36. Campbell regards Booth's conversion as reinforcing an argument about gender roles, in that Booth "turns away from the classical reading which both he and Harrison have treated as a distinctively masculine province" and "from the masculine military code of honor which has repeatedly been presented in specific conflict with Christian belief" (*Natural Masques*, 230). However, the philosophy that Booth learns to renounce—that of the passions—does not appear particularly gendered.

37. Alter argues, for example, "the miraculous recovery of Amelia's estate seems like too easy a way out here because the whole novel has been concerned with the absolute failure of the social system to recognize merit, and the apparently irreversible trend of the whole crooked system is to crush all poor innocents like Booth" (*Fielding*, 165). On the other hand, Rothstein regards the providential ending as deliberately implausible: "Fielding did, after all, need an ending that would continue the broadening of possibilities and knitting together of themes which forms the representational mode of *Amelia*. . . . Given this inclusiveness throughout the first eleven books, the resolution must embrace it. Fortune, which looks like chaos or contrivance to profane eyes, makes its widest sweep; Providence, which informs all reality, reveals itself most clearly" (*Systems of Order*, 204). Rothstein points out that there are actually two endings to *Amelia*, the "providential" and the "prudential" ending, which consists of Dr. Harrison's decision to take the Booths under his care in the country (203).

38. Castle, "Masquerade and Allegory," 205. Paulson discusses Fielding's

alternation between "novelistic and Juvenalian conventions" in "Fielding the Novelist," in *Satire and the Novel*, esp. 157–64.

39. Cross, *History of Henry Fielding*, 2:322.

40. Campbell also refers to this passage, seeing it as indicating that Amelia is "the creation of a man's imagination" (*Natural Masques*, 240). Overall, Campbell regards Amelia as a more autonomous authority than I do. Nevertheless, I find persuasive her argument that "Amelia may slip the moorings of her safely feminine identity, as constructed for masculine ends, and raise at least the possibility of real female moral power" (241). Such an argument is in keeping with my own contention that Fielding's materials get away from him in *Amelia.*

41. Anthony Hassell argues that Dr. Harrison "can usually be trusted to present the author's values with sufficient authority to allow the author to dispense with any supplementary commentary." See "Fielding's *Amelia:* Dramatic and Authorial Narration," 232.

42. Very few readers actually like Dr. Harrison. Alter comments that "one is hard put to think of a character in fiction whose supposed charm is easier to resist" (*Fielding*, 162). Castle calls him "insufferable" (*Masquerade and Civilization*, 221).

43. Hugh Amory, "Magistrate or Censor? The Problem of Authority in Fielding's Later Writings," 514. See also Bender's argument that Harrison is intended to represent "an aspect of the state": "His mistakes glare out as those of Fielding's other disappearing exemplars like Adams and Allworthy do not because he impersonates a means of governance—more an abstract principle than a person, yet not like the allegorical personifications of literary tradition" (*Imagining the Penitentiary*, 192).

44. The nobleman's analogy between the growth and decline of the body and the growth and decline of the nation seems a paraphrase of Dr. Middleton's similar analogy in his *Life of Cicero*, with which Fielding concludes his preface to *An Inquiry into the Causes of the Late Increase of Robbers* (1751): "'this remote country, anciently the jest and contempt of the polite Romans, is become the happy seat of liberty, plenty, and letters; flourishing in all the arts and refinements of civil life; yet running perhaps, the same course, which Rome itself had run before it; from virtuous industry to wealth; from wealth to luxury; from luxury to an impatience of discipline and corruption; till, by a total degeneracy and loss of virtue, being grown ripe for destruction, it falls a prey at last to some hardy oppressor, and, with the loss of liberty, losing every thing else that is valuable, sinks gradually again into its original barbarism'" (*LIR* 73–74).

45. Fielding's friend Hogarth expressed this sort of situation pictorially in Plate 1 of *A Harlot's Progress*, wherein the clergyman is more concerned with getting preferment than with saving a country girl from the hands of a procuress. See Paulson's discussion of the print in *The Art of Hogarth*, 96.

46. Rothstein, *Systems of Order*, 42.

47. Coolidge, "Conservation of Character," 258.

48. In *Masquerade and Civilization*, Castle contends that the masquerade destabilizes the characters, but I see the characters as destabilized throughout the text.

49. Alter remarks that the adultery motif shows the lack of values in society: "adultery itself is a kind of paradigm of all that is wrong in a society where

Christian values have been discarded" (*Fielding*, 153).

50. Trent's selling of his wife's honor to the Noble Lord was apparently not an uncommon situation. Lawrence Stone points out that "it was alleged at the time that some aged husbands married young wives with the deliberate purpose of making money by threats of legal proceedings against the latter's lovers" (*Family, Sex and Marriage*, 506).

51. In his discussions of adultery in *The Covent-Garden Journal* Fielding calls for punishment to be meted out to both women and men engaging in adulterous behavior, but again he is primarily dealing not so much with the man who strays from his wife as with the man who seduces his neighbor's wife (*CGJ* nos. 67, 68, October 21, 28, 1752 [341–62]).

52. Richardson, *Pamela, or Virtue Rewarded*, 4:92.

53. Not all critics agree that Booth is relatively guilt-free. LePage argues that Booth's "infidelity constitutes the major burden of guilt that hinders Booth's relationship with his wife and his minister, Dr. Harrison, through the rest of the novel" ("The Prison and the Dark Beauty," 340). We rarely see Booth manifest that guilt, however. Hunter mentions "Fielding's harshness with Booth for the Miss Mathews affair" ("The Lesson of *Amelia*," 178), but as I demonstrate, Booth is fairly readily forgiven.

54. See Robert Folkenflik, "Purpose and Narration in Fielding's *Amelia*," 168. Rothstein also discusses the Shakespearean allusions, suggesting that Fielding may have taken Booth's name from Barton Booth, the famous stage Othello (*Systems of Order*, 195). The Othello allusions may implicate Booth in a way that the rest of the text does not. Because they make us connect Amelia with Desdemona we begin to see her as Booth's victim.

55. Tony Tanner, *Adultery in the Novel: Contract and Transgression*, 6.

56. Stone, *Family, Sex and Marriage*, 501–2.

57. Bender, *Imagining the Penitentiary*, 180–81.

58. In the glossary to Bakhtin's *The Dialogic Imagination*, Holquist points out that "all utterances are heteroglot in that they are functions of a matrix of forces practically impossible to recoup, and therefore impossible to resolve" (428).

59. Bakhtin writing as V. N. Volosinov, *Marxism and the Philosophy of Language*, trans. Ladislav Matejka and I. R. Titunik (New York: Seminar Press, 1973), 115, 120.

60. Felicity Nussbaum and Laura Brown, "Revising Critical Practices: An Introductory Essay," 5.

6. *Mansfield Park*

1. Lionel Trilling, *The Opposing Self: New Essays in Criticism*, 214.

2. Johnson, *Women, Politics, and the Novel*, 119.

3. Austen's "problem novel" has, not surprisingly, received a good deal of critical attention over the last few decades—perhaps because it mitigates against any facile assumption of a coherent political stance on Austen's part. *Mansfield Park* has divided the critics as to whether it espouses conservative or subversive

values. Duckworth has argued for its status as the paradigm text in the Austen canon—a Burkean affirmation of "improvement" over "innovation" (*Improvement of the Estate*). His chapter on *Mansfield Park* is the first chapter in a study that is otherwise ordered chronologically. Butler, in *War of Ideas*, similarly argues for Austen's essential conservatism, regarding *Sense and Sensibility* and *Mansfield Park* as exemplary. Said makes a case for the text's complicity in "imperialist expansion," arguing that it is "the most explicit in its ideological and moral affirmations of Austen's novels" (*Culture and Imperialism*, 84). Johnson in *Women, Politics, and the Novel* makes her case for a subversive Austen, arguing that *Mansfield Park* parodies conservative fiction and puts forth a consistent argument about the hollowness of the gentry's moral pretensions. I might point out that to an earlier generation of Austen readers the conservatism of *Mansfield Park* was taken as a given (and regarded as off-putting). One of the most recent debates over the novel occurs in Whit Stillman's witty film *Metropolitan*, wherein the Fanny-like heroine defends the novel to the hero, who, citing Lionel Trilling, calls it "notoriously bad" (Whit Stillman, writer and director, Westerly Films, 1991).

4. Nina Auerbach, *Romantic Imprisonment: Women and Other Glorified Outcasts*, 22–37.

5. Tanner, *Jane Austen*, 143, 156. See Trilling's comments on Fanny as a Christian heroine (*The Opposing Self*, 129). Andrew Wright defends Fanny on similar grounds in *Jane Austen's Novels: A Study in Structure* (New York: Oxford University Press, 1961), 124.

6. Auerbach, *Romantic Imprisonment*, 25, 27.

7. Gilbert and Gubar in *Madwoman in the Attic* argue that Austen's heroines are punished for their flights of imagination. None, however, end up adhering to a standard of proper female behavior that the notion of punishment implies.

8. See Jacques Donzelot, *The Policing of Families*, 171.

9. In his biography of Austen, Park Honan implies that the private theatricals the Austen family enjoyed in 1787—wherein they were joined by their glamorous cousin Eliza de Feuillide—may have provided a real-life instance of morally upright young men succumbing to the charms of a worldly young woman: "it is probably true that before the rehearsals of *The Wonder* were over, both James and Henry were in love with [Eliza]. . . . [Henry's] feeling for Eliza might have been predictable, but his behavior was as unusual as James's neglect of clerical decorum. Jane Austen's attitude to theatricals was not that of Fanny Price in *Mansfield Park*, but she did have a chance to see how rehearsals mix with seduction" (*Her Life*, 50).

10. Trilling, *The Opposing Self*, 129.

11. Wollstonecraft, *Vindication*, 111–12.

12. Gilbert and Gubar, *Madwoman in the Attic*, 165.

13. This situation may be akin to the one Austen faced when Harris Wither proposed—a proposal she initially accepted but then turned down. Honan suggests that Austen probably had no idea she was the object of Wither's affections until he actually proposed: "nothing obviously had induced her to view him as a lover before he spoke. Initial attraction, flirtation and a deep, particular concern develop within a social world subject to intense social scrutiny, but neither she

nor Cassandra nor anyone else could have seen that happening in her relations with poor Harris" (*Her Life*, 194).

14. Richardson, *Clarissa*, 40.

15. Ibid., 1466.

16. Bradbrook, *Jane Austen and Her Predecessors*, 123.

17. More, *Strictures*, 2:119. Spencer argues that "Jane Austen is deliberately undercutting the complacent belief in the power of love to reform" (*Rise of the Woman Novelist*, 174). Samuel Richardson himself turned the rake-reformed model on its head with Lovelace in *Clarissa*, but his purpose was not to show the receding power of the exemplary woman but the extraordinary fortitude with which she was possessed.

18. Armstrong, *Desire and Domestic Fiction*, 41.

19. Richardson, *Clarissa*, 1495, 1498.

20. Frances Burney, *Cecilia, or Memoirs of an Heiress*, 585.

21. David Spring argues that "the theme of landed decay and crisis has been taken to extremes" in interpretations of *Mansfield Park*: "It needs therefore to be said again that the world of the rural elite was neither going bankrupt in the early nineteenth century nor disintegrating spiritually and socially." Although he acknowledges that Austen might have "read the nature of her society differently from the way we might," he does not give that notion much credit ("Interpreters of Jane Austen's Social World," 66–67). I would, however, argue that even if there were no actual crisis, Austen perceived one, as the novels indicate.

22. In a letter to Cassandra, Austen noted that their brother Henry, who was then reading *Mansfield Park*, "admires H. Crawford: I mean properly as a clever, pleasant man" (Letter 92, *LSC* 377–78).

23. See Q. D. Leavis, "Jane Austen," *A Selection from "Scrutiny,"* 2:1–80.

24. For Copeland it is not adultery but runaway consumption that poses the greatest threat to the values of Mansfield Park (*Women Writing about Money*, 102–6). Copeland notes, however, the connection between runaway consumption and sexual transgression: "Consumer desire fuels the moral action of *Mansfield Park*, and sexual desire is inextricably intertwined in the struggle" (102).

25. Tanner, *Adultery in the Novel*, 15.

26. Johnson provides a thorough account of the failures of Sir Thomas: "He quiets but he does not quell lawlessness; his children tremble at the detection, rather than the commission of wrongs" (*Women, Politics, and the Novel*, 97). Unlike Johnson, however, I do not find in Austen an overall rejection of the values for which Sir Thomas stands.

27. Wollstonecraft, *Vindication*, 86. For an extended argument about Wollstonecraft's influence on Austen, see Kirkham, *Feminism and Fiction*. Although I think Kirkham exaggerates Austen's feminist tendencies, the connections she makes are provocative. For a discussion of Austen's and Wollstonecraft's methods of dealing with constructions of femininity, see Poovey, *The Proper Lady*.

28. Wollstonecraft, *Vindication*, 83.

29. More, *Strictures*, 2:163. Guest discusses the affinities between the conservative More and the radical Wollstonecraft in "The Dream of a Common

Language." As Guest implies, women who were politically opposed could find a common ground as they considered means for female improvement. Yet, as I suggest, although the means may be the same, the ends are different.

30. Tanner, *Jane Austen*, 173.

31. Johnson regards the incest motif as reinforcing Austen's critique of patriarchy. See also Johanna M. Smith's argument that the motif "demonstrate[s] the constrictions of sister-brother love," in "'My Only Sister Now': Incest in *Mansfield Park*" (13). For an argument on the positive nature of the incestuous marriage see Glenda A. Hudson, "Incestuous Relationships: *Mansfield Park* Revisited."

32. Talcott Parsons, "The Incest Taboo in Relation to Social Structure," 21, 19.

33. Marilyn Sachs notes that Mrs. Francis Brown's 1930 *Susan Price, or Resolution*, a sequel to *Mansfield Park*, features such a cousin marriage. See her essay "The Sequels to Jane Austen's Novels," 375.

34. Tanner, *Jane Austen*, 157. Tanner discusses the main characters in *Mansfield Park* in terms of "guardians," "inheritors," and "interlopers" (142–75).

35. Greene argues that in *Mansfield Park*, "Jane Austen comes as close as she ever does to a thoroughgoing presentation of a Tory democracy" ("Jane Austen and the Peerage," 163). It is a Tory democracy that Fanny envisions.

Afterword

1. Martin Battestin and Ruthe Battestin describe the negative reaction to *Amelia* in *Henry Fielding*, 531–38.

2. Battestin, *Henry Fielding*, 543.

3. The comparatively poor reception of *Mansfield Park* had economic ramifications as well, as Copeland points out when discussing the fate of the second edition: "The second edition of *Mansfield Park*, published on commission with Murray in 1816, brought severe disappointment, producing a loss of £182 8s 3d for the year, and reducing her profits on *Emma* to only £38 18s" (*Women Writing about Money*, 195).

4. For the argument that Emma learns her lesson and becomes a better person as a result, see Butler, *War of Ideas*, 250–74, and Booth, *Rhetoric of Fiction*, 243–66. Gilbert and Gubar offer a somewhat different take on the bildungsroman plot, arguing that Emma's humiliation is negative, signifying a retreat from imaginative activity and self-assertion (*Madwoman in the Attic*, 146–83).

5. D. A. Miller discusses the structure of deferral and open-endedness in *Narrative and Its Discontents: Problems of Closure in the Traditional Novel*, 3–106.

6. In "The Value of Narrativity in the Representation of Reality," Hayden White asks, "could we ever narrativize without moralizing?" (1980); rpt. in *The Content of the Form: Narrative Discourse and Historical Representation* (Baltimore: Johns Hopkins University Press, 1987), 25.

7. Spring argues otherwise, seeing Sir Walter Eliot's renting of his estate as "an ancient expedient for debt-ridden landowners" and as a sign that he is "now being eminently sensible" ("Interpreters of Jane Austen's Social World," 65).

Through Sir Walter's character and actions, however, we see Austen discounting the moral force of the man of property.

8. For a discussion of *Sanditon*'s approach to modernity, see Irene Tayler's "Jane Austen Looks Ahead," the afterword to *Fetter'd or Free? British Women Novelists, 1670–1815*, ed. Mary Anne Schofield and Cecilia Macheski (Athens: Ohio University Press, 1986), 422–33.

WORKS CITED

Alter, Robert. *Fielding and the Nature of the Novel*. Cambridge, Mass.: Harvard University Press, 1968.

Amory, Hugh. "Magistrate or Censor? The Problem of Authority in Fielding's Later Writings." *SEL* 12 (1972): 503–18.

Armstrong, Nancy. *Desire and Domestic Fiction: A Political History of the Novel*. New York: Oxford University Press, 1987.

Auerbach, Nina. "Jane Austen and Romantic Imprisonment." In *Jane Austen in a Social Context*, edited by David Monaghan, 9–27. Totowa, N.J.: Barnes and Noble, 1981.

———. *Romantic Imprisonment: Women and Other Glorified Outcasts*. New York: Columbia University Press, 1985.

Austen, Jane. *Jane Austen's Letters to Her Sister Cassandra and Others*. Edited by R. W. Chapman. London: Oxford University Press, 1952.

———. *Minor Works*. Vol. 6 of *The Works of Jane Austen*. Edited by R. W. Chapman. Oxford: Oxford University Press, 1986.

———. *The Novels of Jane Austen*, 3d ed. 5 vols. Edited by R. W. Chapman. Oxford: Oxford University Press, 1933–1969.

Austen-Leigh, William, and Richard Arthur Austen-Leigh. *Jane Austen, Her Life and Letters: A Family Record*. 2d ed. 1913. New York: Russell and Russell, 1965.

Baker, Sheridan. "Bridget Allworthy: The Creative Pressure of Fielding's Plot." *Papers of the Michigan Academy of Science, Arts, and Letters* 52 (1967): 345–56. Reprinted in *Tom Jones: An Authoritative Text, Contemporary Reactions, Criticism*, edited by Sheridan Baker, 906–16. New York: W. W. Norton, 1973.

———. "Fielding's *Amelia* and the Materials of Romance." *Philological Quarterly* 41 (1962): 437–49.

Bakhtin, Mikhail. *The Dialogic Imagination: Four Essays*. Edited by Michael Holquist, translated by Caryl Emerson and Michael Holquist. University of Texas Press Slavic Series 1. Austin: University of Texas Press, 1981.

Barker, Gerard A. *Grandison's Heirs: The Paragon's Progress in the Late Eighteenth-Century English Novel*. Newark: University of Delaware Press, 1985.

Barreca, Regina, ed. *Last Laughs: Perspectives on Women and Comedy*. Studies in Gender and Culture 2. New York: Gordon and Breach, 1988.

Barwell, Ismay. "Feminine Perspectives and Narrative Points of View." In *Aesthetics in Feminist Perspective*, edited by Hilde Hein and Carolyn Korsmeyer, 93–104. Bloomington: Indiana University Press, 1993.

Battestin, Martin C. "Fielding's Definition of Wisdom: Some Functions of Ambiguity and Emblem in *Tom Jones*." *ELH* 35 (1968): 188–217.

———. "Henry Fielding, Sarah Fielding, and 'the Dreadful Sin of Incest.'" *Novel* 13 (1979): 6–18.

———. *The Moral Basis of Fielding's Art: A Study of "Joseph Andrews."* Middletown, Conn.: Wesleyan University Press, 1959.

———. "The Problem of *Amelia:* Hume, Barrow, and the Conversion of Captain Booth." *ELH* 41 (1974): 613–48.

———. "*Tom Jones:* The Argument of Design." In *The Augustan Milieu: Essays Presented to Louis A. Landa*, edited by Henry Knight Miller, Eric Rothstein, and G. S. Rousseau, 289–319. Oxford: Clarendon Press, 1970.

Battestin, Martin C., and Ruthe R. Battestin. *Henry Fielding: A Life*. London: Routledge, 1989.

Bender, John. *Imagining the Penitentiary: Fiction and the Architecture of Mind in Eighteenth-Century England.* Chicago: Chicago University Press, 1987.

Bliss, Michael. "Fielding's Bill of Fare in *Tom Jones*." *ELH* 30 (1963): 236–43.

Boheemen, Christine van. *The Novel as Family Romance: Language, Gender, and Authority from Fielding to Joyce*. Ithaca: Cornell University Press, 1987.

Booth, Wayne C. *The Rhetoric of Fiction*. 2d ed. Chicago: University of Chicago Press, 1983.

———. *A Rhetoric of Irony*. Chicago: University of Chicago Press, 1974.

Boswell, James. *Boswell's Life of Johnson*. Edited by Humphrey Milford. 2 vols. London: Oxford University Press, 1922.

Bradbrook, Frank. *Jane Austen and Her Predecessors*. Cambridge: Cambridge University Press, 1966.

Braudy, Leo. *Narrative Form in History and Fiction: Hume, Fielding, and Gibbon*. Princeton: Princeton University Press, 1970.

Brooks, Peter. *Reading for the Plot: Design and Intention in Narrative*. New York: Vintage, 1985.

Brower, Reuben. "Light and Bright and Sparkling." In *The Fields of Light: An Experiment in Critical Reading*. London: Oxford University Press, 1951. Reprinted as "Light and Bright and Sparkling: Irony and Fiction in *Pride and Prejudice*." In *Twentieth-Century Interpretations of "Pride and Prejudice": A Collection of Critical Essays*, edited by E. Rubinstein, 62–75. Englewood Cliffs, N.J.: Prentice-Hall, 1969.

Brown, Homer Obed. "The Errant Letter and the Whispering Gallery." *Genre* 10 (1977): 573–99. Reprinted in *Institutions of the English Novel*, 23–50.

———. "The Institution of the English Novel." Section 623. MLA Convention. Los Angeles, December 29, 1982.

———. *Institutions of the English Novel: From Defoe to Scott*. Philadelphia: University of Pennsylvania Press, 1997.

———. "Institutions of the Imaginary: *Northanger Abbey*." Unpublished paper. The Humanities Center of the English and French Departments. Johns Hopkins University, Baltimore, Md., February 1, 1988.

———. "Of the Title to Things Real: Conflicting Stories." Review essay. *ELH* 55 (1988): 917–54.

———. "*Tom Jones:* The 'Bastard' of History." *Boundary 2* 7 (1979): 201–33. Reprinted in *Institutions of the English Novel*, 82–115.

———. "Tristram to the Hebrews: Some Notes on the Institution of a Canonic Text." *Modern Language Notes* 99 (1984): 727–47. Reprinted in *Institutions of the English Novel*, 116–37.

Brownstein, Rachel. "Jane Austen: Irony and Authority." In *Last Laughs: Perspectives on Women and Comedy*, edited by Regina Barreca, 57–69. Studies in Gender and Culture 2. New York: Gordon and Breach, 1988.

Burney, Frances. *Cecilia, or Memoirs of an Heiress*. Edited by Peter Sabor and Margaret Anne Doody. 1782. Oxford: Oxford University Press, 1988.

———. *Evelina*. Edited by Edward A. Bloom and Lillian D. Bloom. 1778. Oxford: Oxford University Press, 1982.

Butler, Marilyn. "History, Politics, and Religion." In *The Jane Austen Companion*, edited by J. David Grey, A. Walton Litz, and Brian Southam, 191–207. New York: MacMillan, 1986.

———. *Jane Austen and the War of Ideas*. Oxford: Clarendon Press, 1975.

———. *Romantics, Rebels, and Reactionaries: English Literature and Its Background, 1760–1830*. Oxford: Oxford University Press, 1981.

Campbell, Jill. *Natural Masques: Gender and Identity in Fielding's Plays and Novels*. Stanford: Stanford University Press, 1995.

Castle, Terry. *Masquerade and Civilization: The Carnivalesque in Eighteenth-Century English Culture and Fiction*. Stanford: Stanford University Press, 1986.

Cervantes Saavedra, Miguel de. *The Adventures of Don Quixote*. Translated by J. M. Cohen. 1604, 1614. Harmondsworth, Middlesex: Penguin, 1950.

Chapman, R. W. *Jane Austen: Facts and Problems*. 1948. Oxford: Clarendon Press, 1961.

Chibka, Robert. "Taking 'The Serious' Seriously: The Introductory Chapters of *Tom Jones*." *The Eighteenth Century: Theory and Interpretation* 31 (1990): 23–45.

Coates, John, and Jane Austen. *The Watsons*. 1958. New York: Signet–New American Library, 1977.

Coolidge, John S. "Fielding and the 'Conservation of Character.'" *Modern Philology* 57 (1960): 245–59.

Copeland, Edward. *Women Writing about Money: Women's Fiction in England, 1790–1820*. Cambridge: Cambridge University Press, 1995.

Cottom, Daniel. "The Novels of Jane Austen: Attachments and Supplements." *Novel* 14 (1981): 152–67.

Cross, Wilbur L. *The History of Henry Fielding*. 3 vols. 1918. New York: Russell and Russell, 1963.

Curtius, Ernst. *European Literature and the Latin Middle Ages*. Translated by Willard R. Trask. Bollingen Series 36. 1953. Princeton: Princeton University Press, 1973. Translation of *Europäische Literatur und lateinisches Mittelalter*. Bern, 1948.

Davis, Lennard J. *Factual Fictions: The Origins of the English Novel*. New York: Columbia University Press, 1983.

Defoe, Daniel. *The Life and Strange Surprizing Adventures of Robinson Crusoe*.

Edited by J. Donald Crowley. 1719. Oxford: Oxford University Press, 1981.

Derrida, Jacques. *Dissemination*. Translated by Barbara Johnson. Chicago: University of Chicago Press. Translation of *La Dissémination*. Paris: Seuil, 1972.

———. "Outwork." Preface to *Dissemination*.

Dickens, Charles. *Dealings with the Firm of Dombey and Son: Wholesale, Retail, and for Exportation*. Edited by H. W. Garrod. 1848. Oxford: Oxford University Press, 1950.

Donzelot, Jacques. *The Policing of Families*. Foreword by Gilles Deleuze, translated by Robert Hurley. New York: Pantheon Books, 1979. Translation of *La Police des familles*. Paris: Les Editions de Minuit, 1977.

Doody, Margaret Anne. *The True Story of the Novel*. New Brunswick, N.J.: Rutgers University Press, 1996.

Duckworth, Alistair M. *The Improvement of the Estate: A Study of Jane Austen's Novels*. Baltimore: Johns Hopkins University Press, 1971.

———. "Jane Austen and the Conflict of Interpretations." In *Jane Austen: New Perspectives*, edited by Janet Todd, 39–52. Women and Literature n.s. 3. New York: Holmes and Meier, 1983.

Eaves, T. C. Duncan. "Amelia and Clarissa." In *A Provision of Human Nature: Essays on Fielding and Others in Honor of Miriam Austin Locke*, edited by Donald Kay, 95–110. University: University of Alabama Press, 1977.

English, Barbara, and John Saville. *Strict Settlement: A Guide for Historians*. Occasional Papers in Economic and Social History 10. Hull, England: University of Hull Press, 1983.

Fielding, Henry. *Amelia*. Edited by Martin C. Battestin with textual introduction by Fredson Bowers. Watertown, Conn.: Wesleyan University Press, 1984.

———. *The Covent-Garden Journal; and, A Plan of the Universal Register-Office*. Edited by Bertrand A. Goldgar. Watertown, Conn.: Wesleyan University Press, 1988.

———. *An Enquiry into the Causes of the Late Increase of Robbers and Related Writings*. Edited by Malvin R. Zirker. Watertown, Conn.: Wesleyan University Press, 1988.

———. *The History of Tom Jones, a Foundling*. Edited by Martin C. Battestin and Fredson Bowers, introduction by Martin C. Battestin. 2 vols. Oxford: Wesleyan University Press, 1975.

———. *Jonathan Wild*. Edited by David Nokes. Harmondsworth, Middlesex: Penguin, 1982.

———. *Joseph Andrews*. Edited by Martin C. Battestin. Watertown, Conn.: Wesleyan University Press, 1967.

———. *A Journal of a Voyage to Lisbon*. In *Henry Fielding: Miscellaneous Writings*, vol. 1. New York: The Literary Guild of America, 1937.

———. *Miscellanies by Henry Fielding, Esq*. Edited by Henry Knight Miller. Watertown, Conn.: Wesleyan University Press, 1972.

———. Preface. *The Adventures of David Simple: Containing an Account of His Travels through the Cities of London and Westminster in the Search of a Real Friend*, by Sarah Fielding. Edited by Malcolm Kelsall. 1744. London: Oxford University Press, 1969.

———. "Preface to *Familiar Letters on David Simple*." In *The Criticism of Henry Fielding*, edited by Ioan Williams, 131–36. New York: Barnes and Noble, 1970.

———. *Shamela*. In Samuel Richardson's *Pamela*. Edited by John M. Bullitt. New York: New American Library, 1980.

Folkenflik, Robert. "Purpose and Narration in Fielding's *Amelia*." *Novel* 6 (1973): 167–74.

Foucault, Michel. "The Discourse on Language." Translated by Rupert Swyer. In *The Archaeology of Knowledge and the Discourse on Language*, 215–37. New York: Pantheon Books, 1972. Translation of *L'Ordre du discours*. Paris: Gallimard, 1971.

———. *The Order of Things: An Archaeology of the Human Sciences*. New York: Vintage, 1973. Translation of *Les Mots et les choses*. Paris: Gallimard, 1966.

———. "What Is an Author?" In *Language, Counter-Memory, Practice: Selected Essay and Interviews*, edited by Donald F. Bouchard, translated by Donald F. Bouchard and Sherry Simon, 113–38. Ithaca: Cornell University Press, 1977.

Frank, Judith. "The Comic Novel and the Poor: Fielding's Preface to *Joseph Andrews*." *Eighteenth-Century Studies* 27 (1993–1994): 217–34.

Frye, Northrop. *Anatomy of Criticism: Four Essays*. Princeton: Princeton University Press, 1957.

Gilbert, Sandra M., and Susan Gubar. *The Madwoman in the Attic: The Woman Writer and the Nineteenth-Century Literary Imagination*. New Haven: Yale University Press, 1979.

Gilligan, Carol. *In a Different Voice: Psychological Theory and Women's Development*. Cambridge: Harvard University Press, 1982.

Goldberg, Homer. *The Art of "Joseph Andrews."* Chicago: University of Chicago Press, 1969.

Greene, Donald. *The Age of Exuberance: Backgrounds to Eighteenth-Century English Literature*. New York: Random House, 1970.

———. "Jane Austen and the Peerage." *PMLA* 68 (1953): 1017–31. Reprinted in *Jane Austen: A Collection of Critical Essays*, edited by Ian Watt, 154–65. Englewood Cliffs, N.J.: Prentice-Hall, 1963.

———. "The Original of Pemberley." *Eighteenth-Century Fiction* 1 (1988): 1–23.

Grey, J. David, A. Walton Litz, and Brian Southam, eds. *The Jane Austen Companion with A Dictionary of Jane Austen's Life and Works*, by Abigail Bok. New York: MacMillan, 1986.

Guest, Harriet. "The Dream of a Common Language: Hannah More and Mary Wollstonecraft." *Textual Practice* 9 (1995): 303–23.

Hahn, H. George. "Main Lines of Criticism of Fielding's *Tom Jones*, 1900–1978." *British Studies Monitor* 10 (1980): 8–35.

Halperin, John. *The Life of Jane Austen*. Baltimore: Johns Hopkins University Press, 1984.

Harding, D. W. "Regulated Hatred: An Aspect of the Work of Jane Austen." In *Jane Austen: Twentieth-Century Views*, edited by Ian Watt, 166–79. Englewood Cliffs, N.J.: Prentice-Hall, 1963.

Harris, Jocelyn. *Jane Austen's Art of Memory*. Cambridge: Cambridge University Press, 1989.

Hassell, Anthony. "Fielding's *Amelia:* Dramatic and Authorial Narration." *Novel* 5 (1972): 225–33.

Honan, Park. *Jane Austen: Her Life.* 1987. New York: St. Martin's Griffin, 1996.

Hudson, Glenda A. "Incestuous Relationships: *Mansfield Park* Revisited." *Eighteenth-Century Fiction* 4 (1991): 53–68.

Hunter, J. Paul. "The Lesson of *Amelia.*" In *Quick Springs of Sense*, edited by Larry S. Champion, 157–82. Athens: University of Georgia Press, 1974.

———. *Occasional Form: Henry Fielding and the Chains of Circumstance.* Baltimore: Johns Hopkins University Press, 1975.

———. "Some Contexts for *Joseph Andrews.*" In *Occasional Form*, 94–116.

Iser, Wolfgang. *The Implied Reader: Patterns of Communication in Prose Fiction from Bunyan to Beckett.* Baltimore: Johns Hopkins University Press, 1974.

Jehlen, Myra. "Archimedes and the Paradox of Feminist Criticism." *Signs* 6 (1981): 575–601.

Johnson, Claudia L. *Jane Austen: Women, Politics, and the Novel.* Chicago: University of Chicago Press, 1988.

Kaplan, Deborah. "Achieving Authority: Jane Austen's First Published Novel." *Nineteenth-Century Fiction* 37 (1983): 531–51.

———. *Jane Austen among Women.* Baltimore: Johns Hopkins University Press, 1992.

Kaplan, Fred. "Fielding's Novel about Novels: The 'Prefaces' and the 'Plot' of *Tom Jones.*" *SEL* 13 (1973): 535–49.

Kirkham, Margaret. *Jane Austen: Feminism and Fiction.* 1983. New York: Methuen, 1986.

Kliger, Samuel. "Jane Austen's *Pride and Prejudice* in the Eighteenth-Century Mode." In *Twentieth-Century Interpretations of "Pride and Prejudice,"* edited by E. Rubinstein, 49–57. Englewood Cliffs, N.J.: Prentice-Hall, 1969.

Kolodny, Annette. "A Map for Rereading: Gender and the Interpretation of Literary Texts." In *The New Feminist Criticism: Essays on Women, Literature, and Theory*, edited by Elaine Showalter, 46–62. New York: Pantheon Books, 1985.

Krieger, Murray. *The Classic Vision: The Retreat from Extremity.* Vol. 2 of *Visions of Extremity in Modern Literature.* Baltimore: Johns Hopkins University Press, 1971.

Lanser, Susan Sniader. *Fictions of Authority: Women Writers and Narrative Voice.* Ithaca: Cornell University Press, 1992.

Leavis, F. R. *The Great Tradition: George Eliot, Henry James, Joseph Conrad.* New York: New York University Press, 1963.

Leavis, Q. D. "Jane Austen." In *A Selection from "Scrutiny,"* edited by F. R. Leavis, 2:1–80. 2 vols. Cambridge: Cambridge University Press, 1986.

Lennox, Charlotte. *The Female Quixote, or The Adventures of Arabella.* 1752. Upper Saddle River, N.J.: Literature House, 1970.

LePage, Peter. "The Prison and the Dark Beauty of *Amelia.*" *Criticism* 9 (1967): 337–54.

Levine, George. *The Realistic Imagination: English Fiction from Frankenstein to Lady Chatterley.* Chicago: University of Chicago Press, 1981.

Litz, A. Walton. "Chronology of Composition." In *The Jane Austen Companion*, edited by J. David Grey, A. Walton Litz, and Brian Southam, 47–51. New York: MacMillan, 1986.

———. *Jane Austen: A Study of Her Artistic Development*. New York: Oxford University Press, 1965.

Lockwood, Thomas. "Matter and Reflection in *Tom Jones*." *ELH* 45 (1978): 226–35.

Maclean, Marie. "The Performance of Illegitimacy: Signing the Matronym." *New Literary History* 25 (1994): 95–107.

McBurney, William Harlin. *A Check List of English Prose Fiction, 1700–1739*. Cambridge: Harvard University Press, 1960.

McCrea, Brian. "Rewriting *Pamela:* Social Change and Religious Faith in *Joseph Andrews*." *Studies in the Novel* 12 (1984): 137–49.

McKeon, Michael. *The Origins of the English Novel, 1600–1740*. Baltimore: Johns Hopkins University Press, 1987.

McKillop, Alan D. "Critical Realism in *Northanger Abbey*." In *From Jane Austen to Joseph Conrad*, edited by Robert C. Rathburn and Martin Steinman Jr. Minneapolis: University of Minnesota, 1958. Reprinted in *Jane Austen: A Collection of Critical Essays*, edited by Ian Watt, 52–61. Englewood Cliffs, N.J.: Prentice-Hall, 1963.

McNamera, Susan. "Mirrors of Fiction within *Tom Jones*." *Eighteenth-Century Studies* 12 (1978): 372–90.

Miller, D. A. *Narrative and Its Discontents: Problems of Closure in the Traditional Novel*. Princeton: Princeton University Press, 1981.

Miller, Henry Knight. "The Voices of Henry Fielding: Style in *Tom Jones*." In *The Augustan Milieu*, 262–88.

Miller, Henry Knight, Eric Rothstein, and G. S. Rousseau, eds. *The Augustan Milieu: Essays Presented to Louis A. Landa*. Oxford: Clarendon Press, 1970.

Miller, J. Hillis. "Preface: Between Theory and Practice." In *The Linguistic Moment: From Wordsworth to Stevens*, xiii–xxi. Princeton: Princeton University Press, 1985.

Moler, Kenneth L. *Jane Austen's Art of Allusion*. Lincoln: University of Nebraska Press, 1968.

Monaghan, David. "Jane Austen and the Position of Women." In *Jane Austen in a Social Context*, edited by David Monaghan, 105–21. Totowa, N.J.: Barnes and Noble, 1981.

More, Hannah. *Strictures on the Modern System of Female Education*. Introduction by Gina Luria. 2 vols. 1799. New York: Garland, 1974.

Moretti, Franco. *The Way of the World: The Bildungsroman in European Culture*. London: Verso, 1987.

Mudrick, Marvin. "Irony versus Gothicism." In *Jane Austen: "Northanger Abbey" and "Persuasion": A Casebook*, edited by B. C. Southam, 73–97. New York: MacMillan, 1976.

Nussbaum, Felicity, and Laura Brown. "Revising Critical Practices: An Introductory Essay." In *The New Eighteenth Century: Theory, Politics, English Literature*, edited by Felicity Nussbaum and Laura Brown, 1–22. New York: Methuen, 1987.

Orr, Leonard. *A Catalogue Checklist of English Prose Fiction, 1750–1800*. Troy, N.Y.: Whitson Publishing, 1979.

Parker, Jo Alyson. "Spiraling down 'the Gutter of Time': *Tristram Shandy* and the Strange Attractor of Death." *Weber Studies* 14 (January 1997): 102–14.

Parsons, Talcott. "The Incest Taboo in Relation to Social Structure." In *The Family: Its Structures and Functions*, edited by Rose Laub Coser, 13–30. 2d ed. New York: St. Martin's, 1974.

Paulson, Ronald. *The Art of Hogarth*. London: Phaidon Press, 1975.

———. *The Beautiful, Novel, and Strange: Aesthetics and Heterodoxy*. Baltimore: Johns Hopkins University Press, 1996.

———. *Satire and the Novel in Eighteenth-Century England*. New Haven: Yale University Press, 1967.

Paulson, Ronald, and Thomas Lockwood, eds. *Henry Fielding: The Critical Heritage*. New York: Barnes and Noble, 1969.

Pocock, J. G. A. *The Ancient Constitution and the Feudal Law: A Study of English Historical Thought in the Seventeenth Century*. 1957. New York: W. W. Norton, 1967.

———. "Authority and Property: The Question of Liberal Origins." 1980. Reprinted in *Virtue, Commerce, and History*, 51–71.

———. "The Mobility of Property and the Rise of Eighteenth-Century Sociology." 1978. Reprinted in *Virtue, Commerce, and History*, 103–23.

———. *Virtue, Commerce, and History: Essays on Political Thought and History, Chiefly in the Eighteenth Century*. Cambridge: Cambridge University Press, 1985.

———. "Virtues, Rights, and Manners: A Model for Historians of Political Thought." 1981. Reprinted in *Virtue, Commerce, and History*, 37–50.

Poovey, Mary. *The Proper Lady and the Woman Writer: Ideology as Style in the Works of Mary Wollstonecraft, Mary Shelley, and Jane Austen*. Chicago: Chicago University Press, 1984.

Powers, Lyall. "The Influence of the *Aeneid* on Fielding's *Amelia*." *Modern Language Notes* 71 (1956): 330–37.

Raven, James. *British Fiction, 1750–1770: A Chronological Check-List of Prose Fiction Printed in Britain and Ireland*. Newark: University of Delaware Press, 1987.

Rawson, Claude J. *Henry Fielding and the Augustan Ideal under Stress: "Nature's Dance of Death" and Other Studies*. London: Routledge and Kegan Paul, 1972.

Rawson, Claude, ed. *Henry Fielding: A Critical Anthology*. Harmondsworth, Middlesex: Penguin, 1973.

Richardson, Samuel. *Clarissa, or The History of a Young Lady*. Edited by Angus Ross. 1747–1748. Harmondsworth, Middlesex: Penguin Books, 1985.

———. *Pamela*. 1740–1741. Edited by John M. Bullitt. New York: New American Library, 1980.

———. *Pamela, or Virtue Rewarded*. Edited by Ethel M. M. McKenn. 4 vols. 1740–1741. Philadelphia: J. B. Lippincott, 1902.

Robinson, Lillian. "Feminist Criticism: How Do We Know When We've Won?" In *Feminist Issues in Literary Scholarship*, edited by Shari Benstock, 141–49. Bloomington: Indiana University Press, 1978.

———. *Sex, Class, and Culture*. Bloomington: Indiana University Press, 1978.
———. "Why Marry Mr. Collins?" In *Sex, Class, and Culture*.
Rogers, Pat. *Henry Fielding: A Biography*. New York: Charles Scribner's Sons, 1979.
Rothstein, Eric. *Systems of Order and Inquiry in Later Eighteenth-Century Fiction*. Berkeley and Los Angeles: University of California Press, 1975.
Rubinstein, E., ed. *Twentieth-Century Interpretations of "Pride and Prejudice": A Collection of Critical Essays*. Englewood Cliffs, N.J.: Prentice-Hall, 1969.
Runge, Laura. "Gendered Strategies in the Criticism of Early Fiction." *Eighteenth-Century Studies* 28 (1995): 363–78.
Sachs, Marilyn. "The Sequels to Jane Austen's Novels." In *The Jane Austen Companion*, edited by J. David Grey, A. Walton Litz, and Brian Southam, 374–76. New York: MacMillan, 1986.
Said, Edward. *Beginnings: Intention and Method*. New York: Basic Books, 1975.
———. *Culture and Imperialism*. New York: Knopf, 1993.
Saunders, David, and Ian Hunter. "Lessons from the 'Literatory': How to Historicise Authorship." *Critical Inquiry* 17 (1991): 479–509.
Scott, Sir Walter. *Sir Walter Scott On Novelists and Fiction*. Edited by Ioan Williams. New York: Barnes and Noble, 1968.
Sherburn, George. "Fielding's *Amelia:* An Interpretation." *ELH* 3 (1936): 1–14.
Showalter, Elaine, ed. *The New Feminist Criticism: Essays on Women, Literature, and Theory*. New York: Pantheon Books, 1985.
Smith, Johanna M. "'My Only Sister Now': Incest in *Mansfield Park*." *Studies in the Novel* 19 (1987): 1–15.
Spacks, Patricia Meyer. "Austen's Laughter." In *Last Laughs: Perspectives on Women and Comedy*, edited by Regina Barreca, 71–85. Studies in Gender and Culture 2. New York: Gordon and Breach, 1988.
———. *Desire and Truth: Functions of Plot in Eighteenth-Century Novels*. Chicago: University of Chicago Press, 1990.
———. *Imagining a Self: Autobiography and Novel in Eighteenth-Century England*. Cambridge, Mass.: Harvard University Press, 1976.
Spencer, Jane. *The Rise of the Woman Novelist: From Aphra Behn to Jane Austen*. Oxford: Basil Blackwell, 1986.
Spring, David. "Interpreters of Jane Austen's Social World: Literary Critics and Historians." In *Jane Austen: New Perspectives*, edited by Janet Todd, 53–72. Women and Literature n.s. 3. New York: Holmes and Meier, 1983.
Steele, Richard. *Essays of Richard Steele*. Edited by L. E. Steele. New York: MacMillan, 1902.
Stephen, Leslie. *History of English Thought in the Eighteenth Century*. 2 vols. 1876. New York: Harcourt, Brace, and World, 1962.
Stevenson, John Allen. *The British Novel, Defoe to Austen: A Critical History*. Twayne's Critical History of the Novel. Boston: Twayne Publishers, 1990.
Stillman, Whit, writer and director. *Metropolitan*. Westerly Films, 1991.
Stimpson, Catherine R. "Ad/d Feminam: Women, Literature, and Society." In *Literature and Society*, edited by Edward W. Said, 174–92. Selected Papers from the English Institute, 1978, n.s. 3. Baltimore: Johns Hopkins University Press 1980.

Stone, Lawrence. *The Family, Sex and Marriage in England, 1500–1800*. London: Weidenfeld and Nicolson, 1977.

Stone, Lawrence, and Jeanne C. Fawtier Stone. *An Open Elite? England, 1540–1880*. Oxford: Clarendon Press, 1984.

Sulloway, Alison. *Jane Austen and the Province of Womanhood*. Philadelphia: University of Pennsylvania Press, 1989.

Tanner, Tony. *Adultery in the Novel: Contract and Transgression*. Baltimore: Johns Hopkins University Press, 1979.

———. *Jane Austen*. Cambridge, Mass.: Harvard University Press, 1986.

Tayler, Irene. "Jane Austen Looks Ahead." In *Fetter'd or Free? British Women Novelists, 1670–1815*, edited by Mary Anne Schofield and Cecilia Macheski. Athens: Ohio University Press, 1986.

Teichman, Jenny. *Illegitimacy: An Examination of Bastardy*. Ithaca: Cornell University Press, 1982.

Thomas, D. S. "Fortune and the Passions in Fielding's *Amelia*." *Modern Language Review* 60 (1965): 176–87.

Thornbury, Ethel. *Henry Fielding's Theory of the Comic Prose Epic*. 1931. New York: Russell and Russell, 1966.

Todd, Janet, ed. *Jane Austen: New Perspectives*. Women and Literature n.s. 3. New York: Holmes and Meier, 1983.

———. *The Sign of Angellica: Women, Writing, and Fiction, 1660–1800*. New York: Columbia University Press, 1989.

———. *Women's Friendship in Literature*. New York: Columbia University Press, 1980.

Tompkins, J. M. S. *The Popular Novel in England, 1770–1800*. 1932. Lincoln: University of Nebraska Press, 1961.

Trilling, Lionel. *The Opposing Self: New Essays in Criticism*. New York: Viking Compass, 1959.

van Ghent, Dorothy. *The English Novel: Form and Function*. 1953. New York: Holt, Rinehart and Winston, 1961.

Volosinov, V. N. [Mikhail Bakhtin]. *Marxism and the Philosophy of Language*. Translated by Ladislav Matejka and I. R. Titunik. New York: Seminar Press, 1973.

Watt, Ian. *Jane Austen: A Collection of Critical Essays*. Englewood Cliffs, N.J.: Prentice-Hall, 1963.

———. *The Rise of the Novel: Studies in Defoe, Richardson, and Fielding*. Berkeley and Los Angeles: University of California Press, 1957.

Weldon, Fay. *Letters to Alice on First Reading Jane Austen*. 1984. San Diego: Harvest-Harcourt, 1986.

Weldon, Fay, adapter. *Pride and Prejudice, or First Impressions*. Directed by Cyril Coke. BBC Video, 1979.

"A Whimsical Writing Lady Displayed." *The London Magazine* 44 (1775): 461–62.

White, Hayden. "The Value of Narrativity in the Representation of Reality." In *The Content of the Form: Narrative Discourse and Historical Representation*, 1–25. Baltimore: Johns Hopkins University Press, 1987.

Williams, Raymond. *Keywords: A Vocabulary of Culture and Society*. 2d ed. New York: Oxford University Press, 1985.

Wollstonecraft, Mary. *Maria, or The Wrongs of Woman.* 1797. New York: Norton, 1975.

———. *A Vindication of the Rights of Woman.* Edited by Miriam Brody Kramnick. 1792. Harmondsworth, Middlesex: Penguin, 1982.

Wright, Andrew. *Jane Austen's Novels: A Study in Structure.* New York: Oxford University Press, 1961.

INDEX